Care Across Generations

Care Across Generations

Solidarity and Sacrifice in Transnational Families

Kristin E. Yarris

Stanford University Press
Stanford, California

Stanford University Press
Stanford, California

Printed in the United States of America on acid-free, archival-quality paper

Library of Congress Cataloging-in-Publication Data

Names: Yarris, Kristin Elizabeth, 1973– author.
Title: Care across generations : solidarity and sacrifice in transnational families / Kristin E. Yarris.
Description: Stanford, California : Stanford University Press, 2017. | Includes bibliographical references and index.
Identifiers: LCCN 2016054546 | ISBN 9781503602045 (cloth : alk. paper) | ISBN 9781503602885 (pbk. : alk. paper) | ISBN 9781503602953 (digital)
Subjects: LCSH: Immigrant families—Nicaragua. | Nicaragua—Emigration and immigration—Social aspects. | Grandparents as parents—Nicaragua. | Grandmothers—Family relationships—Nicaragua. | Women immigrants—Family relationships—Nicaragua. | Children of immigrants—Family relationships—Nicaragua. | Kinship care—Nicaragua. | Intergenerational relations—Nicaragua. | Transnationalism—Social aspects—Nicaragua.
Classification: LCC JV7426 .Y37 2017 | DDC 306.874/5097285—dc23 LC record available at https://lccn.loc.gov/2016054546

Typeset by Newgen in 10/14 Minion

To the memory of my grandmothers: Helen Yarris, my paternal grandmother, who in my early childhood impressed on me the values of faith and humility and the simple joy of reading in a favorite chair, and Madeleine Vastine, my maternal grandmother, for her everyday after-school caregiving and for instilling in me the values of diligence and discipline, as well as for her lifelong commitment to women's higher education

Contents

Illustrations

Figures

Tables

Preface

Entering the Field: Grandmothers, Distress,
and Care

THIS BOOK IS AN ETHNOGRAPHIC EXPLORATION of the experiences of grandmothers who have assumed care for children in Nicaragua after mothers have migrated abroad. This is a story of transnational family life, but one that extends the analysis beyond nuclear families, moving outward from relations between mothers and children to focus on extended kin relations and intergenerational networks of care. By describing the tensions, uncertainties, and ambivalences of transnational life, and the role of grandmother care in responding to these troubles, this book shows how women of the *tercera edad* (third age, or grandparent generation) are central actors in global migration even without crossing national borders. This book therefore argues for the importance of an intergenerational perspective in social science research on migration, transnational family life, and the relations of care that are crucial for family health and well-being in the context of global migration.

Encountering Grandmother Care

In the early 2000s, while studying for a master's degree in public health at the University of California, Los Angeles, I spent approximately six weeks over two summers accompanying groups of medical students and clinicians on trips to Nicaragua. The trips were organized to provide free medical care in rural medically underserved communities. My role in these medical delegations (*brigadas*) was to provide translation between medical students and physicians from the United States and their Nicaraguan patients. These encounters took place in makeshift clinics temporarily set up in schools, churches, and community centers, where the UCLA team was accompanied by Nicaraguan Ministry of Health (Ministerio de Salud; MINSA) staff. As a translator in medical contexts, I encountered all the challenges of making sense of not just what patients *said* to clinicians but the cultural *meanings* contained within patients' embodied complaints. Among the most frequent complaints I heard were expressions of various *dolores* (pains) in different parts of the body, such as *dolor en los huesos* (bone pain) and *dolor en los riñones* (kidney pain). While I felt somewhat competent translating complaints that had apparent equivalents to health problems I was familiar with in the United States, one complaint I repeatedly heard, and which I struggled to make sense of through literal translation, was *dolor de cerebro* (brain pain or brain ache). In the space of our makeshift clinical encounters, providers would treat this expression as analogous to "headache" and often prescribe acetaminophen for the pain. However, given the frequency with which I heard the expression, especially among midlife or older-age women, I sensed that something other than a straightforward headache was being expressed by this complaint. When I asked MINSA nurses about *dolor de cerebro*, they affirmed that it was a common expression, at times attributing it to dehydration or other physical causes, eliding possible social determinants or cultural meanings of this pain. I remained skeptical, reluctant to translate *dolor de cerebro* as "headache" without understanding its sociocultural significance for women in this region of rural Nicaragua. When I returned to UCLA, I scanned the library's holdings for references to *dolor de cerebro*, finding only one citation, to an article written decades earlier by transcultural psychiatrists working with Puerto Rican mental health patients (Abad and Boyce 1979). My interest was piqued, as I found myself wanting to move beyond clinical understandings of this pain into the social world of Nicaragua and the political, economic, and cultural factors shaping expressions of emotional distress for Nicaraguan women of the grandmother generation.

This was the motivation that took me back to Nicaragua in 2006 to conduct fieldwork for my master's degree in anthropology, exploring the central question of the cultural meaning of *dolor de cerebro*. During a three-month study, in which I volunteered with local health nongovernmental organizations, assisted with education campaigns against dengue, and interviewed rural women, I found a consistent pattern of women of the grandmother generation situating the pain of *dolor de cerebro* as a response to their daughters' out-migration (Yarris 2011). While unexpected, this finding pushed me to commit to further research on migration as one important social determinant of health and well-being not only for migrants themselves but also for later-adult women of the grandmother generation. Much existing scholarship on migration and transnational families has sidelined the role of grandmothers, usually focusing on nuclear families or on relationships between parents and children. This book expands our understanding of transnational family life across borders and generations by foregrounding the experiences of family members in Nicaragua living with the consequences of migration, especially for grandmothers and the children in their care.

Care, Solidarity, and Sacrifice

During the year of fieldwork on which this book is based, I made my home in Managua, Nicaragua's capital city and a chaotic urban landscape marked by all the contradictions of late modernity: traffic jams of public buses and *carros blindados* (sedans and SUVs with darkened windows), sprawling low-income barrios and newly constructed middle-class tract homes, ambulant street vendors and upscale shopping centers. The city was difficult to navigate, especially on the typically hot days, without a clear city center (Managua's *centro* having been destroyed by an earthquake in 1972) and with directions given by referring to where buildings once stood, before the earthquake (e.g., "dos cuadras al lago de donde antes era el cine"; two blocks toward the lake from where the cinema used to be). And yet, living in the city, I managed to find my way transiting between the small room I rented, the university where I often worked, and family homes I would visit every day.

One morning, months into my fieldwork, when I was scheduled to visit with a grandmother participating in my study, I woke up feeling incredibly ill. I was not surprised, as the social ecology of sickness in Nicaragua was ever apparent among Managua's inhabitants, and my colds and flus usually followed the hot, humid, and rainy seasonal distribution of sickness around me. Not wanting to miss the opportunity to talk with grandmother Angela about her experience as a caregiver for her granddaughter following her daughter Karla's migration, I pulled myself together with difficulty and made the trip across the city and up into the working-class barrio where her house is located. Sitting in our usual white plastic chairs in Angela's neatly swept dirt patio, I found myself overwhelmed by nausea and unable to continue our conversation. Angela recognized my distress and swiftly directed me to her bathroom, telling me not to worry and to stay calm. Embarrassed to have brought my personal sickness and its attendant messiness into Angela's tidy home, I tried to overcome my symptoms without success. Angela took control of the situation, recognizing my incapacity and kindly leading me into her bedroom, insisting I lie down and rest, and telling me not to worry, repeating, "Estás en casa" (You're at home). After a few feeble protests and one last attempt to get up and get myself back to my rented room, I fell onto Angela's bed and into a feverish sleep that lasted nearly the entire day. Every hour or so, I would wake to find Angela serving me a glass of homemade *suero* (a salt, sugar, and water rehydration remedy) or store-bought Gatorade. She would lay her hands on my head and stomach, pray softly, and encourage me by saying I would feel better soon and not to worry, I could stay at her house for as long as I needed.

Needless to say, I was vulnerable in those moments of sickness, physically weak, geographically distant from my own family and support system, and unable to help myself. Angela's care was a practical and powerful remedy—the way she took care of me with such attentiveness left me feeling emotionally moved and immensely humbled. Later that evening, I finally felt strong enough to get out of bed, and I made my way into the living room, where Angela was seated with her granddaughters, Laleska, Alexa, and Reyna. Angela and the girls encouraged me to stay the night, but I insisted I should go home and soon left, departing with words of thanks and an embrace of gratitude. Angela's granddaughters accompanied me to the street and, as I waited under a streetlight for a taxi, I reached into my bag and pulled out forty córdobas (about two dollars), handing it to the girls and asking them to give it to their grandmother to pay for the Gatorade she had purchased for me earlier in the day. The girls responded with a look both perplexed and disapproving. Thirteen-year-old Alexa broke the awkward moment of silence that followed by saying, in a serious tone belying her usually cheerful demeanor, "No, Kristina, esto no se puede pagar" (No, Kristin, you can't pay for this).

This admonition brought to the fore a considerable cultural mistake—my instinct to monetarily compensate Angela's care. My small gesture ran against the values of care that hold Angela's family, and other transnational families, together. Ever the cultural student, I realized that Angela's caregiving that day, just as all the grandmother caregiving I observed throughout my fieldwork, embodied the practical morality of everyday care, sacrifice, and solidarity that were incommensurable with monetary value. This incommensurability, embodied in Alexa's exhortation, "No, Kristina, esto no se puede pagar," contains a central entanglement of care in families of transnational migrants, in which migrant mothers often attempt to compensate for their physical absence by sending remittances but grandmother caregivers distance themselves from material interests, instead emphasizing the moral solidarity and sacrifice that sustains their caregiving. I return to these tensions throughout this book, attempting to unpack the various meanings and motivations of intergenerational care in Nicaraguan transnational families.

Humbled by Alexa's admonition, I put my money away and boarded the next passing taxi, bidding the girls goodnight and telling them to thank their grandmother again for all her care. I drove home in a hazy, still-feverish, contemplation of the deep cultural value of care, of care's ability to foster health and to forge relatedness in the face of human frailty and through the disruptions of transnational migration.

This book draws on an engaged ethnographic exploration of the lives of Nicaraguan families living with migration to illustrate how grandmother care is a powerful response to the troubles of transnational life. Intergenerational care is a practical resource for children and family well-being and a means of upholding cultural values for unity and togetherness, even as families are divided by time, distance, borders, and immigration policies. In the transnational families whose stories form the basis of this book, grandmothers take care of the everyday needs of children of migrant mothers through social reproductive labor—feeding, clothing, schooling, and nursing back to health—while simultaneously engaging in social regeneration by embodying moral values of sacrifice and solidarity through their caregiving. Grandmother care is thus a moral practice of *caring about* and *caring for*, over generations and across borders, that makes transnational family life possible.

Acknowledgments

THIS BOOK IS THE CULMINATION of over a decade of research, writing, and thinking, which has taken place in several communities of support, guidance, and care.

At the University of California, Los Angeles (UCLA), Linda Garro was my PhD supervisor, and this book reflects her teaching, rigorous empiricism, and example of anthropological scholarship on family health and well-being. I am immensely grateful to Nancy Levine for her mentorship and professional guidance and for pushing me to analyze social structure and kinship and also to account for the value of love and commitment in shaping family relationships. My sincerest appreciation goes to my other advisors and teachers in the Department of Anthropology and the School of Public Health at UCLA: Carole Browner, Michael Goldstein, Doug Hollan, Anne Pebley, and Bonnie Taub. My interests in women and gender in Latin America, transnational families, emotional experience, and the social and cultural determinants of health and well-being reflect their collective intellectual influence.

I extend my gratitude to Claudia Galo (coordinator) and all the women of the Red de Mujeres Familiares de Migrantes in Nicaragua for welcoming me and supporting my research and interest in the experiences of women in transnational families. Special thanks go to Karen Gónzalez for her expert insights into Nicaraguan family life, for inviting me to participate in many important cultural events with her family *como si fuera una hermana* (as if I were a sister), and for her friendship. I also thank Marisol Patiño and Tania Barrantes of the Center for Popular Education in Costa Rica for allowing me to participate in their *talleres* (workshops) in Managua on the feminization of migration and the *ruta critica de migración* (critical migration route) from Nicaragua to Costa Rica, and I thank Ligia Arana, director of the Program on Gender and Development at the Universidad Centroamericana for providing me with an academic home during fieldwork. Many thanks go to Norman Medina for his friendship and for conversations about Nicaraguan grandmothers, mothers, fathers, aunts, uncles, children, and families and to his mother for generously opening her home to me on every return visit to Managua.

My thanks go also to my colleagues at Servicio Jesuita para Migrantes (SJM), Nicaragua: Cándida, for her intellectual camaraderie, keen insights into migration's impact on Nicaraguan society, and colleagueship; José Luis, for his astute analysis of migration dynamics in Central America and the politics of Central American migration to the United States and for providing an example of engaged intellectualism; and Félix Noel Vilchez, for being a wonderful *compañero de campo* (fieldwork partner), for weathering the insufferable Nicaraguan heat to help me obtain that one last interview, for our thought-provoking discussions about the affects of Nicaraguan migration on families, and for his expert help transcribing interviews. Finally, I thank all the other volunteers involved in SJM's Campaña para la Defensa y Protección de la Población Migrante for their *solidaridad* (solidarity) and for working to protect the rights of Nicaragua's undocumented migrant communities in Costa Rica, Panama, Mexico, the United States, Spain, and around the world. ¡Qué la lucha continue! (May the struggle continue!)

The field research on which this book is based was supported by the National Science Foundation (Doctoral Dissertation Improvement Grant) and the Fulbright Institute for International Education. My thanks go to the cohort of 2009–2010 Central America and Caribbean Fulbrighters for their support and feedback during fieldwork, especially Ariana Curtis and Courtney Morris, two inspiring women scholars and activists. Grants from the UCLA Center for the Study of Women and the University of Oregon (UO) Center for the Study of Women in Society supported various phases of this research. A faculty fellowship from the Oregon Humanities Center provided me with a welcome term release from teaching in which to focus on manuscript revisions, and support from the UO Underrepresented Minorities Retention Program was essential in providing me with the time and resources to complete this book.

Different pieces of the material contained in this book have been presented at various conferences and workshops, all of which helped me develop my ideas and arguments further. Among these are the 2010 UC Center of Excellence on

Migration and Health workshop at the University of California, San Diego; the 2013 Cascadia Seminar in Medical Anthropology at Simon Frasier University (thanks go to Janelle Taylor and Susan Erikson for organizing the seminar); and the 2014 UO conference on Globalization, Gender and Development (thanks go to Erin Beck for organizing and to Lynn Fujiwara for her comments in that forum). I am thankful for the wise and insightful comments made on papers I presented at several meetings of the American Anthropological Association, especially those by Robert Desjarlais (in 2010), Jessaca Leinaweaver (in 2011), and Janet Carsten (in 2013). I am grateful to have been a regular participant in the UCLA Mind, Medicine and Culture study group from 2001 to 2011 and in the University of California, San Diego, Psychodynamic seminar from 2011 to 2012; both forums sharpened my interpretive perspective and theoretical approach. Parts of Chapter 3 were published in *Culture, Medicine, and Psychiatry*; I thank the anonymous reviewers and editors at *Culture, Medicine, and Psychiatry* for their comments and the Society for Psychological Anthropology for awarding me the 2015 Stirling Prize for that article.

This book reflects support and exchanges with terrific colleagues—although we are spread across state and national borders, our ongoing communications and collaborations invigorate my thinking and push me to be a better scholar. I specifically thank María Claudia Duque-Páramo, at the Universidad Pontificia de Bogotá, Colombia, for her work with children of migrants and for keeping me grounded and mindful of what really matters about our work; Heide Castañeda for her mentorship and for our shared thinking about migration, humanitarianism, and deservedness; Lauren Heidbrink for her research on Central American children and the inconsistencies of U.S. immigration policies; Jessaca Leinaweaver for her groundbreaking work on kinship, child circulation, and migration in the Latin American context; and Emily Mendenhall for her energy and encouragement to keep academic work fun (ever since our shared summer at the 2008 National Science Foundation research methods camp). I extend thanks to Sarah Willen for reading drafts of chapters for this book and sharing of drafts of her book chapters and for her theoretical insights into the moral economies of migration. Thanks also go to Whitney Duncan for our mutual exchanges of book chapters and for her comments on early drafts of several chapters of this book. Many thanks also go to Ana Paula Pimentel Walker for her indefatigable friendship and for our conversations about Latin American politics and our interdisciplinary work as anthropologists.

I also extend heartfelt appreciation to my colleagues in the Care and the Life Course writing group—Elana Buch, Laura Heinemann, Julia Kowalski, Jessica Robbins-Ruszkowski, and Aaron Seaman—for our exchanges about gender, aging, care, kinship, and reproductive inequalities and for their thoughtful feedback on early versions of nearly every chapter of this book.

At UO, I am most grateful to Iván Sandoval-Cervantes for his research assistance and support during the final preparations of this book, as well as for our conversations about care, relatedness, kinship, gender, and migration. Many thanks go to Lynn Stephen for her expert comments on early drafts of two chapters, for her continued mentorship, and for providing an inspiring example of a politically engaged anthropology of Latino/a America. Thanks go to Lamia Karim for providing useful reminders about remaining focused on book writing during busy teaching terms and while facing all the demands of university service. I thank my students at UO who read and engaged with pieces of this work, most especially Nicolette Dent for her diligent and helpful assistance completing revisions to various chapters. Thanks go to the Américas Research Interest Group for reading and commenting on an early chapter. I also appreciate all my colleagues in the Narrative, Health, and Social Justice Research Interest Group—Daphne Gallagher, Melissa Graboyes, Elizabeth Reis, and Mary Wood—for their astute, critical thinking about the role of history, culture, and power in shaping illness, healing, and medicine and for their practical support and care as I struggled through the various intellectual, emotional, and physical challenges that accompanied the writing of this book.

I am indebted to the anonymous reviewers at Stanford University Press who carefully read versions of this manuscript and provided helpful suggestions for revisions. I am incredibly grateful to my wonderful editor at the press, Michelle Lipinski, who believed in this project from the beginning and provided guidance that helped me make this a stronger book and a more compelling argument about the value of intergenerational care in transnational families.

My sincere wish is that this book authentically portrays the experiences of all the grandmothers I know in Nicaragua. I thank them for sharing their lives, their homes, their tears, and their care with me.

Care Across Generations

Introduction

Solidaridad: Nicaraguan Migration and Intergenerational Care

Vivo en dos mundos, y en cada uno mi vida es diferente pero cruzada por los elementos constantes de mi historia. (I live in two worlds, and in each one my life is different but joined by the constant elements of my history.)
— Gioconda Belli, *El país bajo mi piel*

ON A SPRING MORNING in 2010, I accompanied grandmothers Angela and Marbeya on a trip from their neighborhood in a working-class barrio to the campus of the Universidad Centroamericana in the center of Nicaragua's capital city, Managua. We stepped out of our shared taxi and walked across a scorching hot parking lot into the shockingly cool, air-conditioned studio of the university's radio station, Radio Universidad. In their fifties, Angela and Marbeya are mothers of migrant daughters and primary caregivers for grandchildren in transnational families. (Figure I.1 illustrates the intergenerational relations in Marbeya's and Angela's transnational families.) The women had come to record their stories as grandmother caregivers on a weekly public radio broadcast, called *La mochila viajera* (The traveling backpack), part of the public education efforts of a migrant-serving Nicaraguan nongovernmental organization (NGO). The three of us shared anticipatory small talk as we entered the soundproof room of the recording studio. Despite our hours of preparation in their living rooms, Angela and Marbeya were anxious about sharing their stories publicly, and they sat down in front of the microphones with a combination of nervous excitement and reluctant discomfort. I began to wonder whether it had been a good idea to invite them to be interviewed for this radio program.

Several weeks earlier, I had brought the women's granddaughters, Laleska (age eleven) and Vanessa (age fourteen), into this same studio to share their experiences as children of migrant mothers. Angela's daughter (Laleska's mother) Karla had lived in Miami, Florida, for over ten years; Marbeya's daughter (Vanessa's mother) Azucena had lived in San José, Costa Rica, for more than twelve years, and both girls had a lot to say about living with their mothers' absence,

1

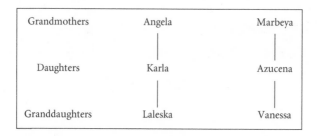

Grandmothers	Angela	Marbeya
Daughters	Karla	Azucena
Granddaughters	Laleska	Vanessa

Figure I.1 Angela's and Marbeya's kin and care relations

their grandmothers' care, and the response of the community around them. While the interview was emotional at times for Laleska and Vanessa, the girls had ultimately enjoyed telling their stories for the radio program and had encouraged their grandmothers to do the same. So it was that Angela and Marbeya came into the studio that day to record their stories as grandmother caregivers in families of migrant mothers.[1]

After introductions, the radio hosts began the program by outlining Nicaraguan migration dynamics. They recounted the facts surrounding the increasing feminization of migration: 51 percent of migrants are women, a majority in their twenties and thirties, and many leave children in Nicaragua when they migrate. The radio hosts described the dynamics of migrant women's labor—that most Nicaraguan women migrants find employment in the domestic service sector in receiving-country economies and thus come to form part of what has been referred to by various scholars as global chains of caregiving labor (Hochschild 2000; Parreñas 2000; Ehrenreich and Hochschild 2004; Yeates 2005).

However, the focus of the radio show that day was not on women who migrate but instead on those who stay behind—grandmother caregivers in transnational families. Marbeya and Angela described how, as grandmothers, they were committed to raising their granddaughters as if they were their own daughters ("como si fueran mis hijas"), investing time and energy toward their grandchildren's well-being in Nicaragua while their daughters labored abroad. In their radio interview, the emotional impact of migration cast a long shadow over Marbeya's and Angela's descriptions of their lives as grandmother caregivers. Marbeya described her daughter's migration to Costa Rica more than ten years earlier as "an emotional blow [un golpe emocional]," her voice interrupted by tears as she recalled falling into a depressive state and then eventually coping with her daughter's ongoing absence. When the radio host asked Angela about her daughter's migration, Angela focused on her distance, describing how for the more than ten years that Karla had lived in the United States, visits home were nearly impossible because of high costs of travel and her lack of legal documentation. When asked by the radio host what this meant for her and her family, Angela reiterated that the migration of her daughter had resulted in a distinct impact on her life, saying, "It's not the same as having her here [No es lo mismo que tenerla aquí]." For both women, transnational migration has upended cultural expectations of gender and care; rather than assuming roles as care recipients, counting on their adult daughters to care for them in later life, these women instead find themselves assuming new roles as care providers, raising another generation of children, in their words, "almost as if we were mothers all over again [casí como si fueramos madres de nuevo]."

And yet despite the disruptions and distresses of migration, Marbeya and Angela's radio interview called attention to the importance of their intergenerational care as a resource for well-being in transnational families. For instance, the women described how they carefully allocate the remittances their daughters send home twice a month to their granddaughters' school fees, food, and health care. As they talked about remittances and caregiving, the grandmothers emphasized their sacrifices—forgoing personal desires and needs for the sake of their grandchildren—which mirror the sacrifices made by their migrant daughters. Care in these transnational families becomes a resource extended across generations, a shared responsibility of mothers, who sacrifice through migration, employment, and the sending of remittances from abroad, and grandmothers, who sacrifice through being present and providing care for another generation of children in Nicaragua.

Care Across Generations takes a close, ethnographic look at grandmother care in transnational families, examining on the one hand the structural and gendered inequalities that motivate migration and caregiving and on the other the cultural values that sustain intergenerational care and give it meaning. This book contributes to migration scholarship by broadening our analysis beyond the parent-child relation, situating care across generations and in the kin networks in sending countries that are so important to maintaining transnational family ties. This analysis of grandmother caregiving also contributes to contemporary anthropological theorizing about care, by asserting that care is best understood as both the gendered labor of social reproduction and the moral value of cultural regeneration across generations. The significance of intergenerational care is located here both within the lives of families divided by borders and within the Nicaraguan cultural values for solidarity and sacrifice. Rather than casting the consequences of women's migration in migrant-sending countries solely in terms of a "care deficit" (Hochschild 2000: 136), this analysis of intergenerational reconfigurations of care shows that care serves as a resource for the well-being of children and other family members who stay behind after transnational migration. Moving our perspective across borders, into migrant-origin communities, and over generations, into extended kin networks, *Care Across Generations* shows the social and moral value of intergenerational care for contemporary transnational families.

Global Care and Grandmothers

Incorporating an intergenerational perspective, we come to see how grandmothers are central actors in the material and moral economies of global migration and care. Grandmothers like Angela and Marbeya participate in global relations of care, even if they never leave Nicaragua, by raising grandchildren while mothers labor abroad in domestic or service sectors. The globalization of the "care economy" (Leinaweaver 2010: 68) results from demographic, social, and economic shifts in migrant-receiving countries—women's entry into the formal workforce, aging populations in need of care, and divestment in public programs that support caregiving for children and other dependents—all of which have contributed to a demand for care that has largely been met by low-paid, immigrant women workers (Ehrenreich and Hochschild 2004; Parreñas 2000, 2001). As women migrate to become paid caregivers abroad in the Global North, they leave behind what has been called a "care deficit" in countries of the Global South (Hochschild 2000: 136). Feminist scholars have described the globalization of women's reproductive labor as constituting a "global care chain" (Yeates 2012: 136; also see Ehrenreich and Hochschild 2004). While analyses of the feminization of global migration highlight the importance of immigrant women's caregiving for domestic and national economies in the Global North (Sassen 1998; Parreñas 2001, 2005), relatively little attention has been focused on the care that women in the Global South provide for children and families left behind by transnational processes of labor migration. In contemporary Latin America, for example, women make up more than 50 percent of contemporary migrants (Pessar 2003), and most of these women work in service industries (such as domestic workers) in destination countries. And yet the care provided by surrogate caregivers in migrant-origin countries has been relatively underanalyzed.

While this framing of care transfer from poorer to wealthier nations through a "global care chain" (Yeates 2005: 232; see also Hochschild 2000) importantly recognizes the drain on caregiving resources that follows women's migration, it fails to acknowledge the care work accomplished through extended kin and intergenerational networks in families of migrant mothers. The care-deficit frame is an illustration of how existing migration scholarship has elided extended families and focused nearly exclusively on the bonds between biological parents and children.

The concept of care circulation offers a way of moving beyond dichotomous views of care transfer in the global economy by highlighting social relations of care in transnational families (Baldassar and Merla 2014: 6). Whereas the care *chains* concept may reify a binary push-and-pull model of migration and care—from sites where low-wage care labor is available (in the Global South) to sites where this care labor becomes exploited (in the Global North) (see Hochschild 2000; Parreñas 2001, 2005)—care *circulation* attempts to capture the ways care connects people across borders through asymmetrical and yet reciprocal flows of caregiving (Baldassar and Merla 2014: 8). This vision of care in circulation mirrors an earlier generation of critiques by migration studies that found binary models of immigration understood in terms of push-pull factors, origin-destination countries, and assimilation and acculturation problematic for their reification of migration as a linear process overly determined by the nation-state. Scholars of transnationalism have instead argued for a framing of migration that captured the circuitous and simultaneous nature of social fields extended across national borders, such as those found in transnational families (Levitt and Glick Schiller 2004; Stephen 2007).[2]

The idea of care in circulation helps reveal the ways intergenerational care in Nicaraguan transnational families is a dynamic resource for social regeneration without losing sight of the structural and gendered inequalities that shape migration and care. First, contemporary Nicaraguan migration flows both North and South, following lines of inequality and relative economic opportunity in historically contingent ways. Therefore, this is not just a study of a chain of care flowing from Global South to North but rather an examination of how care in the migrant-sending country of Nicaragua is reconfigured across generations in response to transnational migration, which is influenced by political and economic opportunities. Second, grandmother caregiving is one dimension of the care that circulates in Nicaraguan transnational families, because mothers continue to care for children and families from abroad, albeit by responding to the realities of migration and renegotiating roles of motherhood. Migrant mothers care for their children in Nicaragua from a distance by remaining *pendiente*, or responsible, for families back home by sending remittances home and using Internet and cell phone communication to stay in touch (Baldassar 2007). Similarly, grandmothers respond to the disruptions of migration by re-configuring cultural expectations and extending care across generations, caring for their grandchildren and in this way supporting their migrant daughters through the embodied values of sacrifice and solidarity. Thus, analyzing grand-mother care in the context of transnational family life reveals the contingencies that shape care provision after mother migration, thereby denaturalizing as-sumptions about gender and care while reinforcing care's value as a means of social organization across generations.[3]

Applying an intergenerational perspective to care in transnational families moves the analytical frame outward, beyond the nuclear family model that has predominated in studies of transnational families.[4] Indeed, when grandmoth-ers have been acknowledged in studies of transnational families, they have of-ten been relegated to the background as "middlewomen" negotiating between children and parents (Dreby 2010: 33). In these analyses, the biological-parent (especially mother) and child tie remains primordial, and grandmother (or grandparent) care is analyzed as a temporary, and perhaps inadequate, sub-stitute. Such a framing further stigmatizes transnational families rather than viewing migration, absence, and distance as central features of contemporary family forms in their own right (Baldassar and Merla 2014: 6). Rather than reify the mother-child tie, or any one family form for that matter, in this book I seek to uncover the gendered cultural expectations that shape motherhood and migration and, by extension, grandmotherhood and care, expectations that women negotiate as they assume responsibilities for another generation of children. Certainly, grandmothers do invest emotional energy in supporting transnational mother-child relationships, in so doing reaffirming the cultural importance of this kin relationship. But grandmothers form strong emotional ties with their grandchildren in mother absence, reconfiguring kin ties that complicate the already-ambivalent prospect of family reunification via chil-dren's migration to join mothers abroad. I seek, then, to decenter the mother-child tie and destigmatize grandmother care and transnational families while still acknowledging the particular stresses and strains of family life extended across borders.

The intergenerational perspective advanced here also engages with migration as a temporal as well as spatial process. As Cati Coe argues, migration reconfigures time and temporalities, because members of transnational families come to reconcile differing cultural expectations for care across the life course (Coe 2015). In their insightful volume on age and globalization, Jennifer Cole and Deborah Durham (2007) argue that the changing cultural scripts of aging and the life course should be central to anthropological analyses of contemporary globalization. Similarly, as we see throughout this book, grandmother care emerges out of temporal disjunctures between how Nicaraguan women anticipated living later adulthood (with the support and copresent care of their adult daughters) and how this expectation is challenged by women's transnational migration and subsequent intergenerational reconfiguration of care. Furthermore, grandmothers experience other temporal dimensions of migration, most centrally the uncertainty surrounding the future of either migrant return or child reunification with mothers abroad.

Nicaraguan Migration Dynamics: Effects on Grandmothers and Families Who Stay

To understand the experiences of grandmothers, children, and other members of Nicaraguan transnational families, it is important to first review the historical and political dynamics shaping contemporary Nicaraguan migration. Migrant destinations matter for members of transnational families, because geographic distance, host-country attitude toward migrants, and immigration policies shape the experiences not only of migrants but also of family members who stay behind. While some of the dynamics around sending and receiving countries described here are particular to Nicaragua (e.g., that Costa Rica is a major destination), other patterns described for this Nicaragua case have much broader, even global, relevance for studies of transnational migration. These include the broader themes of (1) economic inequality as a determinant of migratory flows and (2) migrant illegality as a factor shaping the experiences not only of migrants themselves but also of family members back home.

In this book I use "migrant sending" (i.e., the home country or country of origin) and "migrant receiving" (i.e., the destination or host country) judiciously and cognizant of their limitations. Although pervasive in migration literature, the adjective "sending"—as in "sending household" or "sending community"—implies a sense of volition that is problematic for a number of reasons. First, this phrase reflects a tendency to view migration as the product of a rational, cost-benefit analysis conducted at the level of the household in which members supposedly determine who has the best prospects of success as a migrant and then send this individual, trusting that his or her success will ultimately benefit the entire family (E. Taylor 1999). The choice to migrate is often made not by families as collectives but by individual migrants, albeit through the influence of social networks—peers, family members, and friends, many of whom have also migrated. Second, viewing migration as a choice when migrants are leaving contexts of chronic poverty and social insecurity fails to recognize how migration is always a decision constrained by structural factors in the political economy. On the other hand, as my Nicaraguan colleague José Luis Rocha has argued (2006, 2009), "sending," as in Nicaragua is a sending country, may rightly capture the notion that countries of origin "send" (Rocha uses the verb *expulsar*, "to expel") migrants because of state failure to provide economic opportunity and protect social security for their populations.

For decades, the United States has been a major destination for Nicaraguan migrants. The 1979 Nicaraguan Revolution brought the Sandinistas to power, and many former allies or functionaries of the Somoza regime fled the country and sought political asylum in the United States.[5] After the initial exodus and throughout the 1980s, hundreds of thousands of poor and working-class Nicaraguans continued to emigrate to the United States, fleeing the political violence of the Contra War. These migrants settled in cities such as Miami, Los Angeles, San Francisco, and Houston (Lancaster 1992). Because the U.S. government viewed the Sandinista regime as hostile to U.S. interests, many among this wave of migrants were able to apply for political asylum.[6] In 1997, the U.S. Congress passed the Nicaraguan Adjustment and Central American Relief Act (NACARA), which granted legal residency to some 55,000 Nicaraguans who had entered the United States before December 1, 1995 (Rocha 2006). Migration flows to the United States have leveled off since the 1990s, with an estimated 395,000 Nicaraguans living in the United States as of 2011 (Brown and Patten 2013). Many Nicaraguan migrants who became legal residents under NACARA were subsequently able to petition for residency visas for family members, making this wave of migrants to the United States more stable than subsequent generations, who have had fewer opportunities to regularize their status. (These dynamics of legality and illegality in the United States shape the experience of transnational families across generations, as is illustrated by the story of Angela's family in Chapter 4.)

During the period of research for this book (2009–2010), most Nicaraguans referred to the global economic recession that began in 2008 as La Crisis. This crisis made it difficult to attract foreign investment and find markets for Nicaraguan goods abroad, leading to the loss of jobs and wage stagnation. These dynamics pushed out-migration, positioning most contemporary Nicaraguan migrants into the category of economic migrants, or those who seek greater income-earning opportunities outside their country of origin (Baumeister 2006). Nonetheless, the term "economic migrant" is problematic, both because it glosses over the complicated, intertwined constraints and challenges—political, economic, and social—that shape migration and because economic migrants are deemed to move voluntarily and therefore are often not granted political protection or social support.[7] Approximately forty thousand Nicaraguans have been migrating annually since 2000, with a total of one out of every ten Nicaraguans currently living outside their country of birth (Andersen and Christensen 2009). In this period, and mirroring global patterns, women compose an increasing proportion of transnational migrants. Whereas before 1990, 56 percent of Nicaraguan migrants were men, from 1990 to 2001 the ratios of male and female migrants were nearly equal, a trend that continues (Torres and Barahona 2004: 37).

Contemporary Nicaraguan migration flows are also characterized by what can be called a South–South regional dynamic, with more than three-quarters of a million Nicaraguans residing as migrants in Costa Rica and Panama combined (Servicio Jesuita para Migrantes de Centroamérica 2009). Central American migration is regulated in part through an international agreement of the Central America–4 countries (El Salvador, Guatemala, Honduras, and Nicaragua) that makes it possible for citizens of any CA-4 country to travel to any other CA-4 country with only a national identification card (no passport or work permit is needed). However, and notably, both Costa Rica and Panama have refused to sign on to the CA-4 agreement, instead requiring border crossers to hold passports, work visas, or other legal authorization for entry. What this means is that most Nicaraguan migrants living in Costa Rica and Panama are undocumented—vulnerable given their "illegal" social status. These precarious realities are shared by family members back home, who experience the prolonged and uncertain periods of separation provoked by illegality and the emotional uncertainties surrounding migrant visits or returns.

Costa Rica, Nicaragua's neighbor to the south, is the main destination of contemporary Nicaraguan migrants but is hostile toward them. An estimated half a million Nicaraguans live in Costa Rica, although the actual number is probably much higher, given that the majority lack legal documentation and therefore often go uncounted (Servicio Jesuita para Migrantes de Centroamérica 2009). While male migrants usually find employment in Costa Rica as construction workers, in agriculture, or as security guards, women's employment options are concentrated in the service sector, working as *domésticas* (household domestic laborers) or as *estéticas* (workers in beauty salons). The border checkpoint between the two countries at Peñas Blancas—the only official crossing point—is a small outpost of a concrete building, through which all travelers must pass, waiting in one of several lines to show their passports and visas to border authorities. Nicaraguans without documents avoid this checkpoint and travel illicitly into Costa Rica, risking the dangers of passage, which include robbery, assault, or capture by Costa Rican immigration officials. Some Nicaraguans enter Costa Rica in an authorized manner, often using thirty-day tourist visas (which require filing paperwork and paying a thirty-dollar processing fee at the Costa Rican embassy in Managua, a cost beyond the means of many migrants). Those migrants who enter "legally" with tourist visas or temporary work permits and then stay end up undocumented and vulnerable to the discrimination and exploitation that accompanies their unauthorized status.[8]

Social exclusion of Nicaraguans in Costa Rica is a politically incendiary issue with real impacts for family members in Nicaragua. Nationalist and xenophobic stereotypes stigmatize Nicaraguan migrants, who are accused of taking jobs away from Costa Ricans or taking advantage of publicly funded social services (Baumeister 2006; Rocha 2008; Goldade 2009). Nicaraguan women working in domestic service in Costa Rica are triply marginalized, as undocumented migrants, as women, and by the isolation that characterizes domestic employment (Torres and Barahona 2004: 10).[9] Grandmothers and other family members hear of the discrimination and abuse directed at migrants and worry about the safety and security of their loved ones living in Costa Rica, fretting at even a day's delay in a phone call, text message, or *envío* (transfer) of remittances. Even though their migrant member is living in a geographically proximate, neighboring country, families in Nicaragua experience the distance and uncertainty of prolonged separation, as unauthorized migrants find it difficult to return home to visit, facing the risky prospect of two border crossings (to enter and return).

Increasingly restrictive immigration legislation in Costa Rica has ripple effects for family members of migrants in Nicaragua. In the first decade of the

2000s, Costa Rica passed several immigration laws, largely modeled after restrictive U.S. policies, that increase border securitization and create obstacles for migrants seeking to obtain permanent residency. One such law placed a time limit on applications for adjustment of status and established exclusions to public services such as health care for undocumented migrants (Goldade 2009).[10] As a result, migrants find it ever more difficult to regularize their status, complicating their plans to return to visit Nicaragua or bring family members to Costa Rica using the family reunification visa process. In response, a movement in Nicaragua, particularly among young people, uses popular culture to raise awareness about the threats facing migrants in Costa Rica and create a counternarrative of nonmigration.[11]

Panama is the second major regional destination for Nicaraguan migrants and also presents a complicated case of a host country with a climate of accepting unauthorized migrants to fill low-wage service sector jobs while excluding them from mainstream society. Panama became an important destination country for Nicaraguans especially after La Crisis of 2008 reduced employment opportunities in Costa Rica and pushed migrants farther south in search of jobs. While there are no reliable estimates of the numbers of Nicaraguan migrants in Panama, best estimates are at tens of thousands, many of whom have been lured by friends or family members who emigrated, settled, and sent for others in their social networks to join them (Rocha 2006, 2009). Panama, like Costa Rica, is not a signatory to the CA-4 agreement; therefore, all migrants entering must possess a passport and a temporary visa or work permit to enter "legally." Those without legal documents enter or remain in the country as unauthorized migrants, relegated to lower-paying jobs, their in-country mobility limited to the immigrant enclaves in which they live and the high-rise buildings in which they work as domésticas, construction workers, or security guards. This infrastructure of illegality also shapes the experiences of family members in Nicaragua, as migrants trapped in lower-paid jobs have less disposable income to send home to family members and, since a lack of legal documents makes it difficult to visit home, must endure prolonged absence and separation.

In addition to migration to the United States and intraregional migration, another major destination for Nicaraguan migrants is Spain. Of the approximately eight thousand Nicaraguan migrants living in Spain, the vast majority are women who work as caregivers in private homes for children and elder adults (Pérez 2013). Most of these women were drawn to Spain through the influence of social networks: friends, neighbors, and family members who had emigrated and who encouraged them to do the same, offering them temporary housing and helping them find employment. While Spain offers migrants the attraction of relatively higher-paying work in a Spanish-speaking European country, it also imposes transatlantic distance between migrants and family members in Nicaragua, making visits home nearly impossible and the prospect of reunification highly uncertain. Nonetheless, migration to Spain from Nicaragua is increasing, migrants lured in part by "travel agencies" that specialize in arranging for women to enter Spain with tourist visas and then connecting them to domestic service work, charging exorbitant fees, upward of $6,000, to do so.[12]

The dynamics of migrant illegality augment the worries, fears, and uncertainties of family members in Nicaragua. Nicaraguans traveling south to Costa Rica or Panama and north to the United States face journeys made precarious by restrictive immigration policies and heightened border security, making border transit ever-more clandestine and dangerous (Cornelius 2006). For Nicaraguans and other Central Americans, migration north to the United States requires passing through Mexico, a dangerous middle passage, or transit country, where migrants face extortion by human smugglers, abuse by Mexican immigration authorities, and violence perpetrated by armed parastate actors (Arregui and Roman 2005; Rocha 2006; Vogt 2013). The illegalization of migration also results in large numbers of deportations; approximately 1,600 Nicaraguans were forcibly removed from the United States just in 2009; for these migrants, Mexico becomes a country of transit on their way south, during uncertain returns home (Servicio Jesuita para Migrantes de Centroamérica 2009). Despite these risks, and largely owing to their economic desperation, Nicaraguans continue to *probar la suerte* (try their luck) by migrating north, leaving family members back home in their own state of limbo, worrying about migrants' safety in passage and often suffering prolonged periods with no communication with their migrant member.

Fifteen grandmothers' stories form the basis of this book; all are women living in Nicaragua and are primary caregivers for children of mother migrants. (In fact, there were a total of eighteen mother migrants in these families, since one grandmother had three migrant daughters and another had two.) The grandmothers in this study also have a variety of extended kin relations and household configurations, and they experience different levels of support from nonmigrant adult children. (I describe these kin relations further in Chapter 1.) The destinations of the mothers in the fifteen families reflect contemporary Nicaraguan migration patterns described above: seven live in Costa Rica, three live in the United States, three in Panama, three in Spain, one in Mexico, and one in Guatemala. (See Figure I.2; also see Table A.1 for descriptive information on study families.) The duration of mother migration (time elapsed since initial departure) for the families ranges from less than one year to more than ten years. (See Figure I.3.)

Destination and duration of migration for family members in Nicaragua shape the possibilities of return visits or reunification and contour family members' experiences of distance, absence, and separation. As illustrated in Figure I.2, the modal length of mother migration among families in this study is between one and three years. (Of course, migration continues past the period of this research, and so these figures are only a glimpse of its duration). A few migrants had left within a year of the study, meaning migration was relatively new for family members in Nicaragua. However, most had migrated several years before the study, with three living abroad for more than ten years. In these cases of longer duration of migration, family members become more accustomed to the distance and absence that characterize transnational family life, adapting to the rhythms of uncertain visits and futures. Some families hold on to the possibility of family reunification of children and mothers abroad;

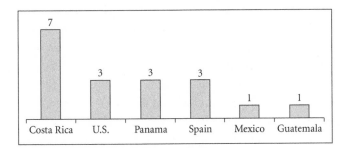

Figure I.2 Number of mother migrants in each destination country

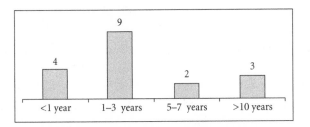

Figure I.3 Number of mother migrants by duration of migration

other families seem more determined that children will not leave Nicaragua. When migration has lasted more than a decade, what was initially assumed to be a temporary shift in care following migration has become a permanent reconfiguration across generations, with grandmothers forming strong ties to children in their care, ties that further complicate prospects and consequences of mother-child reunification.

In addition to destination and duration of migration, migrants' legal status abroad can be a worry to their family members in Nicaragua. About half the migrant members of the families in this book left Nicaragua without legal documents (work permits or residency visas). Other migrants departed with legal documents (tourist visas or temporary work permits) that subsequently expired, leaving them in an "illegal" limbo. At the time of this study, four of the mother migrants (usually those who had lived abroad for longer periods) had secured legal status (three in the United States and one in Costa Rica), either through residency petitions, from marriage-based visas, or on the grounds of reunification with family members abroad. For the eleven families of migrants without legal status, grandmothers' worries about the effect of migration on their family life are exacerbated by concerns over their daughters' safety and security abroad.

In all these families, grandmothers manage their migrant daughters' desires to reunify with their children alongside the prospect of their own emotional loss that reunification between mothers and children represents, given the strong ties they have formed with children in mothers' absence. Confronted with these uncertainties and ambivalences, grandmothers continue to provide care, an embodiment of their commitment to participate in the shared sacrifice of migration. In this way, mother migrants and grandmother caregivers reconfigure relations of care to foster family solidarity despite the tensions and uncertainties of transnational family life.

Solidaridad: A Political Ethos and Cultural Value in Nicaragua

Woven throughout the stories of transnational families told in this book is the importance of solidaridad (solidarity) as a value motivating and reinforced by the assumption of care by grandmothers. Grandmothers draw on solidarity and sacrifice to motivate their care in response to the precariousness of their daughters' migrant lives and to the threats migration poses to culturally valued family unity. While other studies of global migration and family life have referred to the importance of solidarity in shaping family relations, the meaning of solidarity has been relatively underexamined by migration scholars.[13] Solidarity has powerful significance as an orienting value for families facing the threats of political and economic violence and social insecurity and uncertainty. One Nicaraguan intellectual has described *solidaridad* as "a noble feeling that makes us react in the face of the needs and pains of others, in a generous, cooperative, and committed way" (Habed López 2007).[14] Solidaridad in this cultural valence refers to a disposition of, an alignment with, and an attending to the needs and struggles (material and moral) of other human beings that are irreducible to personal or material interests. Instead, solidaridad is understood as a value strengthened in the face of collective adversity. It is in this sense that solidaridad comes to have significance within Nicaraguan families facing the disruption and uncertainty of transnational migration. Solidaridad provides meaning for migrants themselves, who leave Nicaragua to labor abroad, making a personal sacrifice for the sake of their children and families, and solidaridad motivates grandmother caregivers in Nicaragua, who stay behind after migration and assume the responsibility of caring for another generation of children.

Solidaridad, Revolution, and U.S. Intervention

While a complete historical analysis of solidaridad in Nicaragua could go back centuries, I focus here on how this particular cultural value was shaped during the past half century, particularly in response to the Nicaraguan Revolution.[15] In the 1970s and 1980s, solidarity was connected to social and cultural survival, as Nicaraguans fought a war of resistance and independence against a U.S.-backed dictator (Anastasio Somoza) and then struggled to maintain their revolutionary ideals despite U.S. intervention (during the Contra War). In this period, the Sandinistas (Frente Sandinista de Liberación Nacional, or FSLN; Sandinista National Liberation Front) organized as an armed guerrilla insurgency opposing decades'-long control by the Somoza dynasty. Somoza rule was plagued by political corruption and economic control; the government favored large landowners, industrialists, and foreign capitalists, implementing economic policies that marginalized the urban poor and rural campesinos. Inspired by international postcolonial movements and Latin American revolutionary ideologies, the Sandinistas developed a unique political philosophy that combined elements of Marxism, social democracy, feminism, and revolutionary Christianity (Lancaster 1992; Babb 2001a). Throughout the 1970s, many Sandinista leaders and intellectuals settled in exile in Costa Rica, where they strategized and organized to overthrow the Somoza regime. During this period, international solidarity took the form of social justice, religious and leftist groups providing material support to Sandinistas both in exile and inside Nicaragua, a period described in the captivating writing of Nicaraguan intellectual Gioconda Belli (2002). After years of organizing, and despite violent repression by Somoza's infamous Guardía Nacional (National Guard), the FSLN successfully ousted Anastasio Somoza Debayle and took control of Managua on July 19, 1979. El 19 de Julio is a venerated national holiday in Nicaragua, commemorating the victory of popular rebellion and national solidarity over the forces of dictatorship and imperialism.

During the 1980s, solidaridad from the international community continued to support Sandinista revolutionary programs to redistribute wealth and land to the poor and to achieve universal literacy and health care access. Tomás Borge, cofounder of the FSLN and a leader of the Nicaraguan Revolution, has said, "¿De dónde provienen las esperanzas del Tercer Mundo? De la solidaridad internacional, a la que los nicaragüenses hemos llamado la ternura de los pueblos y que reaviva nuestras fuerzas" (From where do the hopes of the Third World come? From international solidarity, from what we Nicaraguans have called the affection of the people, that which reanimates our strength). Indeed, as opposition from the U.S. government to the Sandinista movement mounted, U.S. citizens expressed their solidaridad with the Nicaraguan people—for instance, by forming delegations and traveling to Nicaragua to learn from Nicaraguans' revolutionary process and document the impacts of U.S. intervention.[16] The FSLN also built on Nicaragua's Christian base communities (*comunidades eclesiásticas de base*) and on liberation theology in furthering their commitment to social justice and economic redistribution.[17] Solidaridad thus acquired the moral meanings associated with what Paul Farmer has described as the "preferential option for the poor" characterizing the liberation theology of Vatican II (Farmer 2003: 141). The anthropologist Roger Lancaster describes this period in Nicaragua as a time of hope and optimism, when "Nicaraguans en masse struggled heroically, armed only with class solidarity and collective will, to build the sort of society that would reflect popular interests" (Lancaster 1992: 9). Additionally, during the first years of the Sandinista period, feminists pushed the FSLN to include gender equity as a central part of the revolution, leading to initial reforms to family law and policy granting women and children greater rights (Kampwirth 2004). Solidaridad was instantiated by the FSLN in discourse and in practice as a clear alignment with the less privileged: campesinos, women, youth, and the poor.

However, despite its ideological and pragmatic goals, the Sandinista revolution encountered an enormous foe in the United States, which backed the Contra War. In a climate of Cold War ideological division, the Sandinista revolution was characterized by the United States as communist and hostile to U.S. interests in the region. By 1981, the Ronald Reagan administration imposed an economic embargo on Nicaragua and began to illicitly support military destabilization through *contrarevolucionarios*, or the Contras. Fighting the Contras required the Sandinistas to divert a large proportion of the national budget to military defense, undermining their capacity to invest in popular social programs. As Lancaster describes it, "The will, the dignity, the resolve, and the faith of a people were under attack, and Washington's war inflicted costs that could not be borne" (Lancaster 1992: 7). Weakened by war and a concomitant erosion of popular support, the Sandinistas faced opposition in national elections in 1990, which resulted in Sandinista defeat and the presidency of U.S.-backed Violeta Chamorro. Chamorro implemented economic policies reflecting the Washington Consensus, or economic neoliberal prescriptions, designed by U.S.-backed international financial institutions such as the World Bank and International Monetary Fund to shrink the role of the state, cut social spending, and open markets for foreign capital investment (Babb 2001a, 2001b). Structural adjustment policies slashed public spending on programs such as health care and education that the FSLN had worked to develop. These economic transformations resulted in unemployment, wage stagnation, widespread poverty, and social despair—aptly described by the title of Lancaster's classic ethnography of Nicaragua during the early 1990s, *Life Is Hard* (1992). Many Nicaraguans in the 1990s were pushed to leave their country as migrants in search of security and opportunity abroad.

Solidarity Rebranded: Cristiana, Socialista, Solidaria

Solidaridad has been revitalized as part of official government discourse, implying alignment with the new Latin American left, solidarity with the poor, and a regional development strategy independent of U.S. influence. In 2006, Nicaragua's neoliberal period was ended by the controversial elections that brought President Daniel Ortega back to power.[18] Soon after taking office, Ortega made a clear break with neoliberal policies, allying Nicaragua with Venezuela and the late Venezuelan president Hugo Chávez's Alianza Bolivariana para los Pueblos de Nuestra América (ALBA; Bolivarian Alliance for the Peoples of Our America). Chávez, Ortega, and Cuba's president Fidel Castro positioned ALBA as an overtly anti-imperialist development program that would be a radical departure from the Washington Consensus, independent of international financial institutions, and work in favor of the poorest sectors of society.[19] President Ortega's political discourse is decidedly anti-American; in speeches he refers to the United States as the "imperial power" and to its economic system as "savage capitalism." Ortega adopted the new FSLN slogan *Cristiana, Socialista, Solidaria,* which is plastered all over Managua and the Nicaraguan countryside on posters and billboards in bright pink, the new official color of the FSLN. (At the time of the 1979 revolution and during the decades following the 1990 Sandinista electoral defeat, the official Sandinista colors were black and red. The post-2006 FSLN changed the red to bright pink in an attempt to soften its image.) The use of "Cristiana" illustrates how the new FSLN casts its policies favoring the poor in moral and religious terms, aligning with critiques of global capitalism made by the Catholic Church.[20] The alliance with Venezuela bolstered the Nicaraguan economy through the massive investment of Venezuelan oil revenue, which the Ortega administration used to fund its 21st Century Socialism programs, such as Hambre Zero (Zero Hunger), Calles para el Pueblo (Streets for the People), and Casas para el Pueblo (Houses for the People).

While not all families in my study were overtly aligned with the FSLN (in fact, several were mildly to overtly critical of the government), all were working class and influenced by the FSLN's discourse of solidarity. All Nicaraguans are exposed to the state's public propaganda (through radio, TV, and other media) opposing U.S. imperialism and promoting a particular brand of Nicaraguan nationalism. Most families in this study received tangible benefits from FSLN social programs, such as expanded access to health care, new corrugated steel roofing, or new houses, resulting from their participation in Comités de Poder Ciudadano (Citizen Power Committees), which are the foundation of Ortega's popular democracy. Besides such social programs, including investments in health care and education, the new FSLN has not instituted policies to provide income support to women heads of household; nor has the government adopted programs designed to protect the rights of Nicaraguan migrants, despite pressure and protest from NGOs and civil society. In fact, Ortega is criticized in Nicaragua's progressive sectors, including former Sandinista revolutionaries who have distanced themselves from his rebranded FSLN by saying, "Soy Sandinista, no Ortegüista" (I am Sandinista, not Ortegüista) and critiquing the regime for centralizing political power.[21] However, the United States' active opposition to the FSLN bolsters Ortega and his supporters, as U.S. funding of opposition liberal parties gives substance to the claims made by Ortegüistas of ongoing imperialist intervention in Nicaraguan affairs.[22] In this controversial political climate, solidaridad continues to have significance as an expression of national sovereignty.

Solidarity and Sacrifice

Solidaridad has a deep resonance in Nicaragua as a cultural ethos signifying togetherness in the face of external political threats or existential challenges. In everyday Nicaraguan parlance, "solidaridad" is used not only as a noun (as in "solidaridad entre los pueblos," or "solidarity between peoples") but also as an adjective (as in "eres muy solidaria," an awkward literal translation of which is "you're very in solidarity").[23] These uses of "solidaridad" suggest that the political history of solidarity and the interpersonal quality combine. While one English approximation for this more interpersonal meaning of "solidaridad" might be *empathy*, "solidaridad" implies not just emotional alignment with an "other" but some sort of social action, a gesture of support for the struggles of others, whether a family member or the broader community or nation. In other words, "solidaridad" is not only a political term but also a form of moral action, one of being with and alongside others in their struggles, an orientation toward others' welfare. It is in this sense that "solidarity" comes to mean something similar to *care*.[24]

Solidarity as a form of care calls on an element of sacrifice, another value with particular cultural resonance in Nicaragua. As they assume care for children of migrant mothers, grandmothers like Angela and Marbeya embody solidarity and sacrifice. They are simultaneously supporting their daughters' migration ambitions and assuming responsibility for their grandchildren's care while sidelining their personal desires to have their daughters present. Later— after reunification of children with mothers abroad—grandmothers again sacrifice their desire to have their grandchildren remain in their care for the sake of family unity and solidarity. In this way, grandmothers participate in the shared, gendered sacrifice of mother migration, whereby mothers migrate and work abroad and grandmothers stay and assume caregiving responsibilities back home. Women across generations in transnational families make sacrifices for the sake of social reproduction and cultural regeneration.

In the scene that opens this introduction, grandmother Marbeya recalled responding with ambivalence to her daughter Azucena's migration to Costa Rica, feeling concerned about her daughter's safety and about the effects of migration on herself and her grandchildren. And yet Marbeya overcame these feelings in part through the act of caregiving itself; by assuming her role as a caregiver for her grandchildren, Marbeya was participating in the shared, gendered sacrifice of migration. In this frame, migration involves an intergenerational, parallel sacrifice of women migrants leaving their children and families to labor abroad as transnational workers and send remittances home and of grandmothers assuming care for another generation of children in Nicaragua as a way of supporting both grandchildren and their mothers. Marbeya told Azucena, when she announced her decision to migrate, "As a mother and a woman, I support you. I will take care of your children [Como madre y como mujer, yo te apoyo. Yo me encargo de sus hijos]." Marbeya also situates her expression of solidarity and sacrifice squarely in gendered terms, "as a mother and a woman," reflecting the notion that self-sacrifice for the sake of family members is *what women do*, as mothers and as women.

Providing an adequate historical framing for the value of women's sacrifice in Nicaragua is a complicated undertaking. On the one hand, there is a limited ethnographic record of gender and family life in Nicaragua.[25] On the other, discussions of women's sacrifice must also account for the complexity of male gender roles and configurations of patriarchy and paternalism in Nicaraguan society. While I examine Nicaraguan gender and kinship relations in more detail in Chapter 1, here I present two ethnographic cases that illustrate the values that sustain Nicaraguan women's sacrifices as intergenerational caregivers. The first is the cultural veneration of the Virgin Mary, instantiated in a unique Nicaraguan national holiday known as La Purísima (the Purest One), a popular Catholic celebration held annually during the first week of December. In this tradition, the figure of Mary represents the ultimate sacrifice of a mother for her son, a sacrifice of maternal devotion that offers the possibility of salvation from material wants. While not all Nicaraguans are Catholic,[26] images of the Virgin Mary permeate cultural life and dominate the cultural landscape of major cities like Managua, especially during La Purísima, when families place altars to La Virgin in front of their homes and spend precious savings on offerings of food and dry goods that are distributed to devotees during the culminating event of La Gritería (the Shouting). Celebrated the night of December 7, La Gritería transforms the city's landscape of working-class barrios, filling them with the movement and sounds of groups of people going door to door singing songs of devotion to the Virgin Mary—including exhortations such as "¿Quien causa tanta alegria? ¡La Concepción de María!" (Who causes so much happiness? The Immaculate Conception!) and "¡María de Nicaragua, Nicaragua de María!" (Mary of Nicaragua, Nicaragua of Mary!)—accompanied by elaborate displays of fireworks.

The tradition of La Purísima displays deeply held cultural values for motherhood in Nicaragua, which hold that mothers should be self-sacrificing, devoted to their children, and the foundation of family stability and continuity. While a trope of *marianismo* (Marianism) has been rightly criticized for overgeneralizing Latin American women's roles and identities (Navarro 2002), the cultural ideal of the self-sacrificing mother influences gender roles and relationships between Nicaraguan men and women. Grandmother care in transnational families both embodies and reconfigures these gendered values, extending the ideal of a self-sacrificial mother across generations in families separated by migration. Grandmothers are aware that their intergenerational care embodies cultural values of sacrifice, as expressed in a sentiment I often heard from the women in my study—that they would make every personal sacrifice necessary for the well-being of their families. As grandmother Concepción told me, "However many times it's necessary, I'm going to support my children. . . . This is why we grandmothers are here, to take care of the family in whatever way we can—maybe not economically but a moral support."

The Sandinista revolutionary period also had a lasting impact on ideals and practices of gender roles and women's sacrifice in Nicaragua. The revolution put forward an ideology of the Sandinista "new man," a type of masculinity that was supposed to be bound to a revolutionary consciousness and opposed to bourgeois or materialist values. This "new man" should be willing to take up plows to work the land and arms to defend the nation against U.S. imperialism, embodying the broad ideal of national solidarity that outweighed responsibilities to immediate families.[27] Beyond this symbolic construction of masculinity, the Sandinista period and the Contra War involved the very real fact of forced inscription of tens of thousands of men to fight in a counterinsurgency war, which often required extended periods of separation from children and families. The FSLN also asserted that the revolution would result in a "new woman" (Kampwirth 2004: 25) and mobilized thousands of young women to participate in national campaigns for literacy and health care while feminists were working for gender equity to be institutionalized in law and social policy (Babb 2001a). Solidarity and sacrifice were values associated with national survival despite imperialist incursion, values that required accompanying solidarity and sacrifice by family members, including women of the grandmother generation, who were not themselves on the front lines but rather stayed home to raise the children of men and women involved in revolutionary struggle.[28]

Grandmother care in the contemporary period of transnational migration is motivated by and reinforces these cultural values of solidarity and sacrifice. For women like Angela and Marbeya, who have lived through generations of political and economic violence and hardship—challenges of historic proportion—solidarity has significance not just in political discourse but through the everyday practical action of family caregiving. By sacrificing individual desires, upholding their daughters' migration aspirations, and assuming responsibility for their grandchildren—despite the emotional consequences for themselves of these intergenerational reconfigurations of care—grandmothers' care in transnational families embodies both sacrifice and solidarity.

Grandmother Care as Moral Practice

Grandmother care is a moral and practical engagement with global migration that regenerates Nicaraguan values for solidarity and sacrifice in transnational families. In contemporary cultural anthropology, care has been variously framed as a moral discourse of responsibility (Zigon 2011), a commitment to sustain kin networks despite debt and dispossession (Han 2012; Garcia 2010), a resource to sustain the health of dependent persons (Buch 2014), and a form of biopower used to regulate and control vulnerable populations (Stevenson 2014; Ticktin 2011). Within this blossoming of interest in care as a focus of anthropological analysis, this book grounds care in the ethnographic realities of transnational family life, showing how care is simultaneously practical action oriented toward sustaining children's and families' well-being and also an embodiment of the values of solidarity and sacrifice that support social regeneration in the face of global migration. And yet the dichotomy between caring about and caring for is largely a false division, which reflects the persistence of public-private dichotomies in many debates around care (Thelen 2015: 501). Specifically, I view care as motivated by and embodying a quality of solidarity, which is both a historical and political ethos and a moral and interpersonal value. This cultural analysis collapses the binary between political and (inter)-personal, showing how values that motivate care in families have underpinning in Nicaragua's national history.

In one sense, it is important to acknowledge that grandmothers in transnational families engage in the everyday practice of care*giving*, orienting their efforts and energies toward social reproduction. Grandmother caregiving is focused locally—on children's everyday needs for schooling, feeding, clothing, and well-being—but care is also transnational, supporting social ties between mothers and children and relational ties within families spread across borders and physical distance. This is an important corrective to existing literature on global care chains, since, perhaps unwittingly, the view of care *deficits* in migrant-sending countries such as Nicaragua aligns with stereotypes about surrogate caretakers being inadequate guardians for children of migrant mothers. For instance, in Nicaragua, popular stereotypes situate grandmothers in families of migrant parents as motivated to care mainly for material reasons, accepting economic remittances and using them for personal benefit. Such stigma can have harmful effects, leading to discrimination and harassment not only of grandmother caregivers but also of the children in their care. However, as we will see throughout this book, grandmothers are aware of such stereotypes and insist on their care as a mode of sacrifice, an embodiment of the shared solidarity that sustains Nicaraguan families across generations throughout past threats (e.g., political and economic violence) and present threats (e.g., migration). Grandmothers do this caregiving without state support, as Nicaragua does not currently have legislation in place to protect families of migrants or to support family caregiving. Absent state support, the regeneration of cultural values for family solidarity and sacrifice through intergenerational care becomes all the more important for sustaining the well-being of children and families.

Care is a "fundamentally creative and deeply human endeavor" (J. Taylor 2014) shaped—but not fully determined by—structural inequalities. That is to say, grandmother care is not entirely "freely entered into" but is a responsibility emerging from "embeddedness in familiar and social and historical contexts" (Held 2006: 14), such as the political economy of migration and the gendered inequalities shaping women's responsibilities for children's care. And yet while grandmother care reflects these structural constraints it also reflects and reinforces deeply meaningful values of solidarity and sacrifice, values that motivate care and give meaning to caring. As care circulates in transnational families, migrant mothers sacrifice abroad, working and sending remittances home for children and families, while grandmothers sacrifice through assuming responsibility for children's care in Nicaragua.

Undoubtedly, kin work, care, and domestic labor have always been central to the organization of the global economy, but a focus on intergenerational relationships affords novel, multiscalar insights into globalization, from "the micro-scale of the body, family, and household relations, [to] the larger scale of political and economic transformations" (Cole and Durham 2007: 13). In their analysis of age and globalization, Jennifer Cole and Deborah Durham advance the idea of "regeneration" to refer to the "mutually constitutive interplay between intergenerational relations and wider historical and social processes" (17). On one hand, an analysis focused on social *reproduction* importantly reveals how gender and kinship shape responsibilities for household caregiving labor, which reproduces social life across generations. For Cole and Durham, however, social *regeneration* captures a processual sense of culture changing over time and across generations as people individually and collectively respond to the sociohistorical changes of globalization. I analyze grandmother care in transnational families as both a form of social reproduction (everyday caregiving labor necessary for children and families' well-being) and as a means of social regeneration (a moral practice that embodies cultural values of solidarity and sacrifice in response to global migration).

The moral significance of intergenerational care in transnational families is reinforced by the very precariousness of transnational family life. The anthropologist Michael Jackson has said of migration, "Border situations not only imply a radical break from the known; they presage new possibilities of relatedness" (2009: xiii). The grandmothers in this book are living through a "radical break" between how they expected their late-adult lives to be and the possibilities of caring all over again for another generation of children after mother migration. They had expected their *tercera edad* (third age) to be a period of late adulthood when they would transition to becoming recipients of care provided by adult daughters, but mother migration upended this expectation.[29] Grandmother caregivers in transnational families instead find themselves simultaneously losing their migrant daughters' everyday support and assuming care responsibilities for another generation of children, occupying what has been termed the "care slot" in families of migrant parents (Leinaweaver 2010: 69). Along with the temporal uncertainties of migration—unrealized hopes for migrant returns and ambivalent prospects of children's reunifications—this social disruption is a source of distress for grandmother caregivers (as Chapter 3 illustrates).

With such disruption and uncertainty, intergenerational care becomes a source of practical morality, reaffirming what matters for grandmothers and their families.[30] As intergenerational caregiving reconfigurations once assumed at the outset of migration to be temporary take on the cast of permanence, grandmothers find pleasure and purpose in giving care. The women whose stories are told in this book encounter care as *una carga* (a responsibility or burden) but also as *una diversión* (a distraction), a daily responsibility that helps them focus positively on their grandchildren's well-being and engages them in practical activity to that end. Care, in other words, is filled with ambivalence and contradictions, and yet grandmothers respond to these by reinforcing solidarity and sacrifice, reproducing another generation of children and regenerating moral values in transnational families.

Encountering Grandmothers and Families of Migrants

Finding grandmothers to participate in this study involved the practical problem of identifying women of the grandmother generation who were primary caregivers for children in transnational families. For fuller detail on research methods, see the appendix; here I describe how I came to know Angela and Marbeya, the grandmothers whose stories open this introduction. For the duration of my field research, I lived in a family home in Managua, Nicaragua. While I had worked in Nicaragua before, my previous work focused on public health, and so I needed to develop new networks of colleagues working in migration issues. I spent my first few weeks in Managua reaching out to university researchers, NGO coordinators, and development agencies, having meetings and letting people know about my project. I also sought existing registries of families of migrants but found that, while national-level statistics for Nicaragua provide an estimate of the number of households in different regions that have an out-migrated family member, survey data do not provide information on family-level caregiving arrangements after migration. Therefore, I had to find families in which grandmothers were the primary caregivers for children of parent migrants using my networks of NGO and university colleagues and other interpersonal referrals.

Thus it was that one muggy Managua afternoon in the fall of 2009, at the start of my field research, I attended a meeting of an NGO for women family members of migrants in Nicaragua (Red de Mujeres Familiares de Migrantes; Network of Women Family Members of Migrants; La Red). The meeting was held at the Universidad Centroamericana campus, and several dozen women and children were crowded into a small classroom discussing and planning their upcoming activities. These included a popular education workshop on responses to the feminization of migration and the group's participation in a legislative campaign to support Nicaraguan migrants in Costa Rica through advocacy for safe housing, legal documentation, and employment security. These were all activities I would come to participate in over the year to come, but at this meeting, my first with the NGO, I hoped to introduce myself to the women in attendance and identify grandmothers who might participate in my study. I spoke to the group for several minutes about my research interests, explaining that, while I knew their work focused on the experiences of migrants abroad, I was interested in the experiences of family members in Nicaragua, particularly in grandmothers raising children after mothers had out-migrated. The women in attendance initially responded to my introduction with questions such as "So you want to interview my migrant daughter/sister/niece?" or "My daughter is in Costa Rica/Panama/the U.S., but you can interview her if she returns home to visit." When I clarified that my interest was in speaking with grandmothers raising children of migrant parents about *their own* experiences of migration, the women seemed surprised. Speaking to the collective sentiment, a woman sitting in front of me, her hair dyed reddish brown and her eyes demonstrating the emotion that filled her voice, said, "En fin, alguien se interesa por nosotras" (Finally, someone's interested in us). This was Marbeya, who, along with Angela and two other women I met that afternoon, was one of the first set of grand-mothers to participate in my study. I identified other grandmother participants along the way, through my engagement with NGOs or through word of mouth, as women would tell their friends and neighbors about my study and introduce me to other grandmothers raising children of parent migrants.

The research on which this book is based in many ways reflects my active and ongoing collaborations with two NGOs: La Red and Servicio Jesuita de Migrantes (SJM; Jesuit Migration Service).[31] The aim of La Red is to mobilize women family members to support advocacy campaigns on behalf of Nicara-guan migrants in Costa Rica. The Nicaraguan coordinator of La Red invited me to accompany the group in their activities, including popular education *talleres* (workshops) in Managua focused on the feminization of migration and the status of Nicaraguan migrants in Costa Rica. My involvement with La Red not only helped me identify women participants for my study but also exposed me to important information about the dynamics of Nicaraguan migration, especially to Costa Rica.

All the grandmothers discussed in this book share the experience of caring for children after parent migration; however, meaningful differences in their lives influence their response to migration and caregiving. Among the twenty-four grandmothers in this study, ages range from forty-seven to seventy-five, with an average age of fifty-eight. Notably, that a woman can be a grandmother in her forties reflects the relatively young average age of motherhood in Nicaragua, where roughly half of all births are to women under twenty (Lion, Prata, and Stewart 2009). Age is a factor influencing women's experiences of intergenerational care and of transnational family life, including the physical demands of caring for another generation of children and the emotional consequences of living with a daughter absent because of migration.[32] Obviously, grandmothers in their forties and those in their seventies differ in terms of physiological processes of aging, yet all the women in this book understand themselves to be grandmothers, members of *la tercera edad*. As the lives of the women in this study differ by processes of physiological aging, so do social processes also matter for their experiences of grandmotherhood and transnational family life, including the social and economic hardships they have weathered and the family relationships and other sources of social support they may or may not be able to count on.

My ethnographic research was designed to elicit grandmothers' experiences as caregivers in transnational families, or how mother migration reconfigures relations of care across generations and borders in families like those of Marbeya and Angela. After I met both women at the meeting of La Red described above, I arranged to visit them at their respective homes. On this first home visit, I introduced myself and the purpose of my study and also asked each woman for her agreement to participate in my project. I then began to ask questions about the women's households and about migration experiences of their family members, including destination, duration, communication with migrants, and remittance patterns. I would usually stop the first interview after about an hour, so as not to tire my interlocutor, and then plan subsequent visits to the household to conduct additional interviews. In total, I conducted three semi-structured interviews with every grandmother in my study across at least three separate sittings. After these were completed, I would continue to visit families as they kept the invitation open; for some families, visits stopped shortly after we completed the series of three interviews, for others, like those of Angela and Marbeya, I would visit almost every week during the entire year of my fieldwork. During these visits, I would hang out in family living rooms or front patios, talking to everyone I could, helping children with homework, helping grandmothers with housework, and observing family interactions, including the phone calls or Internet chats with migrant mothers that might occur while

I was visiting. Occasionally, I would receive a call from a grandmother inviting me to a family event, such as a birthday party or church service, and I would attend that as well.

Other times, grandmothers would ask me to visit to help sort out troubles related to transnational family life. For instance, one afternoon I received a call from Angela telling me that I needed to come over, because her granddaughter Laleska had just finished a troubling phone call with her mother, Karla. So I got in a taxi and wound my way up Managua's sprawling urban landscape into the working-class barrio where Angela lives. I then joined Angela and Laleska in an emotional discussion provoked by the phone call between mother and daughter earlier that afternoon, in which we talked about the difficulties of managing relatedness across distance and how Laleska struggled to come to terms with her mother's continuing absence (I analyze this encounter further in Chapter 4). On another occasion, Marbeya's daughter Azucena visited from Costa Rica, and Marbeya invited me to join the family in a *comida* (meal) celebrating her visit, which I did, conversing with Marbeya, Azucena, and other family members for several hours that afternoon. It was through spending time with families that I came to know grandmothers and their experiences of care in Nicaraguan transnational families.

The Chapters That Follow

This book tells the stories of fifteen grandmothers and their families, combining ethnography and anthropological interpretation to describe the importance of solidarity, sacrifice, and intergenerational care in Nicaraguan transnational families. This introduction provides a background for understanding grandmother care within contemporary Nicaraguan migration patterns and within existing literature on global care chains, transnational families, and the anthropology of care. It gives a brief history of the concepts of solidaridad and sacrifice, which are central to understanding the cultural significance of intergenerational care in Nicaraguan transnational families. This review of contemporary patterns of Nicaraguan migration shows how the dynamics of destination and migrant illegality affect not only migrants themselves but also grandmothers and other family members who stay behind. Finally, this introduction analyzes grandmother care as a moral practice, arguing that care regenerates values of solidarity and sacrifice despite the structural constraints and emotional uncertainties of transnational migration.

Chapter 1 describes how grandmothers come to assume caregiving responsibilities for another generation of grandchildren after mother migration. I
describe the cultural patterns of gender and kinship in Nicaragua that partly
structure grandmothers' caregiving roles, leaving them to feel, as one said,
"Tenemos que hacerlo" (We have to do it), referring to their assumption of
children's care after mother migration, because, in their words, "no hay nadie más" (there is no one else) who will assume this responsibility. I discuss
grandmothers' engagements in care and how intergenerational caregiving is
experienced both as burden, or something women have to do, and as a source
of purpose, something that provides meaning in women's everyday lives. Using the cases of two women, Aurora and Olga, I also illustrate grandmothers'
vulnerabilities by describing their fraught relationships with children's fathers
and the legal vulnerabilities—related to Nicaraguan family law and to international immigration policies—that increase the insecurity and uncertainty of
grandmother care.

Chapter 2 analyzes grandmothers' experiences of economic remittances,
which they view as necessary but insufficient compensation for migration. I
describe the material and affective dimensions of remittances, describing how
money sent home by migrants represents a tenuous transnational tie for families back home. Drawing on feminist arguments about the entanglements between love and money in intimate relationships, I argue that grandmothers'
view of remittances, that "no se ajustan" (they don't measure up), is a claim to
the inadequacy of a transactional model of caregiving (remittances for care).
Responding to stereotypes about grandmother caregivers' selfish motivations,
and contributing to anthropological critiques of developmentalist views of remittances, the chapter further illustrates how intergenerational care in transnational families embodies a moral economy of migration that values sacrifice
and solidarity over money or material gain.

Chapter 3 explores grandmothers' emotional experiences of caregiving
through an examination of the idiom *pensando mucho* (thinking too much).
I review the nascent literature on thinking too much as an idiom of distress
in global mental health, showing that—for Nicaraguan women—this complaint registers the uncertainties of transnational migration and the tensions
in their roles as remittance managers and intergenerational caregivers in transnational families. The explanatory model of *pensando mucho* that emerges
from this analysis shows this is a chronic form of worrying or rumination, not

reducible to episodic depression or anxiety. As an idiom of distress, *pensando mucho* shows how grandmothers respond in embodied, emotional ways to the uncertainties and challenges of transnational migration but also is a way for grandmothers to call attention to the cultural value of their care as a source of sacrifice and solidarity in transnational families.

Chapter 4 extends the intergenerational perspective on transnational migration put forward in this book through a discussion of one family's experiences with international migration across generations. By presenting a detailed portrait of Angela's family, I show how grandmothers orient their care for children in the present in ways that reflect their own, past, experiences of migration. More particularly, this intergenerational analysis reveals how grandmother care for grandchildren recalls grandmothers' own past experiences of abandonment and seeks, through regenerating solidarity and sacrifice, to foster family unity and togetherness into the future.

Drawing on my ethnographic engagement with two migrant-serving NGOs, the conclusion offers reflections on the types of social policies that would value grandmothers and intergenerational care in transnational families. I consider the importance of recognizing the value of intergenerational caregiving as a resource, not only for the well-being of children and transnational families but also for the regeneration of cultural values such as solidarity and sacrifice in migrant-sending countries such as Nicaragua.

Tenemos Que Hacerlo

Responsibility and Sacrifice in Grandmother Care

Aquí la mayoría ha pasado así: de que somos las abuelas que quedamos al final. (Here the majority have experienced it like this: that we grandmothers are the ones who are left in the end.)

—Aurora

Assuming and Relinquishing Care

Aurora is an animated, busy, active woman of sixty-three who lives in a small house in a planned residential development near a major interstate transit terminal in Managua. While the terminal is loud, busy, and dusty with the constant traffic of passengers, taxis, and buses, the housing development has a slower pace, with children walking to school in their blue and white uniforms on dirt roads only occasionally crossed by private cars or delivery trucks carrying Bimbo bread or Coca-Cola soft drinks to one of several *ventas*, or neighborhood stores, in the community. Aurora runs a venta out of the converted front room of her cement house, painted lime green. When I first met Aurora, she was awaiting a delivery of ice, and I watched her conduct inventory before she was able to sit down and talk with me. I knew from one of Aurora's neighbors that her daughter, Elizabeth, had left for Spain about two years prior. Aurora talked to me about Elizabeth and about her two granddaughters, Salensca and Daniela, ages seven and five, whom she had raised in this home in their mother's absence. For Aurora, assuming the role of intergenerational caregiver had been a sacrifice, as she had to adjust her schedule at the venta and hire additional help in order to have time for her granddaughters. She also missed the help that Elizabeth used to provide her, at the venta and in her everyday life. Aurora was not receiving either economic or social support from the girls' father, thus her sentiment that "no ha[bía] nadie más" (there [was] no one else) to assume care for the children after their mother's migration. Despite these disruptions to her family life, Aurora enjoyed caring for her granddaughters and viewed her sacrifice as part of the shared sacrifice that her daughter's migration required. Aurora recalled,

> It's what I had to do. She [Elizabeth] had to migrate, and I had to take care of my granddaughters. But I had their affection, and during the time that I had them, I had a routine of getting up in the morning to send them off to school every day. I felt good. In the morning one of the girls went to school, and I got up at four thirty to make her breakfast, her lunchbox. She took her lunch, and I got her ready, bathed her, dressed her, and took her to the bus stop. Then I woke her sister up at nine or ten to give her a bath. . . . They had gotten used to me and wanted me to do all this.

In describing her assumption of caregiving, it is clear how Aurora obtained a sense of purpose, identity, and meaning from her role as a caregiver across generations. Her daily routines for her granddaughters' care "felt good" and helped Aurora adjust to the absence of her daughter. She also grew close to her granddaughters, sharing their "affection" through everyday care. Despite these positive aspects, intergenerational caregiving was a precarious prospect for Aurora, as shown by the reunification of her granddaughters with their mother that terminated her role as a surrogate mother. Just nine days before our first interview, Elizabeth had returned to Managua to reclaim custody of her daughters and take them with her back to Spain. This reunification filled Aurora with ambivalence. On the one hand, she supported her daughter's desire to have her children with her in Spain; on the other, reunification meant that she—Aurora—would no longer enjoy the affection or daily routines of intergenerational care she had grown so fond of. Because of this change in circumstances, Aurora's reflections about grandmothering are framed in the recent past tense.

As a mother, Aurora supported her migrant daughter by caring for her children; as a grandmother, she assumed the responsibility of everyday care for her granddaughters. This reconfiguration of care across generations is a sacrifice structured in part by gendered inequalities, which left Elizabeth's children without the support of their father and Aurora feeling as if there was "no one else" to provide them care. And yet because Aurora found pleasure in her daily routines of care and built strong ties with her granddaughters, their subsequent departure through reunification with their mother abroad is emotionally difficult for her. Despite her personal distress, Aurora makes another sacrifice, overcoming her sense of personal loss of *both* her daughter and her granddaughters for the sake of mother-child reunification. Aurora's story illustrates how solidarity and sacrifice are central in shaping and giving meaning to intergenerational care in transnational families, both in motivating the assumption of intergenerational care and in aiding grandmothers to confront the challenges of transnational family life, including relinquishing care in order to support mother-child reunification.

How do grandmothers like Aurora come to assume care of grandchildren after mother migration? What is the role of gendered inequalities in shaping grandmother care? How do grandmothers make sense of their caregiving in relation to sacrifice and solidarity, and how do these values help grandmothers meet the challenges of transnational family life? I explore these questions by situating grandmothers' roles as intergenerational caregivers within Nicaraguan dynamics of gender and kinship, showing how sacrifice in part reflects gendered inequalities, which place primary responsibility on women as mothers across the generations to care for children. While grandmothering in Nicaragua is not exclusive to transnational families, this discussion shows how grandmothers and the children in their care cope with mother absence and distance and the uncertainties surrounding return and reunification, all qualities of migrant family life that make transnational care particularly challenging. The stories of two women, Aurora and Olga, illustrate these tensions, which include legal vulnerabilities, conflicts with children's fathers, and ambivalence over children's reunification with mothers abroad. Throughout this discussion, we see how grandmothers embody values of sacrifice and solidarity through their care; in so doing, they manage the challenges and uncertainties of intergenerational care in transnational families.

No Hay Nadie Más: Kinship, Gender, and Grandmothers

Grandmothers assume care for children after mother migration because "no hay nadie más" (there is no one else), a sentiment that reflects kinship patterns and gendered inequalities that structure grandmother sacrifice. All the grandmothers in this study assumed care for children after mothers had emigrated through an informal transfer of caregiving, initiated when mothers first left and continuing for the duration of migration. While solid data on the prevalence of grandmothers as caregivers in Nicaraguan transnational families are unavailable, most Nicaraguan women who migrate are young (under forty), and many leave children behind when emigrating.[1] Economic constraints are compounded by a Nicaraguan labor market that actively discriminates on the basis of gender and age, further limiting women's job opportunities.[2] In addition, for some women, factors such as intimate partner violence may influence their decisions to emigrate (Torres and Barahona 2004).

The reasons mothers leave children in Nicaragua upon migration are many but include the dangers of illicit border crossing as well as restrictive immigration policies in host countries that make it difficult for migrants to secure legal documentation for themselves and their children (Dreby 2010; Abrego 2014). During my fieldwork, I found that most parents (mothers and fathers) who emigrate leave children in Nicaragua rather than taking them abroad. The cost of child care abroad is a deterrent for migrant mothers as well; therefore, most mother migrants opt to leave children in the care of their mothers, sisters, or other female relatives in Nicaragua (Centeno Orozco and Gutiérrez Vega 2007).[3] In fact, knowing they can count on their mothers to care for their children may facilitate women's initial migration decisions.

Nicaraguan family life and kinship patterns are perhaps best described as matrifocal but patriarchal. In his ethnography of a working-class Managua barrio in the late 1980s, Roger Lancaster described Nicaraguan family life as "historically patriarchal" and conjugal relations as "brittle and impermanent"; while women organize and sustain the routines of family relationships, men exert control over women's lives and autonomy (Lancaster 1992: 16). Rosario Montoya has also described gender and conjugal relations in Nicaraguan rural communities as patriarchal, arguing that a dichotomy between *casa* and *calle* (house and street) delimits women's movements and reinforces male control by casting the street (and single women) in moral doubt and privileging the house (and women who dedicate themselves to marriage and childrearing) (Montoya 2002). Additionally, ties between family members centered on mothers' kin are strong and enduring. Such kinship patterns look like those described by anthropologists for parts of the Caribbean, where consanguineous ties are stronger than conjugal ties and three-generation, mother-centered households are more prevalent than nuclear family, male-headed households (Safa 2005).

In Nicaragua, heterosexual "marriage" has flexible cultural meaning, often referring to a man and a woman who are sexually involved and cohabitating in the woman's mother's house, even though their union has not been formally arranged through church or state. Nicaraguans often use the term *casado* (married) to refer to someone who is coupled but not necessarily officially married. Women use other terms interchangeably to refer to their male (sexual) partners, such as *marido* (husband), *compañero* or *pareja* (partner), and *esposo* (spouse). For the minority of Nicaraguans who are upper-middle or upper class, the nuclear family model based on heterosexual marriage and coresidence with biological children is a sign of class distinction. This is seen in the ways new, large, private housing developments on the outskirts of Managua are marketed to the upper-middle class on billboards, using pictures of heterosexual, light-complexioned couples with two children standing in front of brightly painted single-family homes, complete with driveways and air-conditioning units. However, none of the families in my study are middle class; all can be considered working class or poor. For these families, stable, heterosexual marriage and nuclear family residence is uncommon.[4]

Nearly all the families in this study follow the pattern of extended family households consisting of maternal grandmothers, their children, and grandchildren. For example, the family of Marbeya (first described in the introduction) consists of twenty members who share a small, four-room, wood-sided house in a working-class barrio on Managua's outskirts. The household consists of three of Marbeya's four adult daughters (the fourth daughter, Azucena, having migrated), two sons-in-law (unmarried partners of two of Marbeya's coresident daughters), her only son and his *compañera*, Marbeya's husband (who works away from the household on construction projects outside the city), and her eleven grandchildren. The large household size was evident by the quantity of laundry often hanging out to dry across the front of the house. Marbeya is the primary caregiver for Azucena's two children and responsible for their feeding, clothing, and schooling. She receives some support in this caregiving from her coresident daughters, the children's maternal aunts, but Marbeya in turn also helps in limited ways with the care for her other nine coresident grandchildren. Marbeya's multigenerational household is typical of many working-poor Nicaraguan families and of the families in this study.

Less typical is Marbeya's husband's presence in the family and in her life. In fact, he was one of only two grandfathers present among the families in this book. Paternal irresponsibility is upheld and justified by gendered ideologies that view men as inherently unable to maintain fidelity in sexual relationships with women, which facilitates multiple partnering.[5] All the mother migrants in this study had emigrated alone, without their children's fathers. In the wake of mother migration, most fathers do not assume primary caregiving responsibilities for children, either because they did not assume responsibility for children before the mother's migration or, less often, because they themselves have emigrated. Of course, there are exceptions to this pattern, and some men in the families in this study—fathers, uncles, and grandfathers—are involved with children's caretaking. However, because fathers are unreliable sources of care, women's migration shifts care responsibilities across extended female kin networks, with grandmothers often the preferred caretakers (Torres and Barahona 2004). Fathers were present in the household and in children's daily lives in just two of the families in my study, and in both families, paternal grandmothers were the children's primary caregivers. Maternal grandmothers were caring for children of migrant mothers in the remaining families.

One of the two paternal grandmothers in this study who are primary caregivers is Isabel, a fifty-four-year-old, confident, and energetic woman who assumed care for her six-year-old grandson, Robin, after his mother Katherine emigrated to Spain. When Katherine left, about two years before my study, she decided to leave Robin in Isabel's care, since she and Robin's father (Isabel's son), René, had lived in Isabel's house for several years. Before emigrating, Katherine had worked full time in Managua, and Isabel had cared for Robin while his mother was at work. After migration, Isabel's caregiving responsibilities shifted, as she became the full-time caregiver for her grandson. Isabel pointed to Robin's calling her *mamá* as a way of showing that her two years of full-time caregiving had left her grandson viewing her as his mom. By comparison, Robin called his migrant mother Katherine. As Isabel and Katherine renegotiated the relations of care for Robin, René remained largely on the sidelines; although he lived with his son, he was not actively involved with Robin's everyday care. On the other hand, Isabel's adult daughter Idelia lives in Isabel's household with her two children. Idelia provides some support to Isabel and assists in a limited way with Robin's care (e.g., by helping prepare his meals or watching him while Isabel is out). Isabel had long since separated from the father of her three children, who is largely absent from their lives. Isabel does have a *compañero*, whom she describes as *medio prestado* (half borrowed), meaning he has another family and visits Isabel only occasionally.

Angela, whom we met in the introduction, is a maternal grandmother, and her family caregiving arrangements are more common among Nicaraguan transnational families. Angela assumed the primary caregiving role for her granddaughter Laleska after her daughter Karla emigrated to the United States, ten years before when Laleska was one year old. Karla had separated from Laleska's father within a year of leaving Nicaragua, and while he lived in the same barrio only about ten minutes' walk from Angela's home, he had limited contact with his daughter. When Karla announced to her mother she was going

to emigrate, Angela assumed she would take over primary caregiving responsibility for Laleska. In Angela's words, "Who else would have done it? [¿Quien
más lo hubiera hecho?]" Her rhetorical question speaks to the sentiment of
women who assume caregiving of children of migrant mothers out of a combined sense of responsibility, inevitability, and sacrifice. As I discuss further in
Chapter 4, Angela has three adult children living in Managua who provide a
limited amount of support to their mother (e.g., visiting on occasion, driving
her to appointments, and sharing meals and special occasions). And yet, when
Karla emigrated, it was to her mother and not to her siblings that she entrusted
the care of her daughter.

While nearly all of the grandmothers in this study receive some degree of
social, material, and emotional support from their nonmigrant adult children,
they remain the primary caregivers for their grandchildren. (See Table A.1 for
descriptive information on families, including grandmothers' adult children
and their place of residence.) After mother migration, gendered inequalities
that reinforce paternal irresponsibility contribute to grandmothers' sense
that "there is no one else" to assume primary caregiving responsibilities for
children. These gendered inequalities further reinforce the sense that intergenerational care by grandmothers embodies women's sacrifice for the sake of solidarity in transnational families.

Intergenerational Care as Shared Sacrifice

Women describe intergenerational care as an instantiation of the value of sacrifice in Nicaraguan families extended over generations and across borders. In
this frame of shared, intergenerational sacrifice, mother migration is a sacrifice
for the sake of children's futures, and grandmothers' care is a sacrifice for the
sake of children's and families' well-being in the present. Before beginning research with the women in these families, I had assumed that the assumption
of grandchildren's care after mother migration reflected a carefully contem-
plated choice, something that was negotiated with mothers before migration,
in a way that mirrored a rational-actor model of migration.[6] Therefore, and
somewhat naïvely, I would ask, "Why did you decide to take on caregiving for
your grandchildren?" My questions were met with grandmothers' counter-
poised "What else was I supposed to do?" This reframing indicates how, for
grandmothers, assumption of grandchildren's care after mother migration is
viewed as a constrained choice, one that reflects their feeling that "no hay nadie
más" to take care of the children. Further, while grandmothers may be involved

in children's care in Nicaragua in nonmigrant households, for all the women in this study, raising children of mother migrants was a qualitatively different experience because of the distance, absence, and uncertainties of transnational family life. As I came to understand, grandmother care in families of migrant mothers embodies the deeply held value of women's sacrifice for children and families, extended across generations. In assuming care for their grandchildren, women are caring for their grandchildren and simultaneously caring about their daughters' sacrifices as migrant mothers.[7]

Grandmothers' assumption of care involves daily activities of social reproduction for another generation of children. Evelyn Nakano Glenn has defined care work as "the relationships and activities involved in maintaining people on a daily basis and intergenerationally," including direct physical care (feeding, cooking, etc.), household maintenance, and the fostering of social ties within families across generations (Glenn 2010: 5). Grandmothers in this study engage in everyday activities of care: bathing, clothing, and feeding children. Even when grandmothers cannot read or write and have only limited formal education, they must oversee children's homework and participate in required school activities, such as parent-teacher meetings. While children are at school, grandmothers clean the house, wash and iron clothes, shop in the market and prepare the midday meal, and engage in other household tasks. Grandmothers also take care of sick children, purchasing medicines and taking them to doctor's appointments when needed. Grandmothers receive and manage remittances from migrant mothers to purchase food and other needed goods for children's care. These daily routines of caregiving occupy the majority of grandmothers' time and energy, constituting the care labor that supports children's and families' welfare in Nicaragua while mothers labor abroad as migrants.

For Marbeya, raising her two grandchildren over the more than ten years that Azucena has lived in Costa Rica had been a struggle. At fifty-two, Marbeya is a vibrant woman, usually dressed in bright colors and wearing her hair dyed red or purple. Despite her outward energetic appearance, Marbeya talked about her role as an intergenerational caregiver as a "really difficult stage [una etapa muy difícil]" of her life, which had left her worn out and weary. Marbeya described caregiving as

> a really hard battle [una batalla muy dura] because at my age, I can tell you, I'm feeling it as a heavy burden, because I wash, cook—I do everything for them [her grandchildren]. . . . If they get sick, I have to run around to take care of

everything [tengo que pegar carreras]. And maybe . . . I have to go to the doctor with them. So I say, whatever, I have to do it, because if I don't, who else is going to?

In addition to washing, cooking, and taking care of her grandchildren's health care needs, Marbeya's daily routine includes securing water for her household. This is an added challenge in homes in poor and working-class neighborhoods of Managua, where water is scarce and its flow controlled by municipal authorities. Marbeya must wake in the early morning, when water flows through her neighborhood's pipes for an hour or two, to fill *pilas* (receptacles) with water for daily washing, cleaning, cooking, and bathing. These everyday challenges contributed to Marbeya's sense of care as a "heavy burden."

Emphasizing the burdensome aspects of caregiving is a way for grandmothers to frame care as part of the shared sacrifice across generations in transnational families. In this framing, grandmother care in Nicaragua is a parallel sacrifice to mother migration and employment abroad. Marbeya explained this intergenerational sacrifice:

My daughter is still over there working for her daughter. . . . You should see how this woman works. Over there she has two jobs. Two jobs. In the morning she works in one; at midday, at two in the afternoon, she leaves one and goes to the other, and that's how the poor little thing—even Sunday mornings this woman works. So I say, no way, I have to—I have to get used to my daughter being over there because if she was here [in Nicaragua], she would live forever in misery . . . because here money and salaries are really messed up.

Marbeya situates Azucena's migration to Costa Rica as a necessary response to economic constraints in Nicaragua, a sacrifice made for the economic well-being of her child. Just as Azucena must migrate to help her household economically, Marbeya feels she must "get used to" her daughter's absence. In other words, Marbeya also makes a sacrifice, forgoing her desires to have all her family together and expressing solidarity with the aspirations of her migrant daughter.

As another example, Aurora, whose story opens this chapter, expressed disagreement with her daughter Elizabeth's decision to migrate to Spain, and yet, Aurora insisted, "And even if I wasn't [in agreement], the poor thing had to go [Y aunque no estuviera se tenía que ir la pobre]." Like other grandmothers, Aurora views her daughter's migration as a necessary response to the lack of economic opportunities in Nicaragua. Although Aurora misses her daughter's copresent support in her life and is concerned about how Elizabeth's absence will affect her two young granddaughters, Aurora's assumption of care responsibilities reflects her willingness to sacrifice her own desires for the sake of her daughter and family. By assuming care of grandchildren, grandmothers are embodying their solidarity with mothers' migration ambitions, overcoming their reluctance to accept their daughters' absences, and providing intergenerational care for the sake of family well-being.

Teresa also expressed resigned support for her daughter Lisdamur's migration to Costa Rica (where Lisdamur lived for two and a half years). Teresa is fifty-six and lives in an economically poor neighborhood on the edge of the polluted Lake Managua, its foul odor often wafting into her home with the afternoon breeze. Teresa has a total of five children, two of whom have emigrated. In addition to Lisdamur, Teresa's son Jorge left for Texas two years prior, leaving his son in Nicaragua in the care of the maternal grandmother. Teresa is aware of her children's vulnerabilities while living undocumented abroad, and this adds to her sense of concern about migration and her family. "I . . . didn't want my children to have to end up doing it [migrating]. It's even worse without papers; it's harder for migrants. I don't agree with them that they should leave their land, their home." Teresa articulates her displeasure and disagreement about migration, but she also assumed care for Lisdamur's two daughters (ages eight and twelve) for nearly a year, until Lisdamur sent for her daughters to join her in Costa Rica. For Teresa, migration is a "mal necesario" (necessary evil), needed to secure family economic well-being, and her caregiving is a necessary responsibility for her family's survival:

> However many times it's necessary, I'm going to support my children . . . and take care of them in the moment that they need me. I'll support them in whatever way. This is why we grandmothers are here, to take care of the family, to support the family in whatever [way] we can—maybe not economically but a moral support.

Teresa frames intergenerational care as an affirmative moral stance, an expression of unconditional support for her migrant children and for the grandchildren in her care. Teresa obtains a sense of purpose through her role as a caregiver; care allows her to participate in the shared sacrifice of migration. That grandmothers like Teresa are able to overcome their overt disapproval of migration and support their children by caring for grandchildren illustrates the intergenerational solidarity that supports migration and care.

Like other women of the grandmother generation facing the realities of poverty and economic necessity in Nicaragua, María Luisa understands "our children have to migrate." In fact, María Luisa and her husband, Miguel, helped their daughter Denia buy a plane ticket to Spain three years earlier by taking out a loan from an agricultural cooperative. The family lives in a rural community in Chinandega, a Nicaraguan state with much out-migration. Upon Denia's departure, María Luisa, in her fifties, assumed care for her three grandchildren, ages thirteen, fifteen, and eighteen. María Luisa has four other children who are migrants or migrated at some point: a coresident daughter who migrated to Spain but was not permitted to enter and was returned from the airport; one son who migrated to the United States, was deported, and then went back; and two sons who live and work in El Salvador, one of whom has a child (with him in El Salvador). Even though María Luisa and Miguel facilitated Denia's migration by purchasing her plane ticket, María Luisa remained deeply ambivalent about her daughter's migration. Her experiences of her other children's unsuccessful migrations and her migrant son's difficulties in the United States as an undocumented migrant, including a short period of detention by immigration authorities and a period of unemployment due to La Crisis, left María Luisa worried that similar harms would befall Denia. She also felt that the difference between having Denia in Spain and having two sons in El Salvador had to do with geographical distance: "It's different, because from El Salvador they can come and go easily; they come and go, but those two who are far away can't come back."

As the permanence of migration settled in, María Luisa was increasingly worried about the separation and distance of her family. She observed her grandchildren becoming inclined themselves toward migration, impatient with their limited options after secondary school in Nicaragua. She worried about her grandchildren and missed her daughter's support in her household, and yet she viewed migration as a necessary response to economic poverty in Nicaragua:

> We were bothered by her departure, but because of the same poverty we experience, we understand our children have to migrate. What else are we supposed to do? [¿Qué más debemos hacer?] Because of this poverty they have to go [por la misma pobreza tienen que irse].

For María Luisa, assuming care of her daughter's children is part of the shared sacrifice of migration; her daughter works abroad and sends money home, and she and her husband assist with their grandchildren's care. Despite her concerns and ambivalence about migration and the separation it has caused in her family, María Luisa feels she has no other option but to participate in the shared sacrifice of intergenerational care; in her words, ¿Qué más debemos hacer?

Grandmothers as Mothers Again

As grandmothers assume care for the children of migrant mothers, they become mothers again, for another generation of children. In their newfound mothering roles women can find pleasure, insofar as they experience a renewed sense of purpose in their lives. The emotional ties that grandmothers form with the children in their care are usually strengthened over time, with longer durations of migration and with the uncertainties of migration. These ties are evident in the kinship terminology children use to refer to their grandmothers, using "mamá" as a descriptive adjective for both their grandmother caretakers and their migrant mothers. For instance, Marbeya's grandchildren refer to her as "mamá Marbeya" and to her migrant daughter as "mamá Azucena."

Norma is an energetic woman of fifty-seven who has been raising her grandson Jeremy (age eleven) since his mother, María José, left for the United States ten years ago. Like other children of migrant mothers, Jeremy referred to his grandmother as "mamá Norma" and to his mother as "mamá Mari." Norma and Jeremy shared a small house in a suburban district of Managua; in the backyard area, Norma's coresident adult son Michal lived in a detached home with his wife and two children. Jeremy enjoyed his cousins' company, and his uncle helped with his caregiving by picking him up from school every day. Still, it was Norma who had been Jeremy's primary caregiver ever since her daughter had emigrated. Norma viewed her relationship with Jeremy as an extension of her role as a single mother for her four children (whose father had emigrated to the United States in the 1980s, when they were very young). Norma described her mothering across the generations of migration this way: "I'm a single mother. I was mother and father [fui madre y padre] for my four children, and now I'm a mother *again* [soy madre de nuevo], for Jeremy" (emphasis mine).

By raising Jeremy, Norma considers herself completing a reproductive cycle that has extended across two generations, four children, and one grandchild. Norma is resolute in her conviction to raise healthy, productive children alone, as a single mother (and grandmother), without the help of their fathers. Years earlier, her husband had sent remittances only in the first few months after emigrating to the United States; after that, he never provided consistent economic support to the family. In Norma's words, after migrating, "he forgot about his children [se olvidó de sus hijos]." As a result, Norma became her children's primary source of emotional and economic support. Following several years of informal employment and economic struggle, Norma completed her university law degree and worked as a family lawyer for the municipal government of Managua. Because of her knowledge of the law and access to legal resources, Norma had completed the administrative process to obtain guardianship for Jeremy, something no other grandmother in my study had been able to do. This provided her a relative sense of security in her caregiving relation with Jeremy. (Jeremy's father has limited contact with his son and does not provide economic support to Norma for his care.) For Norma, mothering and then mothering again is a source of self-esteem and *optimismo* (optimism), as she orients her labors toward Jeremy's well-being. She obtains a sense of pride from her role as a grandmother caregiver.

Over roughly a decade of caring for Jeremy, Norma has grown close to her grandson, and yet she has always been supportive of María José's intentions to reunify with Jeremy in the United States. While María José had not had the opportunity to visit her family in Nicaragua since her emigration (having taken nearly ten years to obtain legal status as a U.S. resident), an opportunity to visit came during my fieldwork. Norma and Jeremy anxiously anticipated the visit, as the family understood that María José was intending to take Jeremy back to New York with her. In the weeks leading up to the visit, Norma took Jeremy shopping for winter clothing, and Jeremy told me he was ready for the *frío* (cold) of New York with his new coats and jackets. As it turned out, Jeremy was not able to leave Nicaragua with María José; essentially, his U.S. visa had not yet been approved, which the family found out only when they showed up for an immigration appointment at the U.S. embassy. Needless to say, everyone was disappointed, including Jeremy, but he tried to put a positive spin on the outcome, telling me a few days later that his "mamá Marí" would return to Nicaragua soon and finally take him to New York.

After this episode, in my conversations with Norma, I asked her how she was able to see the prospect of Jeremy's reunification with María José so positively, seemingly without doubt or hesitation. Norma told me that she had always viewed her daughter's migration in terms of creating this opportunity "for Jeremy to have a better future [para Jeremy tener un mejor futuro]." Yes, I said, I understood that motivation, but how would Norma feel once Jeremy had left to join his mother abroad? Norma replied, "Yes, of course, I'm going to miss him, but it's another necessary sacrifice [Sí, claro, me va a hacer falta, pero es otro sacrificio necesario]." For Norma, her first sacrifice was in assuming care for her grandson; this sacrifice is extended across generations as she sacrifices her personal desire to keep Jeremy physically proximate and instead encourages his reunification with his mother in the United States. Norma's stance on reunification reveals how grandmother caregivers in transnational families usually form strong emotional ties with grandchildren through their caregiving—ties that must be relinquished if and when the children join mothers abroad. Reunification with mothers becomes a further instantiation of grandmothers' sacrifice as intergenerational caregivers in transnational families.

The Ambivalence of Return and Reunification

The prospect of children's reunification with mothers abroad is a source of uncertainty and ambivalence for grandmothers. Even when grandmothers like Aurora and Norma have assumed care for grandchildren over long durations (of ten years or more), their care is made tenuous by gendered cultural expectations for mother-child ties. And it is precisely these longer-term durations of migration and care that shape strong emotional bonds between grandmothers and the children in their care, making reunification that much more distressing for grandmothers. Nonetheless, one important dimension of grandmothers' caregiving is encouraging children to view their mothers as upholding their roles as mothers through migration and its resulting sacrifices. Even after years of migration, grandmothers will relinquish their roles as mothers again, despite the emotional pain this entails for them on a personal level, as a further expression of personal sacrifice for the sake of family solidarity.[8]

Although reunification between parent migrants and children who stay in origin countries has often been addressed unproblematically (i.e., as an ultimate goal for transnational families), focusing on grandmother caregivers' experiences offers a different, more complex, perspective on reunification. Even the term "reunification" reflects a unidirectional view of migration, a seemingly inevitable flow of family members following the first migrant from origin to destination countries. However, focusing solely on children's reunification with migrant mothers (or fathers) sidelines the lived experiences of grandmothers and other surrogates who have cared for children in mothers' absences. As demonstrated here, grandmothers form emotional ties with the grandchildren in their care over years, even decades, of caregiving. The prospect of children's migration to reunify with mothers in destination countries implies yet another separation and yet another loss for grandmothers. A Nicaraguan migration scholar has described this cycle of departures and separations as "una herida resangrienta" (a reopening wound) that festers in the emotional lives of members of transnational families in sending countries.[9]

Marbeya's experience offers an example of grandmothers' ambivalence about reunification and uncertainty about the future of their transnational families. Marbeya understood her daughter Azucena's migration as a necessary measure to support her children and family back home in Nicaragua; Marbeya cared for her two grandchildren in what she assumed would be a temporary arrangement. During her first two years in Costa Rica, Azucena could not visit home because she did not have legal residency documents; by her third year abroad, she had secured a legal work permit, which enabled her to travel back and forth to Nicaragua. In subsequent years, Azucena returned several times a year, on Semana Santa, Mother's Day, and during the December holidays. I dropped by Marbeya's household during one of these December visits and talked with Azucena and the rest of the family. I noticed that Marbeya looked especially energized and happy that day, and when I commented about her mood, Marbeya said, "Well, this is how I am when I have all my family together."

While the visits helped Marbeya and her grandchildren feel connected to Azucena, they also opened up the possibility of permanent return and led to a greater ambivalence about the family's future. As Marbeya explained,

> Well, for us, the uncertainty that we have had for the last two years, every time she visits, is whether she is staying [in Costa Rica] or coming home—because this girl [Vanessa] is getting older. And with the boy [nine-year-old Selso], there are moments when you can see in his face that she—that he needs her. But she [Azucena] tells me, "Mom, if I come back, what am I coming back for if there is no work? And I can't earn here what I'm earning there. What I earn there every two weeks it's rare I'll be able to earn here in a month. So why am I going to come back here?" So it seems that she doesn't think she will be able to be back here [no tiene idea de estar aquí] anytime soon.

Just as grandmothers frame their initial assumption of children's care in response to economic scarcity in Nicaragua, so too does economic necessity shape women's sacrifice through migration and care over long separations. While Marbeya would have liked Azucena to return to Nicaragua, she simultaneously felt that her daughter's return was an ambiguous and indeterminate possibility. This uncertainty left Marbeya feeling frustrated, a frustration she occasionally expressed to her daughter or to interested others. For instance, at one meeting of the NGO La Red, at which I was present, the women in the group were talking about the troubles of Nicaraguan migrants in Costa Rica, including their difficulty accessing health care or traveling home to visit their families. Marbeya shared a recent conversation she had had with Azucena, in which she confronted her daughter about whether she planned to stay in Costa Rica or return to Nicaragua. Seeming to gain confidence from the other women in the room, Marbeya said she was firm in reminding her daughter about the burden of her care work, telling Azucena, "It's fine that you send the monthly remittances, but you're not here, you're not in your children's lives; the washing, the ironing, the breakfasting, making sure they've done their homework, that if they're sick, you take them to the clinic—in all this is me." Marbeya glanced up at her audience and recounted her final exhortation to Azucena: "Tell me the truth, so that I can stop fooling myself into believing you're coming home when you're not." In my field notes from that meeting, I recorded my impression of Marbeya, who was usually somewhat reserved, noting that her tone was confrontational and that her voice filled with emotion as she resoundingly emphasized the ongoing sacrifice of her caregiving and her simultaneous desire for some sense of certainty about the future of her transnational family. I also noted that Marbeya's hopes for Azucena's return seemed to be wearing thin and that she appeared to be assimilating the idea that what she had assumed at the outset of her daughter's migration would be a temporary reconfiguration of care was looking increasingly permanent with the passage of time.

At forty-seven, Juana was among the younger grandmothers in this study. In fact, Juana herself had migration experience (she was the only grandmother who herself had migration experience), having lived and worked as a doméstica in Costa Rica in her thirties. At the time of the study, Juana was caring for her three-year-old granddaughter, Loryi, daughter of one of three of Juana's migrant children (Juana has two daughters and a son living in Costa Rica). Until just a few weeks before I met her, Juana had also been responsible for two other grandchildren, ages nine and five, before their mother sent for them to join her in Costa Rica. Migration had inflicted a series of departures, over generations, on Juana and her family. First, as a migrant mother herself, Juana left her four children behind in their rural community to be cared for by their father and a female neighbor. While Juana had hoped her children would be able to avoid migration, they joined hundreds of others from their community several hours north of the Costa Rican border who cross the border seasonally to work in agriculture and service industries. Before they emigrated, Juana's children and their children had lived with her, so Juana had coresident grandchildren before her children's migrations. When her daughters left, Juana felt their absence as an emotional loss, because they had morally supported her, as well as materially. Still, she and her husband, Pedro, assumed care for her three grandchildren. She found in this responsibility a sense of everyday purpose and usefulness that helped her overcome the sadness of her daughter's absence. Juana grew close to her grandchildren during the time they were in her care, viewing them, she said, "as if they were my own children [como si fueran mis hijos]." She described this responsibility:

> Well, we took on the responsibility, as if they were our own children and not grandchildren. When they are sick . . . we take them to the doctor. [We took on the responsibility] by taking care of their children—that's right—by dedicating this time of our lives to our grandchildren. The children of our children. See, that's where you feel closer to your children; for example, when I care for my granddaughters, I feel like I have my daughter close by because she's part of my daughter—right?—so taking care of my granddaughters brings me closer to her.

Juana describes caregiving as a responsibility, which includes overseeing the health of her grandchildren, and yet she also finds in care a way to maintain solidarity with her migrant children. Caring for grandchildren is a way of feeling proximate to her children, despite their physical absence. Juana grew emotionally close to her grandchildren during the months they were in her care. When her daughter telephoned her from Costa Rica and told her she planned to send for her children to join her, Juana was disappointed and yet relinquished their care to support her daughter's desire for a better life for her children. For Juana, when her granddaughters left, it was as if her "children had left" all over again. Through everyday provisioning of care, Juana's grandchildren had become like her children; their migration left Juana coping with a double absence, that of her children and her grandchildren. In this way, grandmothers' sacrifice is extended over time and across generations—first in the assumption of grandchildren's care and then in its relinquishing to support mother-child reunification.

Care in the Face of Uncertainty

Thus far, this chapter has described how grandmothers come to assume grandchildren's care as an act of sacrifice and solidarity for the sake of their migrant daughters and their transnational families. We have also seen the challenges and uncertainties grandmother caregivers in transnational families face, which include the ambivalence surrounding migration's future, especially the possibility of reunification. To deal with these challenges, grandmothers draw on sacrifice and solidarity to motivate and find meaning in their intergenerational care. In what follows, I illustrate how grandmothers respond to the uncertainties of transnational family life through the stories of two women, Aurora and Olga.

Aurora: Care and Negotiations of Reunification

After her daughter Elizabeth migrated to Spain, Aurora, who we met at the start of this chapter, assumed full-time caregiving for her two granddaughters, Salensca and Daniela. Elizabeth's migration was motivated by economic hardship, including mounting credit card debts and overdue house payments, exacerbated by her daughters' father providing no economic support. Aurora understood the economic motivation for Elizabeth's migration and viewed it as an unavoidable, while undesirable, necessity given the children's father's irresponsibility. Aurora summed up the reason for her daughter's migration in terms of these gendered inequalities: "He [the children's father] didn't help her [Elizabeth], and a mother isn't going to let her daughters die of hunger."

Aurora struggled to make ends meet, since she had to dedicate most of the remittances Elizabeth sent to paying off Elizabeth's debts. The girls' father offered Aurora only limited, sporadic financial help, but Aurora was reluctant to reproach him because he had threatened her and Elizabeth in the past. In fact, during a return visit to Nicaragua, Elizabeth had confronted her ex-partner about not providing child support, and he had reacted violently, running her over with his motorcycle in a major marketplace. Elizabeth's injuries fortunately were not serious, and she recovered and returned to Spain. Still, the episode illustrated to the family, and especially Aurora, how dangerous it could be to provoke this man. A short time after this incident, the children's father showed up at Aurora's house and threatened to take the girls into his custody if Aurora and Elizabeth kept pressuring him for money. This was one of a number of times he showed up at Aurora's house and threatened to take the girls away. While Aurora was troubled by his threats, she also thought he would not follow through because she did not consider him capable of caring for his daughters. Aurora tried to reason with him by reminding him that if he wanted to win his daughters' affection, he had to invest in his relationship with them as she herself had done. Aurora explained her view about the relationship to her granddaughters' father:

When parents divorce, the children will go to the father or mother, depending on the case. In this case, Elizabeth had custody, and he [the father] was supposed to put 5,000 córdobas [about $250] a month into an account as child support for the girls' food. And he didn't do it, not even once. But this didn't matter because I fed them; all I wanted was peace. That's what I told him, that we should talk like adults and arrive at an agreement—end the conflict, I told him. He told me, "Tell the girls they have to come with me." But I told him, "No, you can't force children to love you; you have to win them over with your love." Later he told me that I was making the girls not like him. No, I told him, I just earned their love.

In this passage, Aurora articulates an awareness of her vulnerable legal status in relation to her granddaughters. Elizabeth was awarded legal custody of her daughters after the divorce and their father was to pay child support. After Elizabeth migrated and the girls' care was transferred unofficially to their grandmother, Aurora found herself legally vulnerable and unable to insist that her granddaughters' father provide child support.

When grandmothers assume primary caregiving of grandchildren, they most often do so without legal recognition, because Nicaraguan family law privileges biological mothers and fathers and because families lack the legal resources for transferring children's care officially to grandmothers. In 1992, Nicaragua reformed its national family legal code known as the Ley de Alimentos (Law of Nurture), or Child Support Law, which delineates the responsibilities of biological parents for the sustenance and care of their children.[10] The law specifically outlines mechanisms for mothers to seek financial assistance from children's fathers, even when men have denied paternity and otherwise neglected their paternal responsibilities (Asamblea Nacional de la República de Nicaragua 1992). While this law provides the legal framework through which women can petition for child support, de facto enforcement is infrequent as many women are unaware the law exists. Even when women know about the law, they lack the resources—especially access to legal assistance—needed to file petitions under the law's purview. Unless mothers formally transfer guardianship of their children to grandmothers before migrating, which they seldom do, grandmother caregivers are left without legal protection. Fathers can (and do) take advantage of this liminal legal status to intimidate grandmothers, pressuring them to turn over mothers' remittances and not to challenge fathers' own failure to provide economic support to their children.

Despite her legal vulnerability, Aurora was confident in her role as an intergenerational caregiver, and she even asserted herself in her interactions with her granddaughters' father. She gained this confidence through the very act of her caregiving, through which she felt she had earned her granddaughters' love and loyalty, and she criticized his failure to win his daughters over with love. While Aurora was unsuccessful in getting the girls' father to pay child support, she was able to stem his demands for control of remittances, showing the important role grandmothers play in negotiating relationships with children's fathers after mother migration.

Over the two years of Elizabeth's migration, Aurora developed a strong affective tie with her granddaughters, earning their love through her dedicated caregiving. As she said in the quote above, for her, children's love is earned through care, such as that she gave to Salensca and Daniela over two years of being their primary caregiver. These strong ties of relatedness earned through care made it extremely difficult for Aurora when her daughter returned in January 2010 to take her granddaughters back with her to Spain. Instantiating the intergenerational sacrifice that motivates grandmother care in transnational families, even though anticipating emotional despair after their departure, Aurora helped Elizabeth arrange for them to migrate. This involved processing the legal paperwork required for the girls to leave Nicaragua and convincing the girls' father (something Elizabeth herself had been unable to do) to sign legal documents allowing them to leave the country.[11] Aurora was able to obtain this crucial signature (only after several difficult attempts to communicate with the father), and she proceeded to process all the other legal documents that her granddaughters needed (passports, visas, health and school records). In this way, Aurora actively supported her daughter's desire to reunify with her children, even while she knew that it would mean an emotionally painful separation for her. In other words, she sacrificed her own desire to remain with her granddaughters for the sake of solidarity in her transnational family.

Aurora's case offers insights into the emotional consequences of reunification for grandmother caregivers. For women like Aurora, reunification compounds the initial emotions of mother migration. Grandmothers cope with their daughters' absences in part by dedicating themselves to their grandchildren's care. Then, after years of caregiving, having adapted to their daughters' absence and having grown accustomed to the daily routines of mothering again, grandmothers find themselves having to accept the departures of their grandchildren.

In an interview I had with Aurora about a week after Elizabeth had left with her two daughters, Aurora was visibly distraught and cried on several occasions during our conversation. Aurora related her feelings about her granddaughters' recent departure to how she felt two years earlier, when Elizabeth had first migrated:

> Of course, I missed her a lot—I cried a lot, just like right now when the girls left too [*begins to cry*]. But they give—they gave me strength; they said, "Look, Grandma, don't cry. We are going to come back for you when we grow up." How beautiful they are, my precious girls. They said, "Don't cry, because we are leaving happy." I know, I told them . . . [*breaks into tears*].

In this passage, the past turns into the present and folds into possible futures, as Aurora's present feelings about her granddaughters contain traces of the previous loss of her daughter. In the wake of her granddaughters' departure, Aurora's feelings of sadness and loss expand across time and space, so that what she feels in the present about her granddaughters encompasses what she felt two years earlier about her daughter. In her account, the past envelops the emotions of the present, and one departure becomes the next, leaving Aurora to cope with the grief of two generations of migration.[12]

During my interviews with Aurora, I was struck by the complicated ways mother migration results in (re)configurations of family life and by grandmothers' willingness to sacrifice their own emotional welfare for the sake of their daughters. To secure some semblance of peace in the wake of her daughter's migration, Aurora successfully managed a contentious relationship with an abusive and domineering ex-son-in-law. Aurora formed close emotional ties with her grandchildren through her loving caregiving and then actively supported her daughter's decision to have the children reunify with her in Spain. In one sense, Aurora's case illustrates how transnational caregiving relationships are stratified by generation, whereby migrant mothers leave their children in their mothers' care and grandmothers adapt to these reconfigurations by (re)enacting their moral responsibilities as mothers for another generation of children. Yet in another sense, Aurora also exemplifies the moral commitment and sacrifice that motivates grandmothers' caregiving, a sacrifice oriented toward solidarity in transnational families, even when this involves great personal emotional cost.

Olga: Caregiving, Vulnerabilities, and Uncertainties

Olga has similarly experienced raising her grandchildren following their mother's migration to Panama as a source of pleasure and of potential pain. At seventy-two, Olga is one of the older women in my study, and her life of economic poverty and social hardship (including the premature deaths of two husbands and one adult son) shows on her weathered face. Olga was usually dressed in a simple housedress when I visited her small, two-room home. If my visit was in the morning, I would find Olga washing clothes or preparing the midday meal over her two-burner electric *cocina* (stove); in the afternoon, she would be seated alongside nine-year-old granddaughter Juliana in plastic chairs in their small living room watching afternoon cartoons on TV. On one occasion, I found Olga and Juliana dressed up and waiting at their neighborhood bus stop; Juliana was wearing a pretty yellow print dress and her hair was neatly pulled back in matching barrettes. Olga told me they were going to a *reunión* (meeting) of the Jehovah's Witness church in which Olga regularly participates along with Juliana.

In one of my first interviews with Olga, I asked whether she viewed caregiving for Juliana and her seventeen-year-old brother Dayton after their mother Manuela's migration as an added responsibility in her already-difficult life. (While Dayton was in Olga's care, as a teenager and college student, he was largely independent. He also fell outside the seven–thirteen age range for children in my study, and so I never interviewed him.) Olga quickly responded, "No, no. . . . I take it like fun [a distraction] [No, no. . . . Lo agarro como una diversión]." Indeed, despite her life of hardships, Olga enjoys caring for Juliana. Her daily caregiving routines help her feel active, energetic, and healthy. Olga described her busy morning routine:

> In the morning, I make coffee for both of them. While they're drinking their coffee, if I have a dirty towel to wash, I take the soap and wash it while they are finishing eating. When she's done eating, I make sure she [Juliana] brushes her teeth, then I give her money for a snack, and then, "Vamonos," I take her and drop her off at school. While she's at school, I wash, I cook, and I wait until it's time to pick her up.

Through this and other exchanges, I came to understand how Olga's entire daily life revolved around caring for Juliana. From the time she woke in the morning to the time she went to bed at night, Olga was oriented toward (grand)mothering. She did not experience this as a burden but rather as an opportunity to be a mother again for Juliana and to enjoy the close companionship of her young granddaughter. Olga told me, "It's that, to me, I like going around with Juliana," and that, after Manuela migrated, "I haven't separated myself from her [Juliana]." This togetherness provided Olga with a reason to get up in the morning and the energy she needed to carry on with her day. Like other grandmothers, Olga gained a renewed sense of identity and purpose through caregiving, despite the hardships and troubles of transnational family life.

Over the course of my fieldwork, as I spent time with grandmothers and children, and we discussed the possibilities of migrant returns or children's reunifications, I became aware of their profound uncertainty about the future of transnational family life. Grandmothers might say that their migrant daughters were planning to visit *muy pronto* (really soon), but this did not necessarily mean a visit was imminent. Instead, these claims and temporal referents index grandmothers' desires for family unity, which they hope to achieve through migrant return and family reunification in Nicaragua (rather than through children's leaving to join mothers abroad). This ambivalence is reflected in Olga's experience, as she and Juliana experienced the possibility of multiple return visits that never materialized, leaving Olga unsure about whether her daughter would stay in Panama or return to Nicaragua and whether her granddaughter would remain in her care or join her mother abroad.

The main reason Olga's daughter Manuela had migrated was related to the mounting personal debts she had accumulated in Managua. According to Olga, once Manuela's debts were paid off, "then she would come back [despues se venía]." Indeed, Olga facilitated this hoped-for return by using a portion of the monthly remittances Manuela sent home to pay off her daughter's creditors. With the debtors paid off, Olga saw no reason for her daughter to remain abroad and anticipated her return soon. With this background of expectation, Manuela's visits (including those that were never realized) represented the ambivalence of return or family reunification abroad.

As an example of the ambivalence surrounding visits and returns, Olga told me in October 2009 that Manuela was going to visit for the December holidays. Manuela had told her mother that she would ask for time off from her employer and save the money needed to make the trip. Olga eagerly anticipated this visit, as it would be Manuela's first time home since leaving for Panama two years prior. However, the family's plans seemed to have changed a month later; when I asked Olga in November about Manuela's possible December visit, Olga was less confident that it would occur. Instead, Olga said that Manuela might not visit because she would have to spend money needed for Juliana's school tuition. Olga emphasized the high costs of four international border crossings (Panama into Costa Rica, Costa Rica into Nicaragua, and then the return). While disappointed, Olga explained to me that her daughter's undocumented status made traveling to Nicaragua too risky—she could be detained by immigration authorities in Costa Rica and then deported back to Nicaragua. As if to justify her daughter's continued absence, Olga emphasized that the potential costs—personal, political, and economic—were too high for a visit home. These dangers and risks were of course understandable, real, and apparent, yet it is interesting that Olga framed her daughter's decisions to visit or not in light of these broader political inequalities, almost as a means of upholding the image of solidarity in her family even though disappointed by an unrealized visit.

In fact, Manuela's proposed visit in December 2009 never occurred. Ultimately, Manuela was unable to come up with the money needed, around $180, for round-trip bus fare and the fees she would need to pay immigration authorities at both borders (Panama–Costa Rica and Costa Rica–Nicaragua) for her expired tourist visa. This shows how, even in considerations of short holiday visits, international migration politics are always in the foreground, shaping possibilities of returns and contributing to the uncertainty migrants and their family members experience. Even if Manuela had been able to visit that December, Olga faced a broader uncertainty about her family's future and whether Manuela would stay in Panama or return to Nicaragua. Olga said, "I don't know if she's going to stay here or if she's going to take off again [No sé si se va a quedar aquí o si se va a volar de nuevo]."

In addition to the uncertainties of visits, returns, and reunifications, migration had pushed Olga (like Aurora) into a complicated negotiation with her granddaughter's father. For nearly two years after Manuela's departure, Juliana's father, Johnny, stayed in Olga's household, without contributing to household expenses (such as food or utilities) or Juliana's care. This despite Johnny having work as a chef in a Managua restaurant and earning a steady income (unlike other fathers of families in this study who were unemployed or infrequently employed). Olga recounted to me how, on Johnny's payday, she was astounded to witness him giving Juliana a meager five córdobas (about twenty-five cents) for school lunch money. "What a disaster! [¡Qué barbaridad!]" Olga told me, visibly exacerbated that Juliana's father contributed so minimally to her care. Moreover, Johnny constantly intimidated Olga with threats that he was going to take Juliana away from her, which caused Olga a good deal of stress and anxiety. From Olga's perspective, Johnny was attempting to "steal the girl away [robar la niña]." Olga communicated her problems to Manuela, but from a distance, there was little her daughter could do to influence Johnny.

While the situation was more complicated than this brief summary allows, I present this case because (alongside that of Aurora's) it represents a rather common dynamic in families of migrant mothers. Through my engagements with study families and my work with NGOs, I came across similar complicated and troublesome situations related to the custody of children of migrant parents. Because grandmothers like Olga do not want to relinquish the informal custodial relationship they have with their grandchildren and because they lack knowledge and access to legal resources, they often, understandably, respond to fathers' threats with acquiescence (e.g., fearing that challenging the fathers might provoke these men to remove the children from their custody).

As I became more familiar with Olga's situation and as her frustration with Johnny escalated, I decided to consult with a friend and colleague at the Nicaraguan Ministry of Families (Ministerio de la Familia) about legal options Olga might have. Olga agreed to meet with this lawyer (Karen), who informed us about Olga's limited legal options. Although Olga was not protected under Nicaraguan law, she did have legal recourse, which included using the Ley de Alimentos (Child Support Law) to demand child support from Johnny. She could also formalize her guardianship of Juliana by submitting a legal petition, which would have to be signed by Manuela and was a more complicated process. Olga asked for time to consult with Manuela and her other daughter Ana María (who lived near Olga in Managua) before making a final decision about how to proceed.

A week later, I visited Olga, and she affirmed that she wanted to go ahead with the intervention, which would consist of her processing legal guardianship of Juliana and also pressuring Johnny for child support. Subsequently, Karen drafted documents that would transfer guardianship of Juliana from Manuela to Olga. Karen also set up a formal mediation meeting with Johnny to make the case for his legal responsibility to provide child support (the mediation was an alternative to a court hearing, giving Johnny a chance to respond and avoid legal proceedings). The mediation was successful (in the short term, at least) because, within a week of the meeting, Johnny had responded by paying off the tuition owed at Juliana's school and giving Olga a sum for Juliana's care.

Assisting Olga in this way seemed an appropriate response to the troubles she was having with her ex-son-in-law. After talking with Olga in person and Manuela (via Skype) about how I could help, I arranged to meet Manuela in Panama City so that she could sign the legal documents needed to transfer custody of Juliana to Olga. Olga sent me with a few recent photographs of Juliana and other family members in Nicaragua to share with her daughter. Manuela and I met several weeks later at an arranged location outside a large shopping mall in Panama City. From there, Manuela walked me to the small wood-sided house she shared with four other Nicaraguan women. The house was located in a migrant shantytown in the shadows of the high-rise condominiums where Manuela and other immigrant women worked as domésticas. Sitting on a small twin bed, covered in mosquito netting and surrounded by pictures of Juliana and Dayton and the rest of her family in Nicaragua, Manuela and I sat for several hours talking about her migration experience. Manuela told me how much she missed her children but also about how she found herself, over the years, increasingly tied to her friends and social networks and in an intimate relationship with a Panamanian man. Manuela eventually told me that she was considering marrying this man, obtaining legal status in Panama, and bringing Juliana to Panama to live with her. Knowing that her plans would upset her mother, Manuela asked me not to relay this information to Olga. We also talked about how to support Olga in caring for Juliana and dealing with Johnny in the meantime, and Manuela agreed that our child support intervention was a good idea.

After Manuela signed the custody papers I had brought from Managua and as we prepared to leave her house, she received a phone call from a migrant friend and neighbor that Panamanian immigration authorities (*la migra*) were conducting a raid in the neighborhood where they lived. We sat for another half hour or so, before Manuela confirmed (through a phone call with her friend) that the raid was over and the barrio clear of *la migra*. She then walked me back to the bus stop where we had met, and we parted ways, with my promise to be in touch from Managua and her request that I send hugs to her family back home.

As this example shows, my ethnographic research overlapped with the formation of social ties and relationships with families in complicated ways. Throughout fieldwork, I reflected on whether my intervention in Olga's family might put Olga at greater risk; for instance, by possibly increasing her vulnerability to Johnny's demands. I wondered whether I was doing the right thing by involving myself in Olga's case in this way. My intervention felt right, morally and as a human response to a complicated situation, but I was concerned about unintended consequences that could have followed from overstepping the boundaries of the researcher-participant relationship. I wondered whether my actions were motivated by, or might be understood by the family as, an expression of solidaridad with Olga and her family. And importantly, I pondered the differences in access to power and resources between me and Olga and her family—for instance, those inequalities that permitted me to board a plane and fly to Panama City or to walk out of Manuela's barrio without fear of being detected and deported by *la migra*, because I carried a U.S. passport.

As I write this, I remain somewhat uncertain whether my intervention in Olga's family situation was right or wrong. Moreover, the experience of working alongside Nicaraguan transnational families impressed on me the blurred boundaries that ethnographic research entails but also the importance of these close ties for forming deeper understandings of the complexities of transnational migration and family life. I am certain that my intervention was motivated by a sense of alignment (solidaridad) with Olga's family and a desire to use the resources at my disposal to aid Olga in securing a more stable position as an intergenerational caregiver. Uneasily, I remain aware that if Johnny had turned against Olga or Juliana in a violent response to the child support claim, I would have been directly implicated in—ethically and morally responsible for—any resulting harm. While my intervention felt like an appropriate human response at the time and seemed to shift some of Johnny's pressure away from Olga (he did, after all, move out of Olga's household shortly after he received the summons to appear in family court), it might have been inconsequential for Olga's longer-term situation.

A few months after my visit with Manuela, before the conclusion of my fieldwork (in June 2010), Olga told me that Johnny was delinquent once again on Juliana's school tuition and had not given her money for food or other necessities in weeks. I worried about Olga, about Johnny's renewed threats to take Juliana from her care, and about the possibility that Johnny might physically harm Olga in retaliation for her assertion of Juliana's guardianship. But I also felt there was little more I could do for Olga, other than asking my friend Karen, the lawyer, to call on Olga every so often after I left Nicaragua to check in and make sure she was doing all right. I had already left Nicaragua when, in December 2010, Karen told me that Manuela had returned to Nicaragua for a holiday visit and, without previous notice, taken Juliana with her back to Panama. Olga was left suffering the emotional consequences of another loss, lamenting her granddaughter's absence and missing the everyday companionship Juliana had provided.

A year after Juliana's departure, I visited Managua and stopped by Olga's house to visit. I found her, per her custom, dressed in her simple cotton house robe, doing late-afternoon housework, alone. We sat down to talk for over an hour, with Olga growing emotional as she talked about Juliana's departure and about missing her granddaughter's presence, missing her daily routines of cooking for Juliana, taking her to school, and taking her to church activities. We sat for several moments in silence, the weight of another absence hanging over our heads. I tried to shift the mood by asking how Juliana was doing in school in Panama, but I could see that Olga would not be easily cheered. In that moment, the woman energized by the daily care for her young granddaughter was gone, and in her place was a woman who appeared older, more weary, tired, and uncertain about the future. Olga seemed to hold out hope that Manuela and Juliana would one day return to Managua, but this hope glimmered and seemed to fade with the passage of time.

When I consider Olga's story, I recall how, during an interview in May 2010, before Manuela had come back to Managua for Juliana, Olga had told me she did not want Juliana to leave for Panama. Olga said, "I wouldn't like her to leave. Because here she goes to school on her own, [but in Panama] there are times that her mom is going to go get her [from school], and she'll only stay closed up in [Manuela's] room." Olga had personal reasons not to want her granddaughter to leave but also viewed Nicaragua as providing a preferable childhood for Juliana, one where her granddaughter could play in her neighborhood without fear of being detected by immigration authorities and one where Juliana was surrounded by friends and extended family, rather than being isolated indoors while her mother worked. However, like other grandmother caregivers, Olga was struggling to accept the idea that reunification between migrant mother and daughter was a sort of inevitable future to which she was resigned. In her resignation, Olga embodies the gendered sacrifice of intergeneration caregiving in transnational families, reenacting the original sacrifice of assuming care for her grandchild by relinquishing this very child to her mother's care, even at painful emotional cost to herself.

The turns of transnational family life eventually left Olga alone, after years of caring for her granddaughter, living with the emptiness of Juliana's absence and the growing distance and uncertainty that transnational family life entails. This denouement to Olga's family's story, however fragile and uncertain, leaves me with other, perturbing, questions: Did my connection with Manuela, my conversations with her in Panama, my showing her pictures of Juliana—did any of these encounters influence her decision to send for her daughter? By extension, how much is my intervention responsible for Olga's resultant feelings of loneliness and abandonment after her granddaughter's departure? These questions are unanswerable but raise the messy human interconnectedness that ethnographic engagement involves. Ultimately, it is impossible as an ethnographer to extract oneself from the intricate complexities of human social relationships. And yet it is out of these very intricate, intimate ties and complications that anthropological understanding emerges.

Casí como Madres

Reconfigurations of care in transnational families are shaped by gendered structures of family life in Nicaragua and by global political economies of migration. Grandmother caregiving in Nicaraguan families of migrants is also a concrete expression of deeply held cultural values for women's sacrifice and solidarity in family life, as women take on the responsibility of raising another generation of children in the wake of mother migration. Grandmothers assume care of grandchildren as a concrete expression of these values, framing their care work in Nicaragua as a parallel sacrifice to that made by mothers as migrant workers abroad.

The expression "casí como madre" (almost like a mother) indexes the ambivalence of grandmothers' positions as caregivers in transnational families, for they are *qualified* mothers, "*como*" madres; it is *as if* they are mothers because they engage in all the everyday acts of care necessary for children and families, and yet their roles are temporary and vulnerable. Grandmothers' vulnerability is exacerbated by tensions with children's fathers and when encountering the ambivalent prospect of reunification. That all the grandmothers I worked with expressed a willingness to relinquish their caring roles and relationships with children given the prospect of children's reunification with mothers abroad is another instantiation of how sacrifice is embodied by grandmothers as intergenerational caregivers.

The stories of Olga and Aurora highlight the legal and social vulnerabilities of grandmothers in transnational families. Nicaraguan family law almost exclusively privileges biological paternal and maternal ties to children and does not recognize actual custody or caregiving in determining child guardianship. While Nicaraguan family law does not recognize grandmothers as legal guardians of children without a long, drawn-out process of establishing the absence of biological parents, provisions in the law can still be used to push fathers to provide child support. The problem, for women like Olga and Aurora, is that they are unaware of the legal recourse they might have and lack access to the legal services needed to use the law to remedy their vulnerability. Exacerbating grandmothers' vulnerable social positions as intergenerational caregivers are the often-contentious and potentially abusive relationships they manage with children's fathers. (One source of conflict with fathers is access to economic remittances, which is discussed further in Chapter 2.)

Aurora's and Olga's stories also illustrate how the possibility of migrant visits raise complicated questions about the potential of reunifications between mothers and children and the uncertainties that families living with migration face. Grandmothers are instrumental in upholding the emotional relationships between mothers abroad and their children in Nicaragua and encourage mothers to visit regularly as a means of maintaining these transnational ties. While it is grandmothers who assume the emotional work of mothering across generations and borders over the months, years, and even decades between migrants' visits, grandmothers are willing to relinquish their caregiving roles when children reunite with mothers abroad. Furthermore, despite knowing the emotional cost of reunification to themselves, grandmothers reluctantly support mothers' decisions about reunification. By relinquishing grandchildren to mothers' care, grandmothers reenact the original sacrifice of intergenerational care, reinforcing family solidarity through another instantiation of personal sacrifice for the sake of family well-being.

These examples also reveal how grandmother caregiving is ultimately a temporary kinship reconfiguration, which can be reversed when mothers return or send for their children to reunify with them abroad. While they are largely sidelined from decisions about reunification, grandmothers—given the routines they have developed and the loving care they have provided to grandchildren over many years—have an emotional stake in reunification decisions. To clarify, I in no way intend for this discussion of grandmothers' ambivalent feelings about reunification to undermine immigration policy reform efforts in destination countries like the United States or Costa Rica to streamline parent-child reunification processes and thereby reduce the uncertainty experienced by grandmothers and children in migrant-sending families. Streamlining access to legal immigration status, for migrants and for children and other family members, would go a long way in reducing the time of emotionally costly family separations that have been described in this chapter. (In the conclusion, I discuss additional policy implications emerging from this examination of grandmothers' experiences in transnational families.)

Gendered inequalities reconfigure care across generations in families of migrants, and grandmothers respond to these reconfigurations by embodying values of sacrifice and solidarity through their care. Grandmothers respond with agency to the challenges of transnational family life and to the vulnerabilities of their positions as intergenerational caregivers. While often sidelined from discussions of global migration and global care chains, grandmothers, as this discussion shows, are essential actors in transnational families. As Aurora says at the chapter's beginning, "We grandmothers are the ones who are left in the end [Somos las abuelas que quedamos al final]" to deal with the consequences of migration for children and families and for social reproduction and cultural regeneration.

2 No Se Ajustan

Remittances and Moral Economies of Migration

*Ella me ayuda con cien dólares que manda, pero es mentira; con eso no me
ajusta. (She [migrant daughter] helps me with the hundred dollars that she
sends [monthly], but it's a lie; with that I can't make ends meet.)*

—Marbeya

ONE LATE AFTERNOON in 2009, about two months into my year of field research in
Nicaragua, a national daily TV news program focused its hour-long show on
the "problem" of children and families "left behind" after parent migration. The
program's interviewer-host, whom I will call Celeste, showcased the stories of
two grandmothers raising children of parent migrants in two different Nicaraguan towns. In the first interview, Celeste probed an ostentatiously bejeweled
grandmother, Nora, about her neighbors' allegations that she gambled away
all her remittances at the local casino. "Does your daughter know this is how
you spend her hard-earned money?" Celeste asked, with the camera showing
Nora's teenage grandson hanging out in the barrio, smoking cigarettes, wearing sagging jeans, and seeming to be up to *maldad* (no good). The second interview portrayed a similar state of affairs: well-dressed grandmother Dania
bragging to Celeste about her shopping excursions at a major *centro comeri-
cal* (mall), with the camera following her grandchildren, for whom she was
supposedly responsible, roaming the dusty streets of their *colonia* (neighborhood) poorly dressed and hungry. While an exaggeration, this program contains what are the worst sorts of stereotypes about what happens to children
when parent migrants leave them in the care of grandmothers: they receive
inadequate supervision, do not value the sacrifices their parents make through
migration, and ultimately end up dropping out of school or otherwise failing
social expectations. Whether in Nicaragua or elsewhere in Latin America (for
example, see Duque-Páramo 2010), such images of families of migrants relegate grandmothers to the most self-centered of material transactions: money

(remittances) for love (care) while failing to recognize the intergenerational care grandmothers provide as a valuable cultural resource for transnational families. In part, these are gendered stereotypes that blame mothers for emigrating and then assume that grandmothers' motivation to care is solely material rather than recognizing the structural and gendered inequalities that drive both mother migration and grandmother caregiving.

In this chapter, I explore the material and affective dimensions of remittances to illustrate both the concrete reconfigurations of care in transnational families and the inherent tensions entwined with these reconfigurations. This discussion speaks to feminist and anthropological literature on love in the context of contemporary globalization by showing how self-sacrificing love and material interests are always *both* at work within intergenerational transnational family life, as family members balance expectations for remittances against realities of physical absence (Coe 2011: 9). Grandmothers' acknowledgment of the economic necessity of migration—and by extension, remittances—to household survival exists alongside their distancing of themselves from a material explanation for their caregiving. Further, beyond remittances' importance as material support to migrant-sending households, money sent from abroad signifies the affective implications of transnational migration. Remittances signify intergenerational sacrifice and solidarity: as mothers send money, grandmothers allocate remittances to children's and families' well-being; children in turn uphold these sacrifices by doing well in school. However, this transnational tie through remittances has a more problematic side, for just as remittances are a concrete sign that mothers abroad remain *pendiente* (responsible) for families back home in Nicaragua, remittances also serve as an unavoidable reminder of mothers' absence from everyday family life. Grandmothers' insistence that remittances *no se ajustan* (don't measure up) indexes a moral economy of care and migration that sets remittances against the values of sacrifice and solidarity that grandmothers view as threatened by transnational migration.

The argument advanced here is that an economic or structural perspective does not account for the lived experience of remittances from the perspective of members of transnational families in migrant-sending countries. Exploring these experiences is important, especially given stereotypes in Nicaragua, and elsewhere in Latin America, that hold that families of migrants enjoy relative economic prosperity and that grandmothers who head households after parent migration are motivated solely by the material gains of remittances.

Such a transactional view of remittances for care also pervades much of the extant literature on transnational families, which tends to sideline caregiving in migrant-sending countries and relegate caregivers themselves to roles of dependency rather than agency. Here, I make a different set of claims about grandmothers in transnational families, arguing that their stance toward remittances decenters the material and foregrounds the affective, thereby making gendered cultural values of solidarity and sacrifice central to understanding Nicaraguan transnational families. In asserting no se ajustan, grandmothers are at once pointing to the inadequacy of money as compensation for the tensions of transnational life while also critiquing the global inequalities that push mothers to migrate and shift configurations of care across generations in transnational families.

Remittances: Development or Dependency?

In Nicaragua, as in other Latin American–sending countries, migrant remittances are significant to national as well as household economies, providing a much-needed source of income. In 2008, remittances composed between 13 and 18 percent of Nicaragua's gross domestic product, depending on the source (Bello 2008; Rocha 2008; OIM 2013). From 2006 to 2011, the value of remittances sent to Nicaragua increased from $697.5 million to $901 million, equaling or exceeding total foreign direct investment in the country (OIM 2013). Most remittances are sent from Costa Rica and the United States, in currencies valued much higher than the Nicaraguan córdoba, and are a coveted source of revenue in Nicaragua (Guerrero Nicaragua 2014). Mainstream development organizations, such as the World Bank, along with Nicaragua's Central Bank, cast remittances in a positive light by focusing on their contributions to consumer spending, savings, economic growth, and even public investment in health and education (OIM 2013; Bello 2008; World Bank 2006). Within this discourse, women are often situated as pivotal to maximizing the development potential of remittances, occupying a strategic socioeconomic position as recipients of remittances sent by male migrants (their husbands, partners, or sons). As a result, women are targets of interventions seeking to capture a greater proportion of remittances at the household level on savings and investment, rather than consumption (OIM 2013). Such positivist development discourse can inadvertently reinforce stereotypes of women family members of migrants (e.g., when development programs fail, it must be because women were spending rather than saving remittances).

Critics argue that a reliance on migrant remittances in Nicaragua and other Central American countries hinders rather than benefits national economic development. Instead of a boost to development, remittances are viewed as a crutch, aiding the economy in the short term while discouraging central governments from seeking alternative development strategies that are sustainable in the long term (Rocha 2006, 2009). By extension, such critiques view household economies as becoming dependent on the consumer spending facilitated by remittances, a dependence reinforced via the transformation of cultural values toward individualism and materialism that accompanies neoliberal development (see Escobar 1994). Migration scholar José Luis Rocha disparages the view that Nicaraguan families disproportionately spend remittances on consumer goods identified with North American cultural tastes, including electronics, clothes, and toys (Rocha 2008). Such a shift in consumption patterns and social values may be one adverse aspect of "social remittances," which are the transmission of ways of life that predominate in destination countries back home to family members in sending countries via migrants' shifting experiences, tastes, and values (Levitt 1998). In this view, the initial impulse of migration—to secure household economic survival—gradually shifts to become a vicious cycle of debt and dependency on migration, as migrants and their family members become increasingly dependent on remittances to satisfy new material desires, which are themselves reinforced by migration (Stoll 2010, 2012). Critiques of such developmentalist discourse by anthropologists of migration are many. For example, David Pedersen has compellingly argued that remittances and migrant labor are two overlapping sources of value in the contemporary capitalist economy, values interconnecting migrant-sending villages in El Salvador to large U.S. cities through a moral economy based on inequality, violence, and exploitation (Pedersen 2013).

This discussion also contributes to anthropological critiques of developmentalist perspectives on migration by presenting a gendered analysis of the ways women and children in migrant-sending households exert agency over remittances. As has been argued, an exclusive focus on the material dimensions of migration and remittances "discursively excludes" gender (Ginsberg and Rapp 1995: 3) and particularly women's roles in shaping the social, relational, and emotional consequences of migration. Further, economic overdeterminism reinforces popular discourse in migrant-sending countries such as Nicaragua, which characterizes grandmothers caring for children of migrant parents as motivated primarily by the promise of individual material gain. These sorts of images are not without real consequences at the community level, as children of migrants and their caregivers feel the discriminating weight of stereotypes implying they are selfish, materialistic, or otherwise different from their peers because of migration.[1] Furthermore, these views mask the real emotional consequences of mother absence for sending families and relegate grandmothers, other caregivers, and the children in their care to a position of dependence and passivity in relation to migration. Here I address the questions, What is grandmother caregivers' role in relation to remittances sent by mothers from abroad? How do grandmother caregivers make sense of the economic benefits of remittances in relation to the social and emotional costs of migration? While acknowledging the material benefits of migration to household economies, grandmothers' posture toward remittances prioritizes the affective consequences of migration. In particular, grandmothers' response to remittances through the framing "no se ajustan" foregrounds a moral economy of migration, which responds to the tensions and ambivalences wrought by remittances by reinforcing the value of women's intergenerational sacrifice in maintaining relations of care and solidarity in families living transnationally.

Remittances and Household Economies

The ways grandmothers manage and allocate the money sent by migrant mothers demonstrates the influence of both gender and generation on caregiving relations in transnational families. After describing the material dimensions of remittances, I turn to a discussion of remittances' emotional significance, showing how the cultural values of solidarity and sacrifice are upheld through migrant mothers' remaining *pendiente*, or responsible, for children, caregivers, and other family members who stay. This discussion reveals how remittances are central in the refiguring of relatedness and care that occurs across generations in transnational families but also how remittances embody the tensions in cultural ideals of sacrifice and solidarity in Nicaraguan family life. We see how grandmothers engage with these tensions, attempting to regenerate family continuity despite the challenges posed by remittances.

As part of their caregiving responsibilities within transnational families, grandmothers become remittance managers, receiving the money sent by migrant mothers and spending it on children's care. All the families in this study share economic motives as main factors driving mother migration; most also receive money regularly sent by mother migrants from abroad. Exceptions to the regular flow of remittances do occur and reflect various dimensions of migrants' lives in destination countries. For instance, remittances may be ir-regular or interrupted when migration is relatively recent (less than a year since migrant departure), when migrants have yet to establish regular employment, during periods of unemployment, and when migrants separate, divorce, marry, or have children abroad.[2] Certainly, the regularity of sending remittances home depends on migrants' ability to find and maintain secure employment in desti-nation countries. Furthermore, migrants' documentation status in host coun-tries plays a role in the amount and regularity of remittances by influencing the stability and security of employment. Additionally, when personal debts are a primary factor pushing mothers to leave Nicaragua or when migrants incur debts to pay for their migration journeys, the first several months or even years of remittances may be dedicated to paying off the debts. While I did not explicitly inquire whether debts factored into women's decisions to migrate, grandmothers, mothers, and even children mentioned the role of debt (both personal consumer debt and debt incurred to pay for migrant journeys) in in-terviews with five of the fifteen families discussed in this book.

When I asked grandmothers what they used remittances for, without excep-tion all mentioned three main priorities for spending remittances: education, food, and medical needs for the children in their care. Grandmothers receive the regular *envío* (transfer) of money sent by mother migrants usually every *quincena* (two-week pay period), retrieving the money from a bank account or, more commonly, a private money-exchange company such as Western Union or MoneyGram.[3] For the families in this study, remittances average between $100 and $200 per month.[4] I was struck by this consistency in grandmothers' responses to my questions about how they allocate remittances, a response that reflects both the economic priorities of migrant-sending households and the moral stance that grandmothers take in relation to remittances, which is that the money sent from abroad by mother migrants *no se ajusta* (doesn't measure up). Food and housing are materially necessary but also have a symbolic im-portance in maintaining a sense of family relatedness (Carsten 2000), especially over time and across generations of migration (Constable 1999).

Nonetheless, grandmothers' main priority for remittance expenditures is children's schooling. The priority of investing in children's educational oppor-tunities is evident from the large proportion of monthly remittances that go to school tuition. All the children in this study attend private or semiprivate grade schools, with tuition, books, uniforms, and other fees covered by the remittances sent by their mothers from abroad.[5] Average monthly tuition for one student at one of these *colegios* (grade and high schools) in Managua is about $40; this does not include books, uniforms, backpacks, bus fare, lunch money, and other supplies. Given that most families have more than one child to support, school fees can consume a large share of monthly remittances. The emphasis on children's educational success as a central motivation of mother migration is consistent with findings of other scholars who have demonstrated that education is a key goal of parent migration and a main focus of remittance expenditure (Dreby 2010; Abrego 2014). I return to the importance of schooling as part of the intergenerational sacrifice in transnational families below.

Despite the primary importance of schooling, housing, and feeding children, grandmothers also allocated remittances to secondary priorities, such as making household upgrades or repaying debts incurred by mothers before migration. Usually, these second-order priorities become a focus some time after migration, as household economies stabilize and as grandmothers can afford expenses other than food, shelter, and education. In determining the priorities and allocation of remittances, grandmother caregivers communicate and negotiate with migrant mothers, playing an active role in determining how the money that mothers send is spent in Nicaragua. For example, grandmother Marbeya consistently receives about $150 each month from her daughter Azucena, who has worked in Costa Rica for nearly twelve years. During the first four years of her migration, when she worked in a day care center without legal documentation, Azucena's remittances were inconsistent. However, Azucena gained legal residency after her son Selso was born in Costa Rica, enabling her to secure a better-paying and more desirable (from her perspective) job as a doméstica for a family.[6] During the next eight years, Azucena was able to regularly send about a third of her salary to Marbeya. With this money, Marbeya cares for Azucena's two children, Selso (nine) and Vanessa (fourteen). Marbeya described using remittances to cover the costs of her grandchildren's schooling, food, and health:

> I pay for school, I pay for their bus transportation because they come and take them and they drop them off in the afternoon. I pay for their food, and if they get sick, I take money out of remittances for that. Also if they need anything else for school, from [remittances] I pay for all of that.

As another example, as we see in Chapter 1, grandmother Aurora received remittances (around $200 per month) from her daughter Elizabeth, who migrated to Spain a little over two years before our interviews. Elizabeth had

learned about opportunities for employment as a *niñera* (nanny) through social networks of other Nicaraguan women she knew who had obtained work
in Spain and who found a job and a place to live for Elizabeth there. Elizabeth
began sending money about one month after she left Nicaragua and her remittances had been consistent ever since. Most of the money she sent home
was used by Aurora on school expenses, clothes, and food for her two granddaughters, Salensca and Daniela, ages seven and five. Aurora said, "I bought the
girls what they needed with that [remittance money]: clothes, shoes, milk, and
everything for school." Aurora prioritized care for her granddaughters, even as
she also confronted demands from the girls' father that he have direct access
to the money Elizabeth sent home. Aurora communicated these tensions to
Elizabeth, who grew increasingly exasperated at her ex-partner's attempts to
wrest control of her remittances from her mother. After two years in Spain,
Elizabeth fetched her daughters in Managua and returned to Spain, where they
have remained since. For Aurora, their departure was bittersweet; it meant she
no longer had to deal with conflicts about money but also left her missing her
granddaughters' emotional companionship.

One concrete improvement to household economies that follows migration
is the quality of family diet and nutrition. For instance, when I asked Olga about
her household's budget since Manuela's migration to Panama two years prior,
she emphasized that "things in the family haven't changed much [las cosas en
la familia no han cambiado mucho]," referring to the poverty she still lived in
as evidence that remittances "no ajustan" to cover household expenses. Olga
conceded that "solamente en lo de la comida" (only in things related to food)
was there "mejoría" (improvement) in her household economy since Manuela's
migration. Olga went on to describe how, before migration, she would prepare the typical Nicaraguan *gallo pinto* (fried white rice and black beans) for
all three *tiempos* (mealtimes) of the day. After migration, she was able to purchase a greater variety of foods for her household. Olga noted with discern-
able pride that she now was able to prepare soy-based nutritional beverages for
the children every morning and to include animal protein (such as eggs and
chicken) in meals more regularly (usually two times per week). These changes
were made possible by Manuela's remittances of about $125 every month from
her job as a *doméstica* in Panama City, which helped cover the costs of caring
for nine-year-old Juliana and seventeen-year-old Dayton. Even as she manages
a tight household budget, Olga has invested remittances in the health and well-
being of the children in her care through improved nutrition.

For several families in this study, secondary allocations for remittances had emerged as priorities. In these families, the generational distribution of responsibilities for remittances had come to the fore, as grandmothers find themselves responsible for paying off debts incurred by their daughters to migrate (e.g., to purchase expensive plane tickets to Spain). While such networks of debt were not a focus of my fieldwork, that they were salient to the economies of several households in my study supports David Stoll's claim (based on his research in the highlands of Guatemala) that relations of lending, credit, and indebtedness are central to the causes and consequences of contemporary Central American migration (Stoll 2010, 2012). Debts incurred by the mothers in my study before migration were both formal (loans from banks or other lending institutions) and informal (loans made by loan sharks, informal creditors, or family members). When creditors are informal, grandmothers often must manage tense relationships with unsavory characters to ward off collection threats and keep them satisfied with regular debt payments. Their relationship to remittances and debts places grandmothers in a position of responsibility and vulnerability that precedes, facilitates, and follows migration.

For example, Aurora's daughter Elizabeth owed several thousand dollars to a bank for credit card debts and house payments; in fact, these debts were a main factor motivating her migration to Spain (a trip also made possible by borrowed money). During her two years of caregiving for Elizabeth's daughters, Aurora had to set aside enough money from remittances to make payments on the house in which Aurora lived with her granddaughters (but which was in Elizabeth's name at the time). Aurora also had to interact with informal creditors who had lent Elizabeth funds for her plane ticket to Spain. While managing remittances was a significant source of stress for Aurora, she also viewed it as a concrete expression of intergenerational care, as Elizabeth intended to put the house in her daughters' names once it was paid off, giving them an inheritance in Nicaragua.

As another example, grandmother Isabel allocated a portion of the remittances sent by her daughter-in-law Katherine to paying back the loan she had taken out to purchase her plane ticket to Spain. (She had taken a loan from a microlending agricultural cooperative located in the rural town where her parents lived; it was not clear to me under what pretenses Katherine had borrowed the money.) Katherine had lost her job in Managua about three months before she decided to migrate and was pulled to Spain by a female cousin who had emigrated and who had lined up a job for Katherine in elder care. Before she migrated, Katherine discussed her plans with Isabel, who recalled, "I told her she should go, that I would support her, that over there she could find a better future for herself and her family." In this way, Isabel assumed care for Robin as a gesture of solidarity for her grandson, daughter-in-law, and her son. Interestingly, and reflecting women's care responsibilities across generations, Katherine sent her remittances (about $150 every month) to Isabel (not to the father of her son, Isabel's son René), and Isabel allocated them for Robin's care and, later, to paying off Katherine's debts.

Once debts are paid down, usually in cases of longer duration of migration, grandmothers may invest remittances in a third-order priority: improving or upgrading houses. For example, five years after her daughter Azucena migrated to Costa Rica, Marbeya used remittances to build an indoor bathroom and install a concrete floor in the living room of the small house she shared with twenty other family members. Another example is that of grandmother Concepción, whose daughter Melba had migrated to Costa Rica more than seven years before this study. Melba had found work as a *doméstica* in Costa Rica's capital city and sent approximately $150 every month, which Concepción used to feed, clothe, and shelter the six grandchildren in her care (three of whom, ages twelve, fourteen, and fifteen, are Melba's daughters, and the other three, ages seven, seven, and eleven, children of two other migrant daughters, who live in Guatemala and Mexico). While Melba's two migrant sisters also send remittances home to Concepción, Melba earns more in Costa Rica than her sisters do in Guatemala and Mexico, and so she and Concepción agree that her remittances should be shared among the girls. This spirit of shared responsibility for children, in which migrant mothers' remittances are used by grandmother caregivers as a pooled resource for children's well-being, is found in other transnational families, such as Angela's. According to Concepción, one of Melba's original intentions when she left Nicaragua was to earn enough money to purchase a house for her family in their rural community of origin. Concepción was able to help Melba achieve this goal; beginning several years after Melba's departure, and once her household economy was stabilized, Concepción set aside some of her monthly *envío* for the dreamed-of house.

In the months before I met Concepción, she had successfully completed oversight of the house's construction. Of the small, three-room structure, with brightly painted concrete walls and a corrugated steel roof, Concepción said with satisfaction, "Now we aren't rootless, as Melba says. Even though I went through sacrifices and we all went through sacrifices, now we have a stable little place where we can live." For Melba, Concepción, and their family, migration affords a sense of rootedness through a new home. In cases such as this, it is precisely mothers' departure and ongoing absence that enables transnational families to achieve a secure sense of having a *home* in Nicaragua.[7] Houses built or upgraded with remittances are a concrete sign of the intergenerational sacrifices made by women in transnational families. However, homes built by remittances may also embody the uncertainties of migration insofar as they signify mothers' continuing absences and the illusory promise of migrants' return (Fourrat 2012; Sandoval-Cervantes 2015). Concepción pondered whether, now that Melba's goal of building a house had been achieved, her daughter would return to Nicaragua as promised. The house had been completed for several months, and yet Concepción remained uncertain about her family's reunification.

As these cases show, home improvements may be made when migration lasts long enough for the household's economy to stabilize and permit grandmothers to spend remittances on things other than first-order priorities of education and food. Signaling these priorities, grandmothers would point to their *inability* to make needed home improvements as a sign that migration had not changed their family's economic status much at all. For instance, during an interview with Olga in her home on a rainy Managua afternoon, she pointed to the stream of water leaking through her roof and rhetorically asked, "Don't you think I would have replaced this zinc roof if I could have afforded it?" In posing this question, Olga reinforced the idea that migration had not significantly changed her household's economic status.

Remaining *Pendiente*: Gender, Generation, and Responsibility

As the preceding discussion demonstrates, managing remittances forms an important part of grandmothers' caregiving responsibilities in transnational families. Grandmothers in Nicaragua see their caregiving, including their relationship to remittances, as embodying cultural values for sacrifice and solidarity in families extended across transnational space and into the uncertain futures of return or reunification. Mothers who migrate and their families back home see remittances as a sign of women's concrete sacrifice *as mothers*, albeit mothers who live and work abroad. In short, through remittances, mother migrants are able to remain pendiente for the well-being of their families back home in Nicaragua, just as through their management of remittances, grandmothers participate in the intergenerational sacrifice of migration.

Remittances partly reinforce gender role expectations for women in Nicaraguan transnational families, even while the responsibility for care is reconfigured as it is extended across generations and over space and time. Other migration scholars have argued that gender roles are transformed in the context of transnational migration, as migration permits women greater economic autonomy through employment abroad than they would otherwise have experienced (for example, see Hirsch 2003; Parreñas 2005; Moran-Taylor 2008). Rather than a transformation of gendered expectations for women's sacrifices to their families as mothers, I found that mothers' sacrifice is refigured through migration, work abroad, and sending remittances, while grandmothers' sacrifice is extended over time through intergenerational caregiving, which includes the management of remittances. Instead of being either radically transformed or completely reinforced, gendered values related to women's sacrifice and care for families are reconfigured over generations and across borders in Nicaraguan transnational families.

In this framing, mothers uphold their responsibilities to families through migration and by sending remittances, while grandmothers uphold their end of the intergenerational sacrifice of migration through managing remittances and allocating them to children's care. Grandmothers and children refer to mothers' responsibilities using the cultural trope of pendiente, in which mother migrants are perceived as upholding responsibilities by sending remittances to and keeping in touch with families back home. In this way, while the content of care shifts from mothers' physical presence to their sending money in *ausencia* (absence), children's experiences of transnational family life may be less disrupted to the extent that the regular receipt of remittances and frequent communication with mothers is framed in terms of mothers' sacrifice for children's well-being.[8] In fact, situating mothers' remittances discursively and symbolically as a sign of mothers' sacrifice is one key element of grandmother caregiving. The alternative, undesired possibility is that mothers *abandonan* (abandon) their children and families in Nicaragua by ceasing to remit and otherwise losing touch. Much more than money is at stake in the receipt of remittances, as mothers' envíos become an index of the strength of family ties and the maintenance of relatedness across national borders.

For instance, Norma described her daughter María José's remittances as a concrete sign of her fulfilled responsibilities to her family in Nicaragua. Over nearly ten years of migration (except for a difficult episode during the first few years), María José regularly sent an average of $250 per month to Norma.

Norma managed the remittances María José sent, using them for grandson Jeremy's education in a private elementary school and to cover other costs associated with Jeremy's care. More recently, María José also sent remittances to help Norma make improvements to the home she and Jeremy share. These improvements included adding a bedroom and bathroom and painting the house's interior. In addition, María José sent money so that Norma could purchase a desktop computer and wireless Internet service so that family could regularly communicate. Of María José, Norma said, "She's the one who's maintained the family all this time up until now, she's the one who has made all this happen. All the costs are on her shoulders. She has taken on everything." Norma frames María José as taking on the costs of supporting her family as part of her sacrifice as a transnational mother. Norma reinforces this framing of mother sacrifice with grandson Jeremy, reminding him whenever they receive her envío that his "mamá Marí" is working hard in the United States for his benefit and that she has not forgotten her son but remains pendiente for his well-being.

Grandmothers view the consistent sending of remittances as a symbolic representation of mothers' care, even as remittances fail to fully compensate for mothers' absence. For instance, grandmother Marbeya told me proudly that her daughter Azucena had consistently sent remittances during the eleven years she had lived and worked in Costa Rica. Marbeya has seven adult children, including four daughters, but Azucena is her eldest child and the only one who had migrated. Further, Marbeya shared a particularly close relationship with Azucena, which magnified the emotional impact of Azucena's migration. Marbeya recounted, "I lost my company; I lost it—because up until today I still don't have it. But economically, well, she [Azucena] has always been helping. . . . Thank God she has never abandoned her first daughter or her mother or her other son here." For Marbeya, the regular receipt of remittances confirms that her daughter has not "abandoned" her children or family in Nicaragua. Instead, Marbeya describes how remittances are a concrete sign that mother migrants maintain their intergenerational responsibilities as both daughters and mothers. However, despite Azucena being pendiente, remittances only partially offset the emotional distress of migration, for Marbeya still feels sadness over the loss of her daughter's "company," her everyday supportive presence. Even though she has always received remittances, Marbeya fears her daughter may one day abandon her and the children. In grandmothers' narratives of transnational family life, abandonment remains a threat to family unity and solidarity, an ever-present possibility that represents the antithesis of culturally valued sacrifice and solidarity.

The average length of migration in this study was two years; two mothers—Marbeya's daughter Azucena and Norma's daughter María José—had lived abroad for more than a decade. Despite the length of time, all mothers continued to send remittances and communicate regularly with families in Nicaragua. This consistency persisted even though some mothers formed new families and bore children abroad. This finding concurs with what other studies of transnational families have documented, which is that mother migrants tend to send remittances and maintain relationships over longer periods of migration than father migrants (for example, see Hondagneu-Sotelo 2001; Abrego 2009, 2014). This dynamic illustrates how gender shapes transnational family relationships, whereby women uphold gendered cultural expectations of themselves as mothers, despite the difficulty of their illegality and precarity in host countries. Grandmothers who also had migrant sons (six women in this study) would often compare their sons' and daughters' remittance behavior as a way of emphasizing women's enduring responsibility to their children, further reinforcing gendered cultural expectations for mothers.

Grandmother Juana had one son and two daughters who emigrated to Costa Rica (all three children left grandchildren in Juana's care). Juana made gendered distinctions between her son's and her daughters' remittance patterns, emphasizing that her son's remittances are smaller than her daughters, who know to send enough money to cover basic household necessities, such as food and medicine, for their children's care. Juana told me,

> When my son sends me money and I don't have anything, I can go buy food, [but only a little] because everything is expensive, and he doesn't send much. But when my daughter sends money, it might be enough to pay for things at the store, basic grains, and other things. . . . And if maybe the girl [her granddaughter] needs something, a medicine, whatever, something else, well, we can buy it.

Juana's two daughters migrated six months before this conversation and each sent about $50 per month home, despite their relatively low-paid jobs in beauty salons. On the other hand, Juana's son had lived in Costa Rica for over ten years and had a steady, relatively better-paid job in construction, and yet his remittances were fewer and less consistent.

Juana viewed her son's behavior as illustrative of a broader cultural pattern, explaining migrant fathers' relative inconsistency in sending money as a reflection of gendered norms shaping Nicaraguan men's behavior and irresponsibility for children. Specifically, Juana viewed migrant Nicaraguan men living in Costa

Rica and other destination countries as prone to succumb to *vicios* (vices), such as heavy drinking and infidelity. Juana claimed, "The man assumes many vices over there and forgets about his family here [El varón agarra muchos vicios allá y se olvida de la familia aquí]. This is why the man doesn't send hardly anything." Unlike migrant mothers, who have the fortitude to remain responsible to their families back home, Juana views Nicaraguan men as lacking willpower to resist temptation and thus being vulnerable to *vicios*. This gendered framing, while partly critiquing men, also situates paternal irresponsibility as an almost anticipated outcome for father migrants and reinforces the gendered expectations that mothers remain pendiente, even when fathers fail to do so.[9]

Luisa María offers another example of how grandmothers discursively reinforce gendered expectations of migrant mothers compared to fathers. Luisa María has one son and one daughter living in Costa Rica and sharing a residence there. Luisa María was raising five grandchildren, four children of migrant daughter Salvarita (who had lived in Costa Rica for three years) and one son of migrant father Marcos (who had been in Costa Rica for one year). Marcos's employment in construction was sporadic, and he sent remittances irregularly. Salvarita, on the other hand, had regularly sent $50 every two weeks once she found work as a doméstica shortly after arriving. Luisa María remarked on the difference between her daughter's regular remittances and her son's irregular support, saying, "The difference has to do with the fact that she is a woman and she knows the obligation and she knows the finances, she manages the situation, and this is why. It's always the daughters who know what children cost, they are more responsible than sons." In other words, women and mothers are thought to be more understanding of the costs of maintaining a family and therefore more responsible for meeting these costs with remittances than men and fathers. Luisa María's statement seemed to overlook her son's unstable employment and instead focused on his (almost anticipated) paternal irresponsibility.

To the extent that grandmothers use such gendered assumptions to frame differences between mothers and fathers' remittance behavior, they are in essence upholding a gendered double standard that increases the pressure on mothers while excusing fathers' lack of responsibility for children and families. Thus, fathers who fail to send remittances are in part fulfilling cultural expectations that they are less responsible than mothers. On the other hand, grandmother caregivers expect that migrant mothers will uphold their responsibility by remaining pendiente for children back home through remittances. This double standard most likely adds to the pressure on mothers to send money and compounds mother migrants' stress when they are unable to, such as when unemployed or beset by pressing economic demands.

Schooling and Intergenerational Sacrifice

Not only mothers sacrifice to remain responsible for families back home; grandmothers and children also participate in the shared sacrifice of transnational family life. Grandmothers sacrifice through caregiving, which includes the management and allocation of remittances for the welfare of children and households. Children, for their part, contribute to the shared intergenerational sacrifice of transnational migration by studying and succeeding in school.

The five mother migrants I interviewed as part of this research study all emphasized that a central motivation for their migration was to afford expanded educational opportunities for their children. When Azucena visited Nicaragua for the New Year's holiday, I sat down with her to talk about her motivations for migrating to Costa Rica over a decade earlier and her struggles as a migrant mother. Azucena said her principal motivation for migrating was to give her daughter Vanessa the opportunity to study at the university level, an experience Azucena had not had: "My goal is that she completes her education. . . . I put all my effort toward her studying." For her part, grandmother Marbeya reinforces this emphasis on education by paying for Vanessa's school tuition and supporting her daughter's ambitions that Vanessa attend university in Nicaragua.

One interpretation of this motivation to expand children's educational opportunities is that it reflects and reinforces a particular, Westernized view of childhood as a period of dependency and of children as in need of protection from work or other responsibilities (for example, see Horton 2008: 926; for a critique of this view, see Heidbrink 2014). However, my interpretation of children's experiences in the families in this study is that they are not protected from the difficult realities of migration but rather are keenly aware of, and immersed in, the struggles and sacrifices of transnational family life. Although children in this study were not economically productive, they participated in the shared sacrifice of migration by studying hard and succeeding in school. In my home visits with families, most after-school hours were spent doing homework, with children intently focused on their upcoming exams to ensure they would *pasar de grado* (pass on to the next grade). Of all the children in this study, only one seemed not to be doing well in school.[10]

For instance, children are knowledgeable about the economic motives of their mothers' migrations as well as about the economic costs and benefits of migration (for a fuller discussion of children's experiences than that provided here, see Yarris 2014a). Children (even those as young as six years old) can re- count in detail the circumstances of indebtedness, underemployment, and eco- nomic hardship that prompted their mothers to migrate. For example, Juliana told me of her migrant mother, Manuela, "She had to leave to pay some banks. She had to go and work there and send my grandma [money] to feed me." At nine years old, Juliana was aware that her mother was financially indebted to "some banks," that she was working in Panama to pay off these debts, and that the money sent from Panama to her grandmother Olga is essential to buy food and sustain the household. Fourteen-year-old Vanessa expressed a similarly sophisticated understanding of the economic realities of migration. Vanessa recalled her initial response to her mother's migration over ten years earlier: "I asked myself, 'Why did she leave?' and the answer I came up with is, well, that she had to leave to work so that we could study and because we needed money to live."

Grandmothers reinforce this narrative of remittances as a necessary part of the intergenerational sacrifice of transnational family life by reminding chil- dren that their migrant mothers are working extremely hard for their benefit.[11] As an example, eleven-year-old Laleska described how her mother Karla "is working [over there, in the United States] so that I can be well [over here] [Está trabajando allá para que pueda estar bien aquí]." Grandmothers also reinforce mothers' sacrifice by making sure children are aware of how much money and with what frequency their mothers send remittances. For example, Juliana knew that her mother regularly sent about $125 to grandmother Olga, and could even spell out the detailed process Olga went through to obtain this money from Western Union at each envío. Similarly, grandmothers framed the gifts mothers sent to children as more than mere material presents sent from abroad; they were, rather, another instantiation of their mothers' efforts to up- hold affective ties over space and time. Robin, the six-year-old son of Kather- ine, who had been in Spain for about two years, was happy to receive a toy fire engine and a stuffed bear from his mother one afternoon when I visited, but he told me in a clear voice, "Yes, I like them, but I really want to see her again soon [Sí me gustan, pero quiero que le vuelvo a ver pronto]." Despite his young age, Robin was able to articulate the ambivalence about money and love, presence and absence, embodied by remittances and gifts in transnational families.

For children and their grandmother caregivers, remittances sent from abroad are always about more than material gifts; they are also signifiers of the temporal dimensions of migration, simultaneously indexing mothers' sacrifice, marking their long absence, and indexing the future uncertainty of return or reunification. Like Robin, most children in my study had ambivalent relationships to remittances, gifts, and even their mothers' phone calls from abroad. So it was that Laleska said she usually did not tell her mother about problems she was having at home or school, since, in her words, "What good does it do if she's not here to help me?" Similarly, fourteen-year-old Vanessa, Marbeya's granddaughter, opted not to tell her mamá Azucena about troublesome things her peers told her at school—for instance, when her classmates accused her mother of having abandoned her—because, according to Vanessa, "There are things you can't communicate over long distance." Vanessa's nine-year-old brother Selso added that every time his mother called or sent money or gifts home, he is "happy but also sad [feliz pero triste también]." When I asked Selso to explain, he told me he felt happy to receive the gifts she sent but also sad because his mother was not physically present and he did not know when she would return to Nicaragua. For children, money and gifts do not fully compensate for their mothers' absence, and phone calls fail to collapse the distance between them and their transnational mothers.

Grandmothers and the children in their care simultaneously experience remittances as a symbol of mothers' responsibility and a sign of the uncertainty of the future of return or reunification. Gendered cultural expectations shape the ways that remittances sent by migrant mothers are understood by family members in Nicaragua, particularly through the trope of remaining pendiente for children and families, over time and across borders. However, the ideal of responsibility indexed by "pendiente" is less a stable state of transnational family life and more a status that migrant mothers strive to attain, their striving occurring against the realities of distance and absence and the feared possibility of abandonment. Just as remittances are a sign that mothers have not forgotten families back home, money sent from abroad also marks mothers' absences, further inscribing uncertainty on the everyday experiences of children and grandmother caregivers in transnational families.

Remittances Do Not Measure Up

Despite the material benefits and shared sacrifice surrounding remittances, grandmothers in my study insisted of remittances that "no se ajustan." This is an idiomatic expression that translates approximately to mean that remittances do not make ends meet or measure up. On one level, saying "No se ajustan" is a way for grandmothers to emphasize the difficulty of covering the costs of child caregiving and household maintenance with the money sent by mothers from abroad. By using this expression, grandmothers emphasize their part in the sacrifice of transnational caregiving. However, "no se ajustan" also refers more broadly to the inability of remittances to fill the *vacío* (void) left in the wake of mothers' migration. In this framing, in using the phrase "no se ajustan" grandmothers are giving narrative form to the tensions between love and money, care and compensation, absence and distance in transnational families.

Grandmother Juana described how she used the approximately $50 sent by each of her daughters every two weeks from Costa Rica, "to buy food, to buy the things the girls [her granddaughters] need for school, and we always save for whatever sickness or whatever emergency the girls might have." One of Juana's granddaughters suffers from severe asthma, exacerbated by the hot, dusty climate of her rural community, so covering expenses related to her medical treatment (inhalers, a home respirator machine, and other medicines) is a constant source of concern for Juana. Juana insisted of remittances,

> No, no, it doesn't measure up [No, no, no se ajusta]. You have to make, like they say, other little adjustments to make [ends meet], and even though we are few [in the household], the money isn't anything. That's because everything's expensive. If you have to buy a medicine . . . that takes away [from the food budget], as they say; [remittances] are just not [enough]. . . . You have to limit yourself to not buy some things to be able to buy other things.

Juana emphasizes the material inadequacy of remittances, but she also alludes to her own agency in relation to remittances, as she is the one who has to manage household economies, limiting her spending on "some things to be able to buy other things"—in other words, prioritizing the feeding and care of her grandchildren.

Grandmother Luisa María, who was caring for four children of migrant mother Salvarita, emphasized her gratitude for remittances, saying that, without this money, "Who knows how I would do it? [¿Quien sabe como hiciera yo?]." Still, even as she recognized remittances as imperative to covering the economic costs of caring for her grandchildren, Luisa María explained that remittances are insufficient to cover household expenses: "$50 is for four children and from that I have to buy everything, and sometimes you find yourself in a real bind because $50 doesn't measure up [no se ajusta]."

On a material level, by insisting of remittances that no se ajustan, grandmother caregivers are referring to the economic realities of their households, which are that they continue to struggle to meet household costs, even with remittance income. In a study comparing households of migrants to nonmigrants in Nicaragua, Sang Lee documented how families of migrants "at best cope with (and don't necessarily flourish from) international migration" (Lee 2010: 8). Indeed, in my study, all families of migrants remained living in the same communities and neighborhoods where they had lived before migration, challenging the developmentalist assumption that migration and remittances are automatic pathways to class mobility. While not eliding grandmothers' real concerns about meeting household economic needs and considering the frequency with which grandmothers talked about their difficulties in making ends meet, the phrase "no se ajustan" refers to not just the material dimensions of remittances but also a broader claim by the grandmothers about the moral economies of migration.

In one sense, by saying the money sent by migrant mothers is insufficient, grandmothers are indirectly referring to (and rejecting) popular ideas that caregivers of children in transnational families stand to personally gain from remittances, such as in the vignette that opens this chapter. Instead, "no se ajustan" emphasizes that grandmothers stand in solidarity with their migrant daughters and uphold the shared, intergenerational sacrifice of migration through their caregiving.

As a way of distancing themselves from potential personal economic gain from remittances, grandmothers emphasized that they had to forgo needed medical care for themselves because they could not afford it. For instance, Marbeya had delayed a needed cervical cancer screening because she did not have money to pay for it. Grandmother Angela, diagnosed with high blood pressure, similarly told me she was unable to regularly purchase her prescribed medication because she did not have the money for it after paying for her granddaughters' care. In their conversations with me about remittances, grandmothers would constantly evaluate competing household needs and describe how they carefully calculated expenses to make ends meet and prioritize children's well-being.

In a broader sense, by referring to remittances through the frame "no se ajustan," grandmothers stake their claim about the inadequacy of remittances to compensate for the costs of mother migration to cultural continuity and social regeneration. What fails to "measure up," from grandmothers' point of view, is that money sent from abroad will always be inadequate compensation for the disruption to family unity and solidarity that mother migration provokes. In other words, what fails to measure up for grandmothers is that remittances cannot fill the void left by mothers' continuing absence from everyday family life.

Grandmother Concepción articulated quite clearly these moral economies of migration, remittances, absences, and care. Concepción spoke directly against stereotypes about grandmothers such as herself assuming care for children of parent migrants solely in exchange for remittances. She said, "That's something else. It's not for money that we assume this responsibility. It's not because we benefit from the money . . . because there are moments that I don't even have a peso in hand [no tengo ni un peso en la mano]. Do you understand? So, no, it's not for that." Concepción emphasized the economic limitations she faces as one dimension of what "doesn't measure up" about remittances. Concepción also talked about her grandchildren growing up without their mother and dealing with accusations or teasing from their peers because their mothers have migrated. Referring to her care work in response to these tensions, Concepción said, "That is what we grandmothers respond to. We fill the void for them that mothers can't [Les llenamos ese vacío que las madres no pueden]." For Concepción, this emotional dimension of caring for and caring about is what motivates grandmothers' sacrifice, a sacrifice made in solidarity with the sacrifices made by their migrant daughters.

As another example of the ways grandmothers view remittances as failing to measure up, Juana explained her thoughts about her daughter's migration and remittances:

> Idiay,[12] but the situation and economic necessity make us feel divided. . . . I told my spouse, maybe when the family is all together, sharing a meal, you feel surrounded by your children. Everyone there together, right? But when they leave [migrate], what's left over is that emptiness [vacío], that feeling that says, "You start and you end alone [Uno comienza solo y termina solo]" if there's not—if your children aren't with you.

In Juana's rendering, remittances partially symbolize, and partially stand against, the emptiness (*el vacío*) left after mother migration. For grandmothers, the moral consequences of migration are more important than the economic results.

As another example, in her narrative of her daughter's migration, Marbeya emphasized the emotional consequences:

> You feel you want to cry, you wake up depressed, you want to close yourself off [Se siente ganas de llorar, amanece deprimida, se quiere estar encerrada]; when you are without money and it's time to pay the light bill, the water, school, you get even more depressed. It doesn't measure up, what Azucena sends back [no le ajusta lo que manda la Azucena].

Her feelings of depression and sadness illustrate Marbeya's difficulties in paying household bills, but also, and most centrally, they foreground Marbeya's sense of loss over her daughter's absence. In considering the economic effects of remittances and her difficulties in covering household expenses, Marbeya emphasizes that migration does not measure up—either economically or emotionally.

As these examples show, central to the moral economies of migration from grandmothers' perspective is the threat that migration poses to having *toda la familia unida* (all the family united). *Unidad* (unity), like *solidaridad* (solidarity), is a central cultural ideal for Nicaraguan family life. Remittances are often understood in relation to these cultural values, such that receipt of remittances is, as described above, much more than a mere *envío* of money; it is a way for families to remain affectively tied across national borders.[13] This moral valence means that remittances help transnational families feel that they remain united and in solidarity, despite distance and time. The sacrifices that mothers make, through sending money, and grandmothers make, through allocating remittances, are ways women express solidarity with these moral values for family life. Nonetheless, as the claim "no se ajustan" reveals, family unity and solidarity are always held in tenuous counterpoint to other, undesirable, possibilities— namely, that migrants will forget about, or even abandon, family members back home. The threat of abandonment casts a veil of uncertainty over grandmothers' caregiving efforts.

One concrete way grandmothers draw attention to the threat migration poses to family unity and solidarity is by lamenting that migrant daughters are physically absent at times of sickness. When children are sick, grandmothers feel that mothers should be present and able to take care of them.

When grandmothers themselves are ill, they long for their daughters' presence and their emotional and instrumental support. To emphasize their daughters' absence during these moments, grandmothers would lament, "If she were only here to bring me a glass of water [Si solo estuviera para traerme un vaso de agua]." Whether grandmothers were sick or just in need of emotional support, that their daughters were not present and unable to fulfill this most basic of supportive tasks is a symbolic illustration of the moral impact of mother migration on intergenerational relationships of care. Even though migrant mothers regularly send money home, from grandmothers' perspective this material transfer is inadequate compensation for mothers' physical and emotional absence. In other words, remittances are necessary (to household material economies) but insufficient (for moral economies of migration and care).

In emphasizing grandmothers' experiences, this discussion is not meant to deny or undermine the sacrifices made by mothers. In my interviews with migrant mothers, I was impressed by their struggles and their overcoming the hurdles and precarities of illegality and undocumentation; working long hours, often in multiple jobs; confronting discriminatory working conditions; and sending a large portion of their earnings home for their children and families in Nicaragua. In addition to their own sacrifices, mothers also express gratitude for the sacrifices their mothers make to care for grandchildren.

In an interview that took place shortly after the airing of the television program described in the opening of this chapter, Concepción rejected the view presented by the host Celeste that grandmothers raising children of migrant parents are motivated primarily by remittances. Seemingly frustrated that the public could so greatly misunderstand the reality of her family's life, Concepción said,

> They're wrong because, at least in my case, I don't do it to benefit myself because it's a lie; I do it more humanely—not as a grandmother but out of my humanity, because these children can't go anywhere else. I hear so many cases of mothers who send their children over borders, and they are robbed or even killed.

Concepción articulates grandmothers' moral accounting of mother migration and its consequences for family life. As a grandmother caregiver, she is adamant that her motivation is not the remittances her daughter sends but her "humanity," a desire to protect her grandchildren from possible harm and to share in the sacrifice of migration. The possible harms to migrant children are great, Concepción knows, and her intergenerational care is an embodied form of protection against the dangers of illicit migration. It is not money, in Concepción's configuration, but solidarity and sacrifice that motivate the care she extends across generations in her transnational family.

Money, Love, and Moral Economies of Care

The moral claims grandmothers make about the value of remittances and care in transnational families recall long-standing debates in feminist literature about the economic and social value of women's caregiving. Feminist scholars (for example, see Folbre 2001; Zelizer 2005; Glenn 2007) have convincingly argued that women's activities in the domestic sphere—caring for children and maintaining households—while unpaid or underpaid, have essential economic value in the broader (extrahousehold) economy. In her important work on economics and family values, for instance, feminist economist Nancy Folbre argues that family caregiving activities are founded on three general principles: love, obligation, and responsibility (Folbre 2001). These three principles are embodied by the caregiving of grandmothers in Nicaraguan transnational families, care that both motivates and reinforces gendered cultural ideals of women's sacrifice.

Feminist scholars have also highlighted what has been described as an increasing "commodification of intimacy" (Boris and Salazar Parreñas 2010: 8), or a tendency in postindustrial, globalized societies to negotiate relationships of love, care, and intimacy through the marketplace. To the extent that migrant mothers' relationships with their children back home become focused on sending and receiving remittances and other gifts, these transnational ties might be viewed as one example of this increasing commodification (Boehm 2012; Horton 2008). However, relations of love, care, and emotional intimacy are always, at least partly, influenced by economic exchanges and material interests (Boris and Salazar Parreñas 2010).[14] In one sense, Nicaraguan grandmothers' concerns that economic remittances cannot replace emotional intimacy may be viewed as upholding a false dichotomy between money and love. However, I advance another interpretation for solidarity and unity in family life: that grandmothers' laments about remittances index their views of mother migration as running counter to cultural expectations for physical and emotional closeness between mothers and children. In this way, grandmothers' posture toward remittances reflects their stance that money cannot buy love and that only through committed caregiving can family relationships be sustained, especially in families divided by borders. In this way, the claim "no se ajustan" embodies an ethics of care that is noncontractual (Held 2006), a rejection of the remittances-for-care assumptions built into developmentalist and popular discourses about families of transnational migrants.

Viewed in this way, grandmothers' rejection of the money-for-love trans-actional model of the remittances-caregiving relationship is, by extension, a critique of the marginalization of women's care across generations. Both the remunerated care work of migrant mothers abroad (which becomes neces-sary for social reproduction) and the nonremunerated care of grandmothers (which is necessary for social regeneration) ultimately do not measure up to the moral ideals for family unity and solidarity. Claiming "no se ajustan" cap-tures these tensions surrounding the complex material necessity, but emotional inadequacy, of mothers' remittances and the necessity, but also the imperma-nence and uncertainty, of grandmother caregiving. Grandmothers' tenuous re-lationship to and narratives of remittances articulate an even broader critique of a structural system that pushes mothers to leave Nicaragua in order to sup-port household economies while threatening the moral economies of solidarity and care that sustain families across generations.[15] In this way, grandmothers' claims of "no se ajustan" pose a challenge to discourses—both popular and scholarly—that view remittances as a positive sign that communities are in-creasingly integrated through global capitalist development (for example, see Orozco 2002). Instead, even while acknowledging the material importance of remittances to household economies and while participating in the shared in-tergenerational sacrifice surrounding mother migration, grandmothers lament that migration separates their families and that their intergenerational care is necessary at all. (These tensions, contradictions, and ambivalences surround-ing transnational family life and caregiving as significant sources of emotional distress for grandmothers are the focus of Chapter 3.)

In another sense, the claim "no se ajustan" also reflects grandmothers' desire for recognition of the value (both economic and emotional) of their intergen-erational caregiving within transnational families. This desire for recognition is illustrated by what I witnessed in my visit to La Red described in the intro-duction. Recall that, one afternoon early in my fieldwork, I attended a meeting of an NGO of women family members of migrants to identify women who fit my study criteria. After I had made clear that my interest was in their ex-periences, in Nicaragua, of intergenerational caregiving, Marbeya responded, "Finally, someone's interested in us [En fin, alguien se interesa por nosotras]." Grandmothers viewed their relationship with me as an opportunity to tell their stories and have their experiences made visible, validated, and valued. Grandmother care embodies values of solidarity and sacrifice, which are essential to social reproduction and regeneration within Nicaraguan transnational families. By situating their relationship to remittances within the frame of "no se ajustan," grandmothers are drawing attention to the limited economic benefits of migration and the value of their intergenerational care within the moral economies of migration.

3 Pensando Mucho

Transnational Care and Grandmothers' Distress

> *Pensando mucho, demasiado . . . pensamientos sobre como cuidar de todo . . . la parte económica y todo porque . . . soy la que piensa en todo. Es decir, soy la responsible. (Thinking too much, way too much . . . thoughts about how to take care of everything . . . the economic part and everything because . . . I'm the one who thinks about everything. I mean, I'm the one who is responsible.)*
>
> —Beatriz

The Distress of Transnational Caregiving

Understanding the cultural significance of grandmothers' roles as caregivers in transnational families requires attending to their experiences of embodied distress. Medical and psychological anthropologists have long documented the broader social and cultural significance of pain and illness, especially among women, who may use embodied distress to register complaints about social change on their individual and family lives (for example, see Finkler 1994; Jenkins and Valiente 1994; Mendenhall 2012). As previous chapters have shown, grandmothers respond to mother migration by reconfiguring relations of care across generations, confronting the realities of gender inequalities, and managing the uncertain futures of transnational family life. For grandmothers living with and responding to these social, cultural, and relational changes, embodied distress becomes a way to draw attention to the cultural significance of their caregiving in Nicaraguan transnational families. The meanings of *pensando mucho* (thinking too much) for this group of women therefore have everything to do with how global migration has drawn them into a reconfiguration of care responsibilities across borders and generations. Furthermore, pensando mucho indexes the moral tensions and ambivalences of transnational migration, which grandmothers experience as an economic necessity but which provokes uncertainty and threatens solidarity in family life. Analyzing pensando mucho extends our understanding of the lives and emotional experiences of Nicaraguan women who assume care for grandchildren after mother migration.

I analyze pensando mucho as an idiom of distress, taking seriously its embodied and communicative dimensions. Anthropologists and cross-cultural psychiatrists have defined idioms of distress as "particular ways in which members of sociocultural groups convey affliction" (Hinton and Lewis-Fernandez 2010: 210). In his foundational work on idioms of distress in South Asia, Mark Nichter argues that idioms of distress are especially important for women who may have few other avenues to express their dissatisfaction with social conditions, especially in relation to inequalities of gender and kinship (Nichter 1981). In a recent reconsideration of this approach, Nichter emphasizes the importance of the pragmatic, communicative aspect of idioms of distress—in other words, not just the "whatness" but the "why this," or the reasons "particular individuals and groups embrace alternative means of expressing distress at specific points in time" (Nichter 2010: 403). I approach pensando mucho as a form of embodied distress having particular significance for women of the *tercera edad* (third age) who are living with global migration not as migrants but as intergenerational caregivers in transnational families. Grandmothers feel little ability to intervene in the social conditions that provoke migration, the same conditions they describe as inducing their thinking too much. Still, the expression "pensando mucho" offers grandmothers a means of calling attention (within their families and from this interested ethnographer) to their distress and by extension to their dissatisfaction with the structural causes and the familial consequences of transnational migration. Thinking too much is a way grandmothers make visible their caregiving roles and responsibilities, inscribing their significance through a specific set of somatic symptoms. This communicative aspect of pensando mucho is important, because grandmothers draw attention to their embodied distress, signaling the disruption of transnational family life while emphasizing the cultural value of their caregiving.

This exploration of pensando mucho joins recent research in cross-cultural psychiatry into "thinking a lot" and related linguistic formulations (e.g., "having too many thoughts") across a number of national and cultural contexts. In fact, the most recent version of the American Psychiatric Association's *Diagnostic and Statistical Manual of Mental Disorders (DSM-V)* lists "thinking too much" as one of its nine "cultural concepts of distress," included in an appendix as a guide for clinical practitioners (2013: 833).[1] For example, among Cambodian refugees in the United States, "thinking a lot" has been analyzed as a sign of traumatic experiences of political violence and as an indicator of PTSD (Hinton, Reis, and de Jong 2015). For the urban poor in Haiti, Bonnie Kaiser and her colleagues argue that "thinking too much" (*reflechi twòp*) is an expression of life concerns associated with symptoms such as weight change and insomnia and related to anxiety and depression (2014: 455).[2] Both of these studies situate thinking too much within the broader project of global mental health, associating thinking too much with standard *DSM* diagnostic categories to better account for the burden of mental illness.[3] Elsewhere, I have described pensando mucho as an idiom of distress used by Nicaraguan women to register experiences of death, loss, and abandonment in their families and also as being associated with a particular body pain, *dolor de cerebro* (brain ache or brain pain), felt in the occipital area at the top of the spine (Yarris 2014b, 2011).

This complaint is a mode of social distress in its own right, distinct from other, related syndromes, such as depression and anxiety. For instance, the temporal dimensions of pensando mucho are unique from depression (*depresión*), which women describe as an acute, episodic, emotional response to their daughters' out-migrations. In comparison, pensando mucho is experienced as a continual rumination over the ways transnational migration has reconfigured family relations of care across generations. Pensando mucho is a chronic form of distress for grandmother caregivers, who feel themselves unable to directly alter the circumstances shaping migration or resolve the tensions of transnational family life. This relative lack of control or agency is also a defining characteristic of pensando mucho, evidenced by the clear distinction women make between thinking too much and worrying (*preocupación*), with the latter related to everyday concerns and having more readily apparent solutions. The thoughts of pensando mucho, by contrast, relate to the precarious realities of migrant family life—namely, how grandmothers are situated between the economic necessity of migration and the moral ambivalence about migration's effect on family solidarity. Pensando mucho emerges out of this ambivalence, offering women a way to affirm the cultural value of their care and embody the intergenerational sacrifice of migration while lamenting transnational life's impact on the unity and togetherness they desire within their families.

While the grandmothers in this book do not themselves cross national borders, their emotional and relational lives are extended across space and over time nonetheless (Brijnath 2009; Boehm and Swank 2011; Baldassar and Merla 2014). For these women, thinking too much has to do with the complicated social dislocations of the "care slot" in transnational families, because they are simultaneously mothers who lose the support of out-migrated daughters and grandmothers who assume the care of young children (Leinaweaver 2010: 69).[4] Grandmothers experience the emotions of transnational family life as mothers *and* as grandmothers. Part of the responsibility that grandmothers express through the idiom of pensando mucho is securing the economic welfare of households. However, discussions of pensando mucho simultaneously direct attention toward the moral economies of migration—to the ways transnational migration upends expectations for care in Nicaraguan families. By "moral" I refer not to an abstract ethics of right and wrong but rather to Nicaraguan cultural ideals for family life—namely, solidarity and sacrifice. These are the values threatened by transnational migration, which grandmothers seek to sustain through their caregiving. Thus, grandmothers' care responsibilities figure prominently in discussions of pensando mucho, for caregiving can precipitate but also, inversely, help women cope with their sense of loss by providing a new, affirmative source of social support in children's care. By providing care, grandmothers foster the continuity and unity they value within families, thus partially alleviating their distress. As we see in the descriptions that follow, grandmothers draw attention through this idiom of pensando mucho to the cultural value of their care as a means of sustaining solidarity despite the disruptions of distance, time, and separation in transnational families.

Pensando Mucho and the Moral Economies of Migration

In discussing pensando mucho, grandmothers often referred to economic constraints as a source for and focus of their *pensamientos* (thoughts).[5] For example, Teresa said, "When I get to thinking a lot [Cuando me pongo a pensar mucho], it's about the economic aspect [of migration]." As discussed in Chapter 2, grandmother caregivers receive and manage the remittances sent by migrant mothers, assuming primary responsibility for household economies (even when they share their homes with husbands or other adult children). However, grandmothers also viewed remittances as both materially inadequate to cover household expenses and morally insufficient to make up for mothers' absences, as indexed in the phrase *no se ajustan* (they do not measure up).

Marbeya explicitly associates pensando mucho with her household's economic circumstances, connecting the material aspects of "lo de la casa" (things at home) to her desire for a well-functioning household as an indication of family well-being. Thus, in addition to her thinking about managing the remittances sent from Costa Rica by daughter Azucena, Marbeya thinks too much when she feels unable to maintain control over "things around the house," especially the smooth provisioning of care for her two grandchildren. Marbeya said, "I get desperate [desesperada] when I see that school tuition is coming due, or when the kids ask me for something at exam time, ask me for things up and down, and . . . it's exasperating that the kids ask me for things and the money hasn't arrived." Marbeya ties her responsibility for her household economy and her experience of remittances as not making ends meet to thinking too much, which becomes acute when remittances are stretched thin and she feels unable to meet the demands for her grandchildren's care. Thus, while overtly Marbeya associates pensando mucho to material concerns, her distress also indexes a moral responsibility for "lo de la casa." Marbeya emphasized, "I'm well when everything at home is good; when everything's good, I feel calm about everything. . . . If I'm good, in other words, with things at home, I don't think too much [yo no pienso mucho]." In the context of a household divided by migration, Marbeya frames her caregiving as having the potential to set things right—relationally and economically—in her family and, by extension, to ward off excessive thoughts. This multidimensionality of care—as an everyday responsibility and as a means of alleviating the distresses and of countering the disordering of transnational family life—is central to understanding the significance of pensando mucho in grandmothers' lives.

Grandmother Beatriz also described the onset of her pensando mucho in relation to the emotional stress of her daughter Jimena's departure (Jimena migrated to the United States several months before our interviews). Beatriz, like Marbeya, suffers from insomnia associated with pensando mucho, as she described in this exchange:

KRISTIN: Was there a time when you thought a lot [Cuando se puso a pensar mucho]?

BEATRIZ: Yes.

KRISTIN: When?

BEATRIZ: Well, right now, when my daughter left there was an immense suffering [un sufrimiento bárbaro]. And there I was, thinking a lot [pensando mucho], and I didn't sleep at night.

KRISTIN: You didn't sleep?

BEATRIZ: That's right, I didn't—I was thinking.

When I asked Beatriz what she thought about when she was *pensando*, she talked about missing her eldest and most responsible daughter, the one she "could always count on" to provide consistent economic and emotional support to Beatriz. Beatriz was overwhelmed by tears as she repeated how much she missed Jimena's presence in her home and in her life.

For Beatriz, as for Marbeya, pensando mucho also indexes her responsibilities for her family's economic circumstances, for the management of remittances, and for making do with material circumstances for which remittances "no se ajustan." I asked Beatriz to expand on what she thinks about when she thinks too much, and she responded,

> Well, you see, it depends on the occasion, because there are times that you have thoughts [hay veces uno tiene pensamientos] about how to take care of everything at home. You know, sometimes for the . . . economic part and everything, because what can you do? I'm the one who thinks about everything [Soy la que pienso en todo]. I mean, I'm the one who is—who is responsible.

Beatriz directly associates pensando mucho with responsibilities for her family following migration. Her sense of economic responsibility at the time of the interview was intensified because Jimena had not yet found a job abroad and was not yet sending regular remittances, so Beatriz was struggling to make ends meet and thinking about whether she would be able to finance her granddaughter Alejandra's private school tuition.

However, these economic concerns were inseparable from thoughts of the ways migration had reconfigured Beatriz's family life. As she explained,

> I thought about how I was going to make . . . everything work out. . . . So you can see that we can do it, but because she's [Jimena's] missing, everything is not worked out [no está todo arreglado]. So those were my thoughts [Esos eran mis pensamientos]. You see? I didn't sleep, thinking [too much] [No dormía, pensando]. I said to myself, "How am I going to do it?"

Beatriz connects thinking too much with her increased responsibilities since Jimena's migration and to the disruption that migration has caused in her family. Her thoughts are focused on her family's economic circumstances and on the realities of her daughter's absence, which has left Beatriz feeling that her family life is "disordered [desarreglada]" because of migration. While Beatriz wanted her family to "vivir unidos todos" (live united, all of us together), migration upsets that cultural expectation. Thus, in addition to reflecting concerns about her household's material economy in the wake of migration, pensando mucho indexes Beatriz's broader concerns about migration and what she values for her family's future—namely, unity and solidarity. With her daughter Jimena far away in the United States, Beatriz finds herself unable to sleep at night, her mind focused on the troubling question, "How am I going to do it?" as she ru-minates about her ability to hold her family together after migration.

Like Beatriz, Juana experiences thinking too much as a reflection of her concerns over both the material and the moral impacts of migration. She de-scribed the economic necessity that pushed her two daughters (and one son) to migrate to Costa Rica:

> I am thinking that [Pensando que] . . . if there were a source of work here nearby, there wouldn't be a necessity to go migrate to another country that isn't ours. To be in family [Para estar en familia], they would just go out in the day to work, and we'd know that in the afternoon or the evening, they'd be here. And we would be able to mutually help one another here, all united [aquí todos unidos].

Juana's thoughts refer to the disjuncture of transnational family life, defined as it is by separation, distance, and alienation (in Juana's words, being in "another country that isn't ours"). Through pensando mucho, Juana also presents a cri-tique of transnational migration, as she points to the economic necessity that has pushed her children abroad to find work in Costa Rica and that has simul-taneously disrupted what Juana values for her family, "estar en familia" (being in family), helping one another through unity and togetherness. Once again, we see how pensando mucho allows grandmothers to register their critiques of global migration's consequences on their lives. Even as they simultaneously acknowledge the necessity of migration for household economies, grandmoth-ers use thinking too much to register their distress over the consequences of migration for family moralities of unity and solidarity.

Pensando Mucho, *Depresión*, and Somatic Symptoms

Pensando mucho indexes the chronic uncertainty of transnational caregiv-ing and is associated with other forms of emotional and embodied suffering. For instance, women talk about their immediate short-term responses to their daughters' migrations in terms of two other embodied reactions: *enfermarse* (to become sick, or to get oneself sick) and *deprimirse* (to become depressed, or to get oneself depressed). Grandmothers would use the expression *me enfermé* (I got sick or I fell ill) in the days after their daughters' departures, experiencing physical symptoms such as headaches, body aches, exhaustion, fever, and stom-ach upset, which would usually dissipate within a week or over a few weeks.[6] In fact, nearly all the women I interviewed described *enfermedad* (malaise or sickness) in relation to the immediate emotional consequences of migration, leading me to understand *enfermedad* as a way grandmothers embody their feelings of loss and sadness following the out-migration of their daughters.

Grandmothers may also experience *depresión* as an acute reaction to mother migration, usually following the period of *enfermedad* and continuing for weeks, months, or even more than a year. When women experience depression in this context, their symptoms may be quite debilitating and include a lack of interest in everyday activities, an inability to get out of bed, and a loss of sense of purpose. In fact, six of the grandmothers explicitly mentioned feeling depressed after their daughters migrated. Further, nearly all grandmothers described feeling some variant of sadness (*tristeza*) in relation to the immediate aftermath of migration.

In developing this analysis, I am wary of overinterpreting women's feelings of distress or of collapsing cultural experiences of pensando mucho into a universal diagnostic category such as depression. For one reason, depresión has a temporal register distinct from pensando mucho, as Juana explained:

> Well, [when I'm] depressed [deprimida], I feel like I don't want to go out. I only want to be inside, and I don't want to go out. A lot of times I didn't even feel like bathing, I didn't feel like eating, I didn't have an appetite. I'm completely depressed, and in general if I give space to depression, it will get stronger until I say, stop already, and I try to go out and stop being closed up inside. But sometimes I take two or three days with depression [before I can overcome it].

In Juana's description, depression encompasses both a somatic state (loss of energy, loss of appetite) and an emotional state (sadness, feelings of detachment and isolation). These symptoms look much like those of the *DSM-V* criteria for depression (American Psychiatric Association 2013). Further, Juana's explanation also reveals the moral dimension of depresión, as she expresses an ability to overcome this sort of temporary sadness and even describes a moral responsibility to not "give space to depression," to reestablish her emotional well-being and thus her ability to care for herself and others. Thus, depresión in this cultural framing is an episodic, immediate response to the emotional trauma of out-migration. Importantly, however, it is an emotional state that women view themselves as capable of overcoming.

In some cases, depresión and pensando mucho share similar symptoms. For instance, Teresa said, "Thinking too much, yes, is related to depression," and she went on to describe how, after her daughter Lisdamur migrated to

Costa Rica (more than two years ago), she experienced "sadness, depression, symptoms of loneliness, sadness . . . that situation of feeling that you are alone, depressed, sad [tristeza, deprimida, los síntomas de soledad, tristeza . . . esa situación de sentirse uno solo, deprimido, así, triste]." These feelings were associated with Lisdamur's status as an undocumented migrant and the attendant risks to physical safety, potential for deportation, and possible consequences for her mother and family. Teresa said that "problems like that" lead her to feel "thoughtful . . . grief-stricken [pensativa . . . uno se aflige]."[7] By using the generic third-person *uno* (one), Teresa situates such feelings with grandmother caregivers in general rather than being particular to her personal situation. Teresa's emotional response indexes the actual and the imagined consequences of illicit migration on herself and her family; in particular, "thinking too much" or being "thoughtful" is a way of describing the distress associated with the uncertainties of migration, deportation, and long-term family separation.

Marbeya experienced depresión and enfermedad following her daughter Azucena's migration to Costa Rica (eleven years ago). Marbeya explained, "When she left, after a time I suddenly started to feel depression, like a sadness [una tristeza]." She also told me, "Me caí enferma" (I fell ill). Similar to Teresa, Marbeya used the terms "depression" and "sadness" almost interchangeably, as in this exchange:

> MARBEYA: Ay, yes. It was as if they had pulled out a little bit of my heart, as if they had taken out half my heart when she left.
> KRISTIN: How long after her migration did you feel this way?
> MARBEYA: Almost a full year. Almost a year I spent like that, depressed. I closed myself up all the time. It was sadness. It was depression. I felt really—like nothing they told me helped, I just kept crying. Almost a year I spent like that.
> KRISTIN: So what do you think was the cause of your depression during this time?
> MARBEYA: Her [Azucena's] migration.

Marbeya situates her daughter's migration as a precipitating, even causal, factor for depression. However, whereas Marbeya viewed her sadness and depression as an understandable or even inevitable response to her daughter's migration, her immediate family might not have shared this view. Marbeya refers to the futile efforts of family members to encourage her to feel better, saying, "Nothing they told me helped." Marbeya recalled her three coresident daughters telling her, "What are you worried about if we are here and she [Azucena] hasn't died; she's working. What else do you want? She's going to send you money. What are you worried about?" While Marbeya recognized that her daughters were trying to lift her mood (as they were also emphasizing that they were still present in her life), she did not feel their encouragement acknowledged her emotional reality. Instead, as a mother of a migrant daughter, Marbeya feels entitled to her sadness. Thus, her response to her daughters was, "Yes, it's all good. I know what you're saying, but I still miss my daughter." Through her experience of loss and depression, Marbeya claims her right to grieve her daughter's absence and asserts that the promised economic benefits of migration are not what matter to her most but her actual loss, the loss of the emotional support and solidarity of her migrant daughter.

Beatriz was the only woman I interviewed about pensando mucho who viewed it as nearly the same as depresión. For Beatriz, this is because "depression comes—I'd say it comes from thinking so much [de estar pensando tanto]; you get sad. To me, well—it's the same." For Beatriz, depression comes from pensando mucho, and thinking too much leads to sadness. Like other women, Beatriz pointed to migration as a causal factor for her depression:

> BEATRIZ: And when she left, it wasn't the same, so for me that was terrible. Because I thought she was going to go away, and I wondered when I was going to see her again. That's what got me.
>
> KRISTIN: So in your view, what was the cause of your depression?
>
> BEATRIZ: Her departure; directly, her departure.

Beatriz's sense of loss is both tangible and intangible, real and imagined, because Jimena has left Beatriz without the emotional and instrumental support she once provided and because Beatriz is uncertain when she will see her daughter again. Both these dimensions of her loss—the certain and the uncertain—contribute to Beatriz's emotional experience of depression and, by her explanation, are therefore also related to pensando mucho.

Two somatic symptoms frequently mentioned by women in conversations about pensando mucho were insomnia and *dolor de cerebro*. Expressions women used to describe insomnia included *tuve insomnia* (I had insomnia), *me quitó el sueño* (it took my sleep away), and *no puedo dormir* (I can't sleep). *Dolor de cerebro* is described as a pulsing pain felt at the back of the head or base of the skull, top of the neck; distinct from, but possibly co-occurring with, *dolor de cabeza* (headache) and *migraña* (migraine). While *cerebro* can be translated literally as "brain," women use *cerebro* almost interchangeably with *mente*, which can be literally translated as "mind." Thus, *dolor de cerebro* could be translated literally as "brain ache" or "brain pain" but can also be glossed as "mind pain."

Beatriz explained the association between pensando mucho and dolor de cerebro in the following exchange:

> KRISTIN: Do your thoughts [pensamientos] hurt you? Is there anyplace in your body that—
>
> BEATRIZ: In the brain [en el cerebro], yes, in the brain. Because that wears you out, the brain. Well, it's the circumstances that we live in. If you had the [economic] means, ahh, you'd live well! But . . . being poor, you have to think about how you're going to get by.

In Beatriz's explanation, she "thinks too much" about the circumstances of her life, specifically her economic poverty. Thinking about how she's "going to get by" produces a physical sensation of pain in her brain or mind.

Similar to Beatriz, Marbeya described dolor de cerebro as a somatic reflection of pensando mucho, a response to her family's economic circumstances. She said,

> I'm thinking [Estoy pensando], how is money going to last me? What am I going to spend it on? If the boy [her grandson Selso] gets sick today, tomorrow I can't buy him shoes, because I have to take him to the doctor. So there is the brain [cerebro] going; it's the mind [mente] and the brain [cerebro], and everything is working. It's like being super worried [súper preocupada].

Marbeya portrays the experience of pensando mucho as a sensation that her brain/mind is working, processing thoughts and worries related to her role as a caregiver and remittance manager. In her description, pensando mucho is "like being super worried"; *pensar* (to think) is different from and more intense than *preocupar* (to worry). In addition to associating pensando mucho with dolor de cerebro, Marbeya connected pensando mucho with symptoms such as sleeplessness:

> If I don't think too much, I sleep well [Si yo no pienso mucho, yo me duermo tranquila]. But if I lie down, thoughts invade, like going "riqui, riqui" [*makes machinelike sounds and points to her head*], the cassette going around, that tape is going around and around. . . . If I don't think too much, my brain is calm.

Marbeya describes sleeplessness as a result of thinking too much. When Marbeya is thinking too much, her mind processes thoughts like a cassette tape playing over and over and thus making it difficult for her to rest. Other nights, when she is not distracted by thinking too much, Marbeya feels her "brain is calm," and she can sleep well.

In her discussions of pensando mucho, Marbeya described feeling that her cerebro (brain-mind) is working machinelike, processing her thoughts. In this view, the brain or mind is experienced as a distinct object, organ, or site of the body that is an agent of thinking (*pensando*) and of thoughts (*pensamientos*). The brain/mind "working too much" causes dolor de cerebro and insomnia, and in Marbeya's portrayal, it seems she is separated from her brain/mind, unable to intervene and calm her thoughts. Another time, Marbeya said about pensando mucho, "It's when you are wearing yourself out [se está desgastando], you put yourself—I feel like my brain [cerebro] is tired [cansado]." Beatriz, just above, also mentions this feeling that the thoughts in the brain can "wear out [the brain]" (*desgastarse*).[8] Beatriz and Marbeya share with other interviewees an emic understanding of the brain and mind as partly separate from the self, because as the brain or mind actively responds to social stressors and produces thoughts, this is framed as occurring partly outside the bounds of individual control. Furthermore, with the content of thinking too much reflecting the moral dilemmas associated with migration, the brain/mind appears in these descriptions as the body site for registering moral distress. In these ways, it makes sense that the brain (or mind) is the site for pensando mucho, since the thoughts about which women think too much are fundamentally tied to social disruption and therefore exceed women's individual control.

Pensando Mucho and the Care Slot

One particular aspect of transnational caregiving that grandmothers refer to in their discussions of pensando mucho is the care slot. As discussed in the introduction, this term describes the positions of women of the *tercera edad* who experience transnational migration both as mothers of migrant daughters and as grandmothers of children in Nicaragua. The emotional impacts of migration for grandmothers are thus compounded by their thoughts on their daughters' safety and security as (usually undocumented) migrants abroad and on their grandchildren's well-being. The reconfigurations of care and responsibility that follow mother migration thus suspend grandmothers' emotional lives across space and time, as their thoughts extend over national borders even though they themselves do not migrate. Pensando mucho indexes the moral ambivalence of grandmothers' positions as transnational, intergenerational caregivers, an ambivalence associated with grandmothers' support of mothers' migration aspirations and their simultaneous lament over migration's effects on their family life. This ambivalence is magnified by the near-constant reminders of the distance that separates them from their migrant daughters. Juana described another example:

> [You feel] really, really sad. Sometimes during the daytime you can pretend [you don't feel it] because there's so much to do, but when nighttime arrives even sleep escapes us [hasta el sueño se nos quita], as they say, because we get to thinking a lot [nos ponemos a pensar mucho] about the fact that they're not here, about how they're doing, about what's happening, about when they may call us. We say they will call us, but [when they do] they won't tell us the truth so that we won't worry. We get to thinking because, well, all this happens. Then you can't sleep calmly. It's something that you're already thinking [que ya estás pensando]; maybe you can't even eat right, because you're eating and you're thinking [estás pensando]: How is she doing over there? What is she doing now? How is my daughter?

Juana uses the plural pronoun "we" in her description of filling the care slot: worrying about migrant daughters' safety abroad and simultaneously suffering negative emotional consequences associated with their ongoing absence from home. It is not only a physical sense of absence that Juana is expressing here, however; she also refers to an emotional separation, a feeling of detachment from her daughters associated with the physical distance of transnational family life. Juana is aware that her daughters alter their representations of life abroad so as not to worry her with the troublesome side of migrant life.[9] These realities of transnational family life provoke Juana's thinking too much, which is particularly debilitating at night, when she is unable to distract herself with daily activities and lies awake, sleep escaping her, her mind filled with *pensamientos*. This detail about the temporality of pensando mucho also reminds us how caregiving can be an antidote for grandmothers like Juana who fill their days with care activities and thus, even if temporarily, offset the distress of thinking too much.

Juana's example also illustrates the in-betweenness that grandmothers in transnational families experience: even as they themselves do not physically cross national borders, they feel their emotional lives extended by the realities of migration nonetheless. In a sense, Juana and other grandmothers feel that a part of them leaves Nicaragua when their daughters migrate, causing their emotional lives to become suspended over national borders and between migrants' lives and the lives of those in Nicaragua. Grandmother caregivers feel themselves occupying the ambivalent affective space between "here" (family homes in Nicaragua) and "there" (the new spaces occupied by their migrant children).[10] This emotional experience is often embodied through difficulties eating (as Juana described) or through related expressions such as heartache (as when Marbeya said migration has "taken out half my heart").

One of the things most at stake for Juana in her description of pensando mucho is an inability to mother her children as she desires, because the separation of migration makes it impossible for her to protect her migrant daughters from the dangers and troubles they will encounter in Costa Rica. Pensando mucho indexes the emotional and instrumental support that is missing as grandmothers occupy the care slot after mother migration. Juana not only wants to be present in her daughters' lives; she wants them to be present in her life in ways made impossible by migration. This becomes clear in Juana's description of what, explicitly, she thought about when she thought too much:

> I think about the economic part, about the health of my family, and about my children who aren't here—you can feel the loneliness. You feel alone. After being [in a house] full of people, you find yourself alone. And sometimes you need someone—even if it's just for them to bring you a glass of water when you're sick.

Here, Juana refers to having her house "full of people," surrounded by her three children before they migrated to Costa Rica. Even though she continues to share her household with her husband, Pedro, and her grandchildren and although a daughter and son-in-law live nearby, Juana feels lonely. For Juana, her family's "health" is a reflection of both economic and emotional realities, and the "economic part" of migration reminds her of the moral impact of her children's absence. Juana's pensando mucho thus indexes the gap between the expectation for her life at *tercera edad* and the realities consequent to migration, which has left her without the support of her children, illustrated concretely through their inability to "bring . . . a glass of water" when Juana is ill.

As mentioned in Chapter 2, this desire to have adult children present to bring a glass of water at times of illness was articulated by several women as a way of reinforcing the vacío in family life their daughters' absences created. Norma, for example, said she longed for her migrant daughters' presence when she was feeling sick, "if only it were to bring me a glass of water." Bringing a glass of water in these narratives of pensando mucho has symbolic meaning as a concrete example of the kinds of instrumental and emotional care that are no longer available to grandmothers from their daughters because of transnational migration and physical separation.

This sort of nostalgia, or longing for family unity and solidarity, plays through other aspects of grandmothers' discussions of pensando mucho. For instance, the idea of living in a time when "toda la familia era unida" (all the family was united), seen above in Juana's and Beatriz's descriptions, was echoed in other women's narratives. Marbeya described her *pensamientos* as including a longing for times before migration and the reconfigurations of care that characterize transnational family relations:

> There are times . . . when a longing [una nostalgia] takes hold of me, and I say to myself, "Ay, if my daughter were here with me I might feel in good health [bien de salud]," or I would feel calm because I would be relieved of a burden that I have now. . . . It's like an obligation I have right now with her children. And if she were here, I wouldn't have this obligation; I would pass it off to her hands. It would be fewer thoughts for my brain [Sería menos pensamientos para mi cerebro].

In Marbeya's account, "nostalgia" is a way of rendering memories of her past (before migration), when the order of caregiving responsibilities in her household was undisrupted—when mothers cared for children and grandmothers counted on the support of adult daughters. Reestablishing a culturally expected ordering of care across generations would help Marbeya feel "bien de salud" (in good health) by removing one of the main sources of her *pensamientos*. Marbeya's account of pensando mucho connects an idealized past (when "toda la familia era unida") with a longed-for (postmigration) future, when she will be relieved of her intergenerational care responsibilities, when her grandchildren will be cared for by their migrant mother, and when the order of caregiving will be set right.

In our conversations about her two daughters' migrations to the United States, Norma also referred to a nostalgia for having her family united. While she assured me that she did not currently suffer from pensando mucho, Norma admitted to feeling debilitating depression in the months immediately following her daughters' migration. In recounting this period, Norma talked about her "nostalgia" for her daughters' physical and emotional presence in her life: "I felt the longing of not having them [una nostalgia de no tenerlas a ellas] and because they couldn't be here to embrace me [para darme un abrazo]." Norma suffered a good deal after her daughters' migrations; she was bedridden with depression for several months and unable to get up, go to work, or engage in her other usual activities. Her longing for copresence is illustrated in the reference to "darme un abrazo" (give me a hug), an embodied reminder of Norma's sense of loss following her daughters' migration and separation from their family in Nicaragua. Norma's distress comes despite actively encouraging her daughters to migrate and supporting their intentions of staying in the United States and trying to make better lives for themselves and their children. It was in part her support for their migration and its promise of opportunity that helped Norma overcome the episode of depression that followed her daughters' departures. Norma recalled that her daughter María José noticed during a telephone conversation how sad her mother was and said she would return to Nicaragua if Norma did not recover her usual energetic, positive self. Norma remembered this conversation as a moment when María José was "an angel God sent to me," because it served to jolt her out of her feelings of helplessness and depression. In fact, Norma did not want her daughters to return, but she had to overcome her initial sadness at their absence to match the sacrifices they had made in migrating with her own sacrifices as an intergenerational caregiver. For Norma, like other grandmothers, staying home in Nicaragua, assuming care for grandchildren, and sidelining personal emotional distress is a way of sharing in the family project of migration. Caregiving, while partly a burden and a responsibility, is how grandmothers participate in the intergenerational sacrifice of migration and thereby also overcome personal feelings of emotional distress for the sake of their children and grandchildren.

Nonetheless, despite their sacrifices, grandmothers' desire to have their families united persists. Nostalgia in grandmothers' accounts of their daughters' migrations expands the temporal frame surrounding thinking too much, broadening the emotional experience of transnational family life beyond the present, into the past and future. Thus, grandmothers' thoughts are ruminations over longed-for pasts, before migration, just as they are projections about hoped-for futures, when daughters might return and family solidarity might be reestablished. For Norma, such nostalgia is especially poignant at special occasions, such as Mother's Day and her birthday, when she is painfully reminded of her daughters' absences. Even though they consistently send money and gifts from abroad to help celebrate such holidays, Norma told me, "Don't believe it; the gifts and parties are insufficient. They don't make me miss them less." As long as families are separated by migration, remittances will not measure up to grandmothers' desires for unity and solidarity in families, producing the distress of thinking too much.

Pensando Mucho and Transnational Uncertainties

The ambivalences and uncertainties of transnational family life that provoke pensando mucho are reflections of the complex moral economies of migration, in which economic remittances cannot compensate for the moral and emotional costs of migrant mothers' absences. However, the ambivalence provoking pensando mucho is also a reflection of the realities of transnational caregiving, because along with grandmothers' support of their daughters' migration aspirations (in part embodied by the very act of assuming care for grandchildren) and their longing for reunification of their families come profound uncertainties surrounding the future. The thoughts of pensando mucho are exacerbated by these uncertainties, for while grandmothers form strong emotional attachments to the children in their care, they are unsure how long their primary caregiving responsibilities will endure and unclear about the prospects for child-mother reunification. These temporal uncertainties in family care relations are generative thoughts for grandmothers' thinking too much.[11]

Angela provides an illustrative example of the relation between the temporal uncertainty of migration and pensando mucho. While I discuss Angela's and her family's migration experience in detail in Chapter 4, here I focus on those aspects of their story most relevant to thinking too much. Angela is quite clear that, for her, pensando mucho is caused by the uncertainty surrounding her granddaughter Laleska's potential reunification with migrant mother Karla in the United States. In part, Angela's uncertainty about Laleska's potential migration reflects the complexities of the U.S. immigration bureaucracy and Karla's difficultly navigating the legal processes required to obtain a family reunification visa for Laleska. While Angela had at one moment felt that her granddaughter's departure was imminent, over the years it became much less clear to her whether Karla had even initiated the paperwork for her daughter's residency visa. Thus, Angela found herself living with the profound uncertainty of not knowing whether the granddaughter with whom she had grown so close over the previous ten years would stay or leave for the United States at a moment's notice.

For Angela, such uncertainty about her family's future is a clear provocation for pensando mucho. Angela thinks too much about what will happen to granddaughter Laleska, whether she should or will stay in Nicaragua or go to

Miami with her mother Karla. While Angela does not view the decision about Laleska's future as hers to make (she feels it is largely up to Karla to decide the fate of her daughter), she worries about Laleska's possible future in the United States. Angela is concerned that Laleska will not adjust well to living with her mother after more than a decade of separation and that her granddaughter will miss her two coresident female cousins, who are "like sisters" to her. As she described these uncertainties to me one afternoon in her shady front patio, Angela connected one thought to another in a litany of anxiety and distress; finally, sighing deeply, she said, "You see, I get to thinking a lot about all of those things [Ya ves, en todas esas cosas yo me pongo a pensar mucho]."

Part of the complexity of Angela's thinking too much is that decisions about her family's future are not squarely within her control. First, there is the complex and burdensome U.S. immigration bureaucracy, which makes reunification a long and expensive process and which Karla is attempting to navigate with insufficient legal or financial resources. Second, family decisions about reunification lie in Karla's hands since, as a U.S. resident, she is the one who will submit a residency petition for her daughter to join her. These realities leave Angela feeling marginalized from the actions that determine her own and her family's future. She explained,

> It's this that has me—all the time—it's something that she [Karla] has already thought about; it's a situation that's presenting itself and that I think about all the time: How am I going to do it? How can she leave here? So I get to thinking [me pongo a pensar].

Angela situates her pensando mucho within a complicated, transnational, temporal frame. She finds the complications of migration unfolding along the lines of an uncertain future, a future largely out of her control, leaving her thinking too much. Further, according to Angela, the possible futures of her family's life are things that her daughter Karla "has already thought about." Angela portrays Karla as the protagonist, who has already made the decisions that shape Angela's family's future. As a grandmother caregiver, Angela finds herself ruminating "all the time"—in the *present*—about the potential *future* consequences of reunification for her and her family. Her thoughts are exacerbated by her relative lack of agency, because Angela feels sidelined from the realities of migration and the uncertainties of her family's future that she thinks too much about.

The uncertainties of transnational life that underlie thinking too much are exacerbated by international immigration politics. As another example, Olga's daughter Manuela has lived undocumented in Panama City for the past two years. Olga knows of other migrants from her Managua neighborhood who have been deported from Panama, and she thinks a lot about the risks of this potential future fate for Manuela. Olga told me that while Manuela's departure precipitated her pensando mucho, her thoughts since were focused on the uncertainty and insecurity facing her daughter and her family. Olga said, "¡Idiay! I think about the fact that migration [Panamanian immigration authorities] can grab her at any time, and they can send her back. Like they say, they'll send her back without anything; they say that everything [Manuela's belongings] will stay where she lived. Migration—yes, I get to thinking [me pongo a pensar]."

Olga's fear of Manuela's possible deportation reflects a very real threat. I had occasion to visit Manuela in Panama City in the small house she shares with other Nicaraguan migrants in an immigrant community. As I describe in Chapter 2, during my visit, Manuela received a phone call from a friend who also resided in the neighborhood, telling her that la migra (immigration authorities) were conducting a sweep of the barrio, asking people to show their immigration papers and taking those without documents into custody. Manuela seemed accustomed to such immigration raids and told me they happen all the time (the ways Manuela and her friends use social networks and cell phones to protect each other is revealing of the frequency of these raids and immigrants' resourcefulness in responding to them). While her daughter had grown accustomed to the risks of her undocumented status, Olga, back home in Nicaragua, feared the worst, thinking that Manuela might be detained and deported at any time. Thus, when Olga does not receive one of her regular twice-monthly phone calls from Manuela, anxiety sets in and she gets to thinking, "Could it be that immigration detained her? I become grief-stricken [Yo me quedo afligida]." For Olga, then, the vulnerabilities and uncertainties of transnational family life provoke deeply felt afflictions and sorrows (afliccciones), which contribute to her pensamientos.

As these examples demonstrate, grandmothers' discussions of pensando mucho highlight the uncertainties of transnational family life, in which mother migration represents a direct threat to family well-being because of the dangers of undocumented migration and the precarities of living in the shadow (whether as grandmothers and grandchildren in Nicaragua or migrants abroad) of complex, international immigration bureaucracies. By narrating their experiences of pensando mucho, grandmothers articulate these broader concerns about the effect of mother migration on their individual and family lives. Further, women's narratives of pensando mucho contain a temporal dimension, connecting present thoughts both to nostalgia for longed-for pasts and to ambivalences about possible futures.[12] Grandmothers wonder whether migration is temporary or permanent, whether they and their grandchildren will stay in Nicaragua or join migrant mothers in host countries, and whether their migrant daughters will be deported or return voluntarily. All these concerns about international migration and transnational family life form the content of grandmothers' thoughts in pensando mucho.

Thoughts, Worries, and Women's Agency

In their discussions of pensando mucho, women often compared thinking too much to worrying (*preocupación*). Whereas preocupación is a common, acute type of worrying about everyday problems with relatively straightforward solutions, the intensity and chronicity of pensando mucho is associated with thoughts that have no apparent or easy resolution. Angela explained this distinction:

> Yes, I think they [pensando mucho and preocupación] are different, because worrying [preocupación], you have it all the time, right? For example, you worry about "What am I going to cook?" Or if you [happen to] have money, [it's] "Let's see, what am I going to do [with it]?" It's a worry, but it's already over. On the other hand, thinking too much is about a problem that you maybe don't know how to resolve. It's different.

In Angela's description, preocupación is related to the everyday activities of running a household, such as preparing meals on a limited budget. Pensando mucho, on the other hand, is a more profound form of worrying about problems without apparent resolution. Angela in particular associates pensando mucho with what she describes as "the problem of being a mother in this situation," a problem embedded in her caregiving role in a transnational family. Of such *pensamientos*, Angela says, "You're always going to have these thoughts. I feel like these are the things that sometimes drive you to—well, you'd like to find a solution, so you don't stop having this problem in your mind [no deja de tener ese problema en la mente]." Angela admits that she'd "like to find a solution" to these problems but emphasizes that the problems about which she ruminates are continuous, embedded in her roles as a mother and grandmother in a transnational family.

Pensando mucho is a persistent worrying about social and even transnational problems without simple solution, while preocupación is a more immediate or short-term form of worrying about problems that women feel they can control, usually at the household level. As another example, Juana described how she responds to her granddaughter's illness (the three-year-old is asthmatic and has recurrent episodes) by saying, "Me preocupo" (I worry)—about the cost of her granddaughter's examinations and medicines. However, if she spends money on medical treatment for the girl, this provokes a qualitatively different form of distress; Juana said, "Me pongo a pensar" (I get to thinking)— about how to afford the cost of food to feed her family. "Thoughts are more out there [son más allá]. If I spend on medicine for her today, what are we going to eat tomorrow? It's a problem without a solution. We're—as we Nicaraguans say—between the sword and the wall."[13] As we have seen, the temporal dimensions of pensando mucho are central to this expression of distress, which is associated with concerns about transnational family life that lack an apparent or easy resolution.

Thinking too much therefore reflects the complexities of absence, distance, separation, care reconfiguration, and future uncertainty in transnational families. According to Juana,

> I don't feel there's an exit or a solution to my problem. I don't have an answer or a way out of my problem, so this makes me tense. . . . In other words, it's like a continuous desperation because I can't resolve my problem. . . . For that reason I said that, with several people, it's more possible—my daughter told me when she was here [on a recent visit], "Don't worry, Mom, we are going to open a store, or we'll find a way to do something." There, you see, there are two heads thinking, not just one. We can do this or that other thing, and there we go. But when there's only one person, then I'm like, "What am I going to do tomorrow?" I don't know. I feel I don't have a way out; I can't figure out which way to go.

Juana relates a visceral sense of "continuous desperation" associated with this perception of having no way to resolve her problems, for at their base is the absence of her migrant children, who are unable to be physically present and aid her in resolving her everyday life difficulties. The lament of pensando mucho— what women like Juana are thinking too much about—is how migration has separated and upended the unity and solidarity they desire in their families. Juana gave the example of her daughter, on a recent visit home, offering to solve the family's economic problems by setting up a small store to generate income. This example illustrates how pensando mucho results from a sense of solitude, since if her daughter were to return to Nicaragua, Juana would have companionship and be able to address her problems with the help of her daughter. Alone, Juana finds herself stuck in a cycle of thoughts without apparent resolution, unable to "figure out which way to go."

Beatriz also described the difference between pensando mucho and preocupación in terms of the gravity or seriousness of the things being thought or worried about. Beatriz explained that preocupación is about "something light," such as her son coming home late on a weekend night. This is something (related to her son's drinking and partying) that Beatriz worries about, but it is also something that has "una solución," according to Beatriz, because when she hears him come in the front door she feels better and stops worrying (she also believes this is just a phase of early adulthood that he will outgrow). For Beatriz, pensando mucho is distinct and often related to her role as head of an economically poor household and a manager of remittances within the moral and material economies of migration and care. As she explained, "When I'm thinking about something like that, it's something that doesn't have a resolution. Because, you see, it's when I can't make ends meet [que no me ajusta el dinero] that I get to thinking, how am I going to do it?" For Beatriz, economic limitations do not have a simple solution, she thinks about them repeatedly, and they form the basis of her pensando mucho.

Unlike *pensamientos*, which have no apparent solution, women can intervene in their preocupaciones. Since worries are related to the everyday aspects of life women encounter as grandmothers, mothers, and heads of household, they can address these immediate challenges and alter the circumstances producing worries or, at least, change their responses to these circumstances. As Teresa described it, "And being worried—we're always going to be worried; worries are always going to be a part of our lives. So it's up to us how we are going to respond to them." Worries are largely under women's control, whereas the thoughts involved in thinking too much exceed the bounds of individual autonomy, because they are inexorably tied to the troubles and uncertainties of transnational social relations and intergenerational care responsibilities.

Responding to Distress: Acknowledgment and Care

While grandmothers' control over the economic circumstances pushing their daughters to migrate is circumscribed, and although they cannot resolve the profound uncertainties of transnational family life, they can draw attention to the cultural and moral value of their caregiving. It is this communicative dimension of pensando mucho that is so powerfully significant in grandmothers'

distress, given their social location in relation to the ambivalent moral economies of intergenerational, transborder caregiving. Like other culturally meaningful forms of distress, thinking too much may index a rupture in cultural
expectations for individual lives, a disjuncture between an anticipated life and
the actual, lived circumstances.[14] On one hand, pensando mucho refers to ruptures in a culturally expected order of care across generations in Nicaraguan
families, in which women of the *tercera edad* expect to receive social, emotional,
and instrumental support from their adult daughters as they enter later adulthood. Instead, grandmothers find themselves occupying the care slot, missing
their daughters and lamenting the ways migration undermines their desire to
have "toda la familia unida" (all the family united) in physical copresence, emotional support, and solidarity.

The grandmothers in my study express pensando mucho in a distinct way
because of the particular moral, temporal, and agentive dimensions of their
experience of migration. As this chapter illustrates, and as is summarized in
Table 3.1, women's narratives connect pensando mucho to nostalgia for longed-
for pasts of family unity, to fears about the present dangers facing their migrant
daughters, to the emotional consequences of migration on their grandchildren,
and to the profound uncertainties of transnational life. Precisely because pensando mucho is provoked by these troubling structural realities of global migration, there is no simple resolution for this form of distress. Certainly, if a
solution were to be proffered, it would not lie in clinical spaces but rather in the
social relations of care with which grandmothers engage in their families and
communities. As we have seen, while grandmothers lament the consequences of
mother migration on family separation, they also extend their own caregiving
as an expression of solidarity and support for their migrant daughters and in
so doing partly alleviate—through the very practices of care on which transnational families depend—their distress. Therefore, acknowledging and supporting intergenerational care helps offset the emotional pain of thinking too much.

Table 3.1 *Pensando mucho*: A Nicaraguan explanatory model

Associated causes	Associated symptoms	Associated syndromes	Coping
• Economic hardship • Family separation • Generational disruption in care • Uncertainty about the future	• Insomnia • Rumination • "Brain ache" or "brain pain" • Malaise or sickness (*enfermedad*)	• Depression (*depresión*) • Worrying (*preocupación*) • Suffering (*aflicción*)	• Social support • Acknowledgment • Recognition • Family support • Caregiving

Because of the lack of a simple solution, thinking too much is a chronic source of embodied distress for women that reflects the disruptive realities of transnational family life. This is part of the moral ambivalence that is captured through pensando mucho, for grandmothers find their emotional lives partly extended across national borders and over time as they think about their daughters' migrations and the effects on their families now and into the future. In this way, one interpretation of the prevalence of pensando mucho among this group of grandmother caregivers is that thinking too much emerges as a way of filling the emotional space migrant daughters once occupied through physical presence. As Norma told me, "You feel the emptiness, the space that remains where they no longer are [Se siente el vacio, el espacio queda donde ellas no están]." Grandmothers are left thinking too much about their daughters' absence, with thoughts like emotional echoes of family togetherness, traces of the migrant women now removed by transnational migration.

This discussion of pensando mucho only partly supports the conclusions of a body of health research linking caregiving to chronic illness and other health problems for caregivers. Studies in the United States, for instance, have examined the health toll of caregiving for key relatives caring for ill family members, suggesting that caregivers experience depression, pain, and other chronic conditions as a result of the burdens of caregiving (for example, see Sales 2003; Saunders 2008). Extending this argument to global migration, Mary Alice Scott has argued that the women of the grandparent generation who provide care in families following out-migration, what she terms "care substitutions," often suffer from complications of unmanaged diabetes and other chronic health conditions because they neglect their personal health to focus resources on the children in their care (Scott 2012: 149). In part, this analysis of pensando mucho can be read in a similar vein, as illustrating the negative consequences of caregiving on Nicaraguan grandmothers, including the short-term episodic depression they experience following their daughters' migrations. However, I extend this argument about the health costs of caregiving to consider how thinking too much embodies all the moral and social troubles of transnational life—the economic strains, the stresses of separation, and the uncertainties surrounding the future—not only the physical burdens of caregiving. Furthermore, the caregiver-burden perspective largely fails to acknowledge that caregiving not only is experienced as a health-deteriorating burden but can be a means of coping, a way of achieving social support, and a source of affirmation and purpose for caregivers.

In this way, while the causes and consequences of migration are largely beyond their control, grandmothers find a way of asserting their agency through caregiving, (re)encountering a sense of life's purpose and affirming cultural values of unity and solidarity in their families. By assuming care for grandchildren, women align themselves with their daughters' migration ambitions, offering concrete support by caring for their children and thus making migration an intergenerational project. While these complex reconfigurations of care contribute to pensando mucho, caregiving itself dialectically offers grandmothers a means of coping with the troubles and uncertainties of transnational life. Being responsible for children keeps women occupied and engaged in everyday routines, which help ward off thinking too much. Further, as we have seen in previous chapters, caring for grandchildren offers women a sense of purpose, because they contribute not only to children's well-being and daughters' migration ambitions but also to the maintenance of family togetherness and solidarity. Despite the social hardships and uncertainties of transnational family life, grandmothers are actively and affirmatively participating in the re-creation of cultural values for family life through their caregiving. While pensando mucho evidences the troubling uncertainties of transnational family futures, everyday caregiving also represents a concrete instantiation of what grandmothers value. Care can be brought under women's control, even as the causes and consequences of global migration exceed the bounds of their agency.

Therefore, while I could leave an analysis of pensando mucho at the level of social suffering or embodied distress, doing so would represent an incomplete interpretation of women's experiences. Nor is my intention to advocate for a clinical response to pensando mucho, although, as with other idioms of distress, an awareness of the cultural significance of this embodied expression would likely improve clinical communication and efficacy (Hinton and Lewis-Fernandez 2011; Nichter 2010). However, women are unlikely to take complaints of pensando mucho to health care settings. Instead, by expressing pensando mucho, grandmothers seek both social recognition and social support in family and interpersonal networks. As a form of embodied distress, pensando mucho makes visible the work of intergenerational care that grandmothers do in transnational families. That grandmothers' thinking too much reflects the moral economies of migration also leads to an interpretation of it not only as an embodied idiom of distress, pointing inward to women's individual suffering, but also as an expressed critique, pointing outward, toward the ways transnational migration threatens unity and solidarity in family life. Thus, appropriate responses to pensando mucho are most likely compassionate listening, an acknowledgment of the strains of transborder caregiving and the stresses of transnational life, and an expression of solidarity and support for grandmother caregivers.

4 Care and Responsibility Across Generations
A Family Migration Portrait

*Pero yo sé que ese vacío, yo, por mucho que la quiera, por mucho que la
sobreproteja, por mucho que yo sienta por ella, ese vacío no lo lleno yo. (But
I know that emptiness, for as much as I love her, for as much as I overprotect
her, for as much as I feel for her, I don't fill that emptiness.)*

—Angela

Transnational Family Life in Intergenerational Perspective

One of the families with whom I grew particularly close during fieldwork was
that of grandmother Angela. Angela, in her early fifties, was the primary caregiver for Laleska (eleven), whose mother Karla had migrated to Miami in 1999,
when Laleska was just over a year old. Also sharing the family's tidy, three-
room home in a working-class barrio of Managua were Laleska's two maternal cousins, who were *como hermanas* (like sisters) to her, Alexa (thirteen) and
Reyna (sixteen). I spent a good deal of time in Angela's home, sitting in the
shaded, neatly swept patio, kept cool by the hillside breezes and the ice-cold
fruit drinks Angela always prepared for my visits. Although we would eventually become close, early in my fieldwork I stumbled through several awkward
interviews with Angela. On the occasion of my first formal interview, which I
had designed to review basic household demographic information and details
about migration histories, Angela interrupted my line of questioning about her
daughter's migration by saying, "You know, this is not the first abandonment
I've lived through [Sabes, esto no es el primer abandono que he vivido]," and
went on to discuss the migration of her husband, Carlo, to the United States
in the late 1980s. This shift in focus from the present to the past, into the story
of a previous intimate encounter with migration, reveals the importance of an
intergenerational perspective on transnational family life.

While migration is recognized as a spatial process, it is less often conceived
of in terms of its temporal dimensions. The spatiality of migration is evident in
migrant movements over space—across territories and beyond borders—and

as family members back home experience the physical separation of distance. And yet space itself has a temporal dimension, for migrant crossings take time and family members' experience of separation is often compounded by time's passage. Caregiving embodies this temporal dimension, as family members provide care in ways that reflect their own past experiences receiving (or failing to receive) care and as care in the present is oriented toward hoped-for (or feared) futures.[1] Often, stories of migration and transnational family life are told cross-sectionally, in the present tense, as if migration's impacts could be removed from time and disengaged from life courses. Here I craft a family portrait of migration embedded in time and imprinted across generations, showing how the experiences of those living with transnational migration are always filtered temporally and accumulated intergenerationally. This perspective engages with temporality by showing how transnational migration as lived experience in the present always contains shadows of meaning cast in the past; this perspective widens our analytical lens across time, cumulatively, and over generations.

Angela's family story reveals the temporal and intergenerational dimensions of migration, with previous experiences of migration shaping the ways care is provisioned in the present and the ways the future of family life looms large and uncertain. Telling this family's story across generations reveals how Angela's hopes and fears for her children's migrations and for her granddaughter Laleska reflect her personal experience living through her husband's out-migration a generation before. Furthermore, Angela's perception of the threat migration poses to her family's unity and her response—providing care and fostering equity and solidarity—must be understood across time, emerging from her past and profoundly marking her caregiving in the present. Situating our anthropological lens to focus on one family can reveal the microcultural dynamics—relational, moral, and emotional—affecting family members' overall health and well-being (for example, see Garro 2011; Garro and Yarris 2009). My aim in this chapter is to present a family migration portrait, an in-depth look at the histories and experiences, causes and consequences, of migration over generations within one transnational family.

Migration and a First Abandonment

Like others fleeing the Contra War and its concomitant violence and economic insecurity, Angela's husband, Carlo, emigrated in 1989 and settled in Miami,

Florida. While Angela understood the motives for her husband's departure and even supported his initial desire to secure a better future for their children via migration, her ultimate experience of Carlo's migration as an abandonment of his responsibilities to his family in Nicaragua has cast a long shadow over subsequent generations of migration.

At the time of Carlo's departure, Angela had been married to him for over fifteen years, and the couple had five children. When Carlo left, he told Angela that his sole intention was to find work in order to support her and their children: Carlos, Lidia, Noelia, Karla, and Jonathan, ages sixteen to seven at the time. Angela supported her husband's decision because she believed his promise to send money so that their children could complete school and they could improve the family house. Angela was willing to manage the household and raise her children alone because she wagered that her husband's migration would help their children get ahead; she placed her hopes on migration's tenuous promise.

While Carlo called his family and sent money from Miami fairly regularly during his first two years of migration, his communication and remittances ceased soon thereafter. Initially, Angela missed her husband and looked forward to his calls; as his support trickled to a stop, she began to dread the telephone's ring, dreading having to confront him once again about his irresponsibility. Angela recounted the range of excuses Carlo would give for losing touch with his family in Nicaragua: job loss, economic recession, his declining health. Gradually, Angela realized that migration was not going to be "all that he had promised [todo lo que él prometió]"; past promises of migration as improving family circumstances clashed with Angela's looming sense of her husband's abandonment in the present.

With her money running out, Angela sought paid employment, working as a seamstress, an administrative assistant, and in other odd, part-time jobs to support her family. Receiving word of her employment, Carlo accused Angela of "hanging out in the street prostituting herself," a criticism that stung, seeing that Carlo and his failure to provide for the family had forced Angela to take responsibility for the economic stability of her household. In this case, remittances did not measure up (no se ajustaron) to Angela's expectations and Carlo's promises, neither materially nor morally.

This first generation of migration split the loyalties of Angela's children and produced division and discord within the family. Noelia and Lidia defended their father, Karla and Jonathan tried to see both sides, and Carlos (the oldest

son) supported Angela.[2] Angela remembers her family life in the years following Carlo's migration as fraught with tension and mistrust, because her older
daughters blamed her for their father's absence, and she struggled to hold the
family together, economically and emotionally. The friction between Angela
and Noelia built to such a point that, in her late teens, Noelia migrated to Costa
Rica with her boyfriend, returning to the household nine months later when
that relationship had come to an end. Angela viewed Noelia as acting out her
father's abandonment, migrating as a means to punish Angela for what Noelia perceived to be her mother's failure to hold the family together. All these
problems only deepened Angela's sense of migration as abandonment and as
a rupture to family ties of solidarity, because it was Carlo's departure that had
initiated the family's problems, and in his absence Angela was left alone to deal
with the consequences.

Broken Promises Across a Second Generation

A decade after Carlo emigrated, Angela's daughter Karla and son Jonathan decided to leave Nicaragua and join their father in the United States, although
their contact with Carlo had been irregular. Jonathan was seventeen and child-
less and Karla nineteen and already mother of a young daughter (Laleska),
whom she left behind in Angela's care. As Angela describes it, her children made
the decision to migrate largely without her input, believing they would reunite
with their father once they arrived in Miami and that he would help them establish their lives abroad. Jonathan and Karla were influenced by their father's
positive description of life in the United States, which shaped their belief that
they would be able to achieve economic success and send money home to support Angela and the rest of the family. They imagined reuniting with Carlo in
Miami and sharing a house with their father as they once had in Managua.

Jonathan and Karla's migration experiences were far from what they imagined, and they suffered one hardship after another. Their plan had been to
attend school in Miami (Jonathan had completed high school in Nicaragua
and wanted to attend college; Karla wanted to complete high school) and then
work, participating in their version of el Sueño Americano (the American
Dream). Angela expected that her husband would economically support Karla
and Jonathan: "I thought when they left here that they would have the total
support of their dad, which is exactly what they did not have." Shortly after his
children arrived, Carlo informed them they would not be able to study because
he needed them to work in order to support his household. Angela remembers

their disillusionment: "All this was really sad, because it was a very big pain for my children to know that the reality wasn't anything like what he had said, that he was going to bring them [to the United States] to help them. None of that—they couldn't study; they only just had to work." Jonathan and Karla found whatever employment they could as undocumented migrants: in fast food, child-care, janitorial, and other service industry jobs.

Contributing to their disillusionment in Miami, Jonathan and Karla discovered that their father was living with another woman (a Honduran immigrant) and her two U.S.-born children. While Angela and her children had had suspicions about Carlo's infidelity over the years, he had successfully hidden his affairs from his Nicaraguan family.[3] In discovering this reality of their father's life, Jonathan and Karla understood that their Nicaraguan family was fractured beyond repair. Back home, Angela was holding on to a different temporality, a sense of hope that Carlo would one day come back and that their life would return to its premigration configuration. Jonathan and Karla knew they needed to let Angela know the painful truth, even though it would confirm her worst fears about how migration had undermined their family's solidarity. As Carlo's new wife grew impatient with having to share her home with his Nicaraguan children, Carlo pressured Jonathan and Karla to move out, which they did about a year after they had arrived.

After moving out, Jonathan and Karla survived by supporting each other, finding a shared apartment and working in a variety of jobs until landing positions as full-time janitors for a major hotel chain. While their tie with their father was broken, their sibling tie strengthened, at least temporarily. Soon thereafter, Jonathan went through a period that Angela describes as his *rebelión* (rebellion), when he spent a lot of time and money in fiestas and lost touch with his mother back home. This worried Angela, concerned that her son, like his father before him, would fall into the easy pleasures of *la vida allá* (life over there)—partying, consumption, and prioritizing individual desires over family responsibilities. This is another illustration of the fears of grandmothers, like Juana's earlier, that their migrant sons will fall into *vicios* (vices). In fact, for several years Jonathan did not regularly communicate or send remittances home, seeming to follow in his father's footsteps of the gendered expectations about male migrants' irresponsibility that contained Angela's fears of another generation of abandonment. However, eventually, Jonathan found a steady girlfriend and settled down; at the time of this writing, he and Angela communicate regularly, he visits about once a year, and he has taken his Ecuadoran-born girlfriend to Nicaragua to meet the family.

For her part, Karla suffered through a strained relationship in the United States with the father of her U.S.-born twins. According to Angela, this man was physically and emotionally abusive. While Karla tried to conceal her troubles so as not to worry her mother, Angela became aware of her daughter's predicament and pensó mucho (thought too much) about her plight. Eventually, with Jonathan's help, Karla left her boyfriend and married a Cuban American, with whom she has a third U.S.-born child. Given these struggles, Karla was unable to visit her daughter and mother in Nicaragua for more than ten years, a difficult and prolonged period of separation.[4]

When Karla and Jonathan sent word home confirming her worst suspicions about her husband's adultery, Angela was emotionally devastated. His promises to support their family would never be fulfilled, and his affair magnified her sense of abandonment: first, Carlo had emigrated, and then he had absolved himself of all responsibility for his Nicaraguan family. Shortly after learning this news (in 2004), Angela was hospitalized and underwent heart-catheterization surgery. Angela indirectly attributes this hospitalization to her husband's affair, seeing her illness and hospitalization as an outcome of an acute episode of depression. In Angela's words,

> It was like little by little with the passage of time I was falling into a depressive state, and this led me to the hospital. The problem is that these things don't just happen; instead they come along little by little, little by little. And the doctor told [my children], "Your mother is falling into a depressive state" and that if they didn't pay attention, I was going to die, because a moment would arrive when I would no longer be able to recover.

Angela's account of her hospitalization is particularly interesting for the way she frames depression temporally as a progressive state of decline that did not "just happen" but accumulated over time. Since her husband's migration, Angela's emotional state had declined, "little by little." In Angela's account, depression functions as an idiom of distress, giving warning signs and calling for the attention of her adult children, who are exhorted to "pay attention" to their mother's distress. Angela's narrative frames depression as an emotional and temporal response to migration, similar to the model of grandmothers' emotional distress presented in Chapter 3. Further, Angela positions herself as the main recipient of the consequences of migration, using depression to communicate her distress to her adult children by reminding them of their responsibility to support her emotionally. As an idiom of distress, depression in this case calls attention to what matters most for Angela, which is that her family come together in solidarity, despite the hardships consequent to migration.

In talking about this depression and hospitalization episode, Angela asserts that the uncertainty and ambivalence that characterize transnational ties become unbearable, causing caregivers like herself in migrant-sending households to fall ill. Angela compares out-migration to the hypothetical death of a spouse, saying the latter is more bearable because of its certain, finite nature: "He died, and from there you can't do anything." On the other hand, Angela describes the out-migration of her husband and her growing suspicions about his infidelity as "golpeando" (beating [down]) and "dañando" (harming) her, continually, over time, like a chronic assault without apparent end. When Angela's suspicions were confirmed, she remembers feeling a moment of acute realization that "his obligation to us [Angela and her children in Nicaragua] was definitely over."

Angela remains resentful of Carlo for not living up to his promises to his family. She attributes this in part to the self-centered lifestyle he developed as a migrant, which Angela views as part of the transformation of values that migration to the United States entails:

If he really had wanted to, he could have thought more about his children. He would have thought more about us, which was what he didn't do; instead, he dedicated himself to living his own life. They say that he—ever since he began his life with that woman—went to play cards, to drink. Everything was about vice. So that's why it was easier for him to be alone over there and work and make his own life and forget himself.

Angela's reflections on Carlo's migration contain a strong critique about the life he has lived as a migrant, a life Angela describes as self-centered, individualistic, and "forgetful" of obligations to kin back home. This excerpt highlights what Angela most values, which is a sense of family unity, responsibility, and solidarity—values that are threatened by migration. These values prioritize responsibilities to others, especially family members, over and above individual desires. Carlo's migration ruptured not only his ties and obligations to family back home but also relations with other family members. It is as if migration situated Carlo in a different temporal register, where selfishness is valued over commitment and responsibility to family. For Angela, the change in Carlo's values is crystallized in the way he treats his Nicaraguan children: first, putting them out of the house because they displeased his new wife and, second, denying paternity and further complicating Karla and Jonathan's ability to obtain legal residency. For Angela, the ultimate abandonment is not that Carlo was physically absent but that he relinquished his responsibilities to care for his family.

Further, Carlo's migration provoked separation and fissure throughout the family, fraying the ties between Angela and her children. By migrating, Carlo induced his children to also emigrate, making it impossible for Angela to be the kind of mother she desires to be. In her words, "He took away my right to see my children . . . my right as the mother of my children [Me quitó el derecho de ver a mis hijos . . . el derecho que yo tengo como madre de mis hijos]." Separation from her migrant children continues to be a source of emotional distress for Angela. The despair over the physical distance separating her from her children is most pronounced at times of trouble, as when Jonathan and Karla have gone through difficulties in the United States. During these episodes, Angela longs for the physical proximity that would allow her to provide emotional support to her children, but instead she has felt estranged and incompetent as a mother because her children are far away. She describes this feeling this way: "Emotionally, you would like to be close to them [your children]; you would like to be able to help them, and this is the most difficult thing—that it's not within your reach to be able to help them and be able to support them." Angela describes the physical and emotional distance that characterize transnational family life, an experience she has had firsthand, as a spouse and mother, and that therefore sensitizes her to Karla's experience as a migrant mother and Karla's daughter's experience as a child of a migrant parent. Angela works to counter this distance, separation, and potential fracture through the sacrifices she makes as a caregiver, which are aligned to promote solidarity in her family across generations.

Carlo's migration provoked disunity among Angela's children. For instance, Angela's daughter Noelia recalled her mother's hospitalization as a time when the distance between her migrant siblings and family back home was magnified. Noelia contacted Karla and Jonathan to tell them their mother was in the hospital and recalled that their response was to send money to cover medical expenses. While Noelia and Angela (and her other two children in Nicaragua) certainly appreciated this gesture of material support, it simultaneously

reminded them of Karla and Jonathan's physical absence from the family Noelia recalls her mother saying, "My poor children . . . because they try to replace
the 'I'm not there,' 'I can't see you,' 'I can't pick you up,' 'I can't bathe you' with
money." Once again, the trade-offs in transnational migration crystallize in the
inadequacy of material gain to compensate for the absence of emotional support and solidarity within families.

Despite the distance and more than a decade of separation consequent to
migration, Angela retains a hope and even an expectation that her children will
return home to Nicaragua. Angela often says, "This will always be their home. . . .
They have to return to Nicaragua; this will be their home [Ésta siempre será
su casa. . . . Tienen que volver a Nicaragua; ésta sería su casa]." Angela and her
older son Carlos have begun to invest some of Karla and Jonathan's remittances
in a parcel of land near the coast, which they imagine as a family residence
for sometime in the future. As we see in Chapter 2, migrant remittances are
often used to renovate or construct houses, especially in families like Angela's,
in which the duration of migration is long enough that the priorities of remittance expenditures (food, schooling, health care) have been met. Nonetheless,
it is not clear that Jonathan and Karla have any intentions to return home to
settle in Nicaragua, and given their newly formed relationships (in Karla's case,
partnerships that produced three U.S.-born children) in the United States, their
orientations are likely shifting away from Nicaragua. In the recent past, immediate present, and near future, Jonathan and Karla's migration will complicate
the physical and emotional closeness that Angela desires for her family. Nonetheless, Angela responds to these tensions and uncertainties of transnational
family life by emphasizing values of unity and solidarity, particularly with re-
spect to her care for her granddaughter Laleska.

Moralities of Care in a Third Migrant Generation

Karla's impermanent union in Nicaragua with Laleska's father had ended after his irresponsible and abusive behavior led Karla to move back in with her
mother, taking her daughter with her.[5] Karla worked several temporary, part-
time jobs before deciding to leave Managua in search of greater economic opportunities abroad. Angela had provided care for Laleska in the first year of her
life while her mother was at work, but assuming primary responsibility after
Karla's migration was a significantly different experience, requiring a reconfiguration of care across generations.

Angela responded to Karla's migration through the lens of her own first-hand experience with migration. Angela recalls her reaction to Karla's decision to leave:

> I told Karlita, love, remember that you have your girl; you are going to miss your girl. It's not the same to say as it is to feel. It's not the same to say, "I'm going to be over there." You're going to be thinking about your child. This girl is going to grow up. "Yes, Mom, but I want to go. I know that by working over there I'm going to help out more; we're all going to be better off and everything." I didn't have another option. . . . If they [her children] said yes [to migration], I say yes too.

As Angela describes it, the decision to migrate was made by Karla, and Angela was left to adapt to the consequent changes in her family's life. This rendering of migration decision making runs counter to the household decision model often put forward in developmentalist or other social science analyses of migration. Scholars working from a new household economics perspective suggest that migration decisions are made collectively at the household level, according to shared assessments of available resources and opportunities (for example, see Donato 1993; Massey 1990). However, Angela's story suggests something different—a pattern of decision making seen throughout other families in this study. In this model, a migrant mother's decision to leave is made, and a grandmother assumes care for grandchildren as an act of embodied solidarity for the family's well-being. Further, grandmothers often experience their daughters' migrations through the perspective of their own troublesome past experiences of migration. Angela views her adult children's desires to migrate and *mejorarse* (improve themselves) as a reflection of their father's similar desires a generation prior. Furthermore, she has concerns that migration will rupture her family's solidarity in the present, just as it did in the past.

Not wanting to be the obstacle to her children's hopes for a better life, Angela overcomes her doubts about migration and offers her support to her adult children as she did previously to her husband. This intergenerational support is most concretely instantiated through Angela's assumption of care for her granddaughter, Laleska. Through this intergenerational care, Angela is lending support to her daughter's migration ambitions and to the moral bargain that Karla is making, which is that migration will pay off in terms of improved conditions of life for Laleska and for the entire family. Angela is also, moreover, embodying the solidarity and care that she expected from her husband a generation earlier and continues to expect from her migrant children in the present.

Angela was concerned about how mother migration would affect her granddaughter's life, not only at the moment of Karla's departure but also over time. As she states above, Angela foresaw a growing emotional distance between mother and daughter and encouraged Karla to consider that "this girl is going to grow up" and that Karla would miss being present during her daughter's development. Of course, Laleska did grow up and experienced critical life transitions without her mother present. One of these was menarche, which occurred when Laleska was ten years old. Aunt Noelia was the female figure Laleska turned to in her mother's absence and who helped her learn about managing her "special time of the month." [6] Not being able to share this culturally significant physiological change with her mother was emotionally painful for Laleska, who told her grandmother, "I had wanted the first to know to be my mom [Yo quería que la primera que supiera fuera mi mama]." The cultural expectation that daughter and mother would share this important rite of passage went unrealized because the temporality of her mother's migration was asynchronous with Laleska's life course in Nicaragua.

Over the more than ten years of Karla's migration, Angela has assumed the primary everyday caregiving role for Laleska in ways that reflect her emphasis on solidarity in family relations. This ethos of solidarity is most explicitly embodied in Angela making sure to share her care equally with the three granddaughters in her care: Laleska, Reyna (sixteen) and Alexa (thirteen). All three girls were their mothers' first-born children and have lived with Angela since birth, even as their mothers have moved on to form separate households. Reyna's mother, Lidia, and Alexa's mother, Noelia, both live in Managua in households shared with male partners and younger children. Angela cares for her three granddaughters "como si fuera su mama" (as if I were their mother), treating all three with parity and equity. This has meant sharing the remittances Karla sends home equally among the three girls. Once she established herself financially in the United States, Karla has consistently sent money back home (on average, about $300 per month). All three granddaughters attend the same neighborhood Catholic school, where tuition runs about $75 per month per child. Angela uses the remaining money to buy food, clothing, and any needed medical care for her *niñas* (girls). Angela describes the distribution of remittances this way: "Karla has helped all three [of the girls]: in their studies, their nutrition, in everything, in their sicknesses. Karlita is the one who has taken care of everything." Using Karla's remittances to equally support her daughter and her nieces embodies the ethos of responsibility and solidarity that Angela works to uphold in her family. Ever since her husband's migration led to ruptured ties and unrealized responsibilities, what matters most for Angela is preventing the same consequence for her granddaughters.

Laleska, Alexa, and Reyna, as maternal cousins, have formed strong ties of relatedness through years of sharing a household and everyday relations of care for one another and for their grandmother Angela. (For an illustration of Angela's kinship and migration relations and more discussion of kinship migration maps in general, see the appendix.) These strong kin bonds are indicated by the kin terms the girls use to refer to one another, as *hermanas* (sisters), and to Angela, as "mamá." Angela describes her care for her granddaughters this way:

> What is my struggle? I do this; I do the other; I do washing, cooking, making them their little meals for when they come home from school, cleaning their house so when they come they find their little house clean. Doing everything. You see that they have come out well.

As we see in Chapter 1, for grandmothers like Angela, caring for grandchildren is indeed a responsibility, or struggle (*lucha*), to use Angela's words. The struggle is in the everyday caregiving labor of cleaning, washing, and cooking. And yet Angela's pleasure comes in the results of her care: that her granddaughters "have come out well" gives her a great source of satisfaction. Angela's household is indeed orderly and clean in the way she describes here. I saw this during my morning visits, after the girls had left for school, when Angela would be washing clothes, cleaning house, and preparing the midday meal. In the afternoon, after the girls returned from school and had lunch, they might rest for a while and then get busy doing their homework. In the evenings, the girls would help Angela with the many church-related activities she was responsible for, setting up chairs for a Bible study or buying snacks to take to a meeting.

While I did not explore Angela's religious beliefs in depth, it is clear to me that her religious views and activities play an important role in her moral orientation toward intergenerational care. She is a practicing evangelical Christian and leader of a *célula* (cell, or neighborhood group) of her church. Angela distinguishes her church as being more *abierta* (open) than other, more conservative Christian churches in Nicaragua, since women are permitted to wear pants and short skirts (unlike in other evangelical churches), and the church also actively encourages women such as herself to take on leadership roles in church and community life.[7] In addition to these rather progressive tendencies, Angela's religious beliefs influence her child-rearing practices in other apparent ways. For example, Angela strictly controls her niñas, telling them where and with whom they can be after school and discouraging them from being alone with boys or men. On more than one occasion, Angela told me that she felt it was her responsibility to protect her girls from sexual abuse or assault by men.[8]

Furthermore, Angela's intergenerational care is motivated by values of shared responsibility and solidarity, which is expressed in her moral commitment to uphold an egalitarian ethos in her family. As Angela explains of her granddaughters, "I love all three the same; with the three of them we always share the same. If I have enough for one, I have for all three. If I don't have enough for all three, then I say to the others they have to wait; when I have enough for all three, then we will buy [it]." Angela imparts a sense of gratitude to her granddaughters, ensuring they recognize both the sacrifices she makes in caring for them and Karla's sacrifices as a migrant working abroad and sending money home. Angela even uses Karla's *remesas* (remittances) as leverage to motivate her niñas to study hard, to share in the intergenerational sacrifice of migration by doing well in school.[9]

Angela positions her care against popular stereotypes of grandmothers raising children of parent migrants solely for material gain. In this way, Angela's story illustrates the moral economies of migration and care presented in Chapter 2. For instance, during one of my visits to her household, the television was tuned to a program about migration's effects on Nicaraguan families. A child psychologist was talking about grandmothers who raise children of migrant mothers, saying they either are too lax and unable to discipline their grandchildren or treat their grandchildren like servants, forcing them to do household chores and then taking in remittances for personal use. Angela was angered by this stereotype, saying, "I hear a whole lot of things, but thank God, that's not how it is with me and my girls. It's not like that." Angela distances herself from stereotypes of grandmothers who are self-interested, divert remittances for personal use, and neglect the children in their care. She has worked hard over the decade since Karla's migration to create an orderly, fair, and harmonious household, one characterized by mutual support and solidarity and wherein each member, even those who have migrated, uphold their responsibilities to one another.

Despite Angela's best attempts to shape her family's receipt of remittances through an ethos of shared sacrifice and solidarity, tensions surround the money Karla sends home. For instance, every time Karla sends remittances, the money painfully reminds her daughter of her absence. Angela refers to this pain as the concrete difference between Laleska's experience as a daughter of a migrant mother and Alexa's and Reyna's experiences as children whose mothers live in Managua and can be physically present when needed. For Angela, this distinction is central to the impact of mother migration on children and families left behind. She emphasized, "It's not the same [when] having to contact her mom, having to call her; it's not the same talking over the phone as having a face-to-face talk." Furthermore, Angela has perceived that Karla's relationship with Laleska has frayed over time, with absence and distance. Angela and her daughter Noelia sense that Karla has responded to these reconfigurations of relatedness by trying to compensate for her absence with material gifts. The women discussed this dynamic with me one warm late afternoon as we sat in Angela's living room drinking fresh fruit-infused water that Angela had prepared.

> NOELIA: With Laleska, she [Karla] tries to appease her, in whatever way she can. Even Karla has that wall, like she doesn't want to break that ice, because in the bottom of her heart, she once told me over the phone, crying, that she felt bad about Laleska. But I told her, "But why do you feel bad? If you have her in school, she doesn't want for anything; Mom is taking care of her." She told me, "It's that here I can take Kathy [her younger U.S.-born daughter] out. I can take her shopping. We go out to eat chicken, and sometimes when we're out eating chicken, I ask myself, 'I wonder what Laleska's doing now?' What happens is that I try to detach myself," she told me. So I told her to send money to Laleska so she can go out to eat chicken too. . . . It's like a game, this "I am going to give you [things] so that you don't suffer."
>
> ANGELA: It's like exchanging feelings for money.
>
> NOELIA: Yep: "I'm going to give you things so you don't suffer."

This exchange illustrates the tensions in transnational families surrounding love and money, or the "transubstantiation of love into things" in mother-child relationships divided by borders (Horton 2008: 927). Noelia is concerned that Karla seeks to use material goods to fill the void left by her absence. For Noelia this is a serious game of "I'm going to give you things so you don't suffer." The risk, as Angela puts it, is in "exchanging feelings for money [cambiar el sentimiento por el dinero]." (I myself succumbed to this risk, in an episode I recount in the preface, in which I found myself a recipient of Angela's care during fieldwork and attempted—naïvely—to compensate care with monetary payment.) What is at stake in these relational exchanges over time and space are the moral economies of care and migration that grandmothers in this study embody through their intergenerational care.

Angela's care for Laleska is oriented to prevent such a rupture in the trans-national mother-child tie and in the values of sacrifice and solidarity that she has strived to uphold in her transnational family, over generations. While sending money home for children's education may be a principal motive for mothers to emigrate (for example, see Dreby 2010; Horton 2008; Hondagneu-Sotelo and Avila 1997), caregivers in migrant-sending countries must manage the transnational tensions in mother-child relationships that persist, despite remittances. For her part, partly because of Carlo's abandonment and fail-ure to send financial support in the previous generation, Angela feels that, as long as Karla continues to send money home, she remains—at least in part—responsible (*pendiente*) for her Nicaraguan family. Still, Angela observes the troubles in Laleska's relationship with her mother—the increasing emotional distance that compounds over time—and orients her care toward fostering connection in these transnational ties. Whether her intergenerational care can succeed in sustaining solidarity despite the troubles of transnational life is a question hinged on the balance between past experience, present realities, and future uncertainties.

Care Against Abandonment

Through my volunteer work with the NGO Servicio Jesuita para Migrantes, I helped coordinate activities on a national campaign to raise awareness about violations of Nicaraguan migrants' rights abroad. One activity was radio pro-grams, such as that in which Angela and Marbeya participated, which is de-scribed in this book's introduction. I was in the recording studio when Angela and Marbeya were interviewed by the radio host about their experiences as grandmothers raising children of mother migrants. The women answered the host's questions with candor and honesty, even when the questions touched emotionally troublesome topics. At one point, as she described Laleska's rela-tionship with Karla, Angela's voice choked with tears. She told the host that La-leska occasionally spoke of not wanting to talk to or see her mother ever again and went on to describe how, as an intergenerational caregiver, she experiences her daughter's struggles and her granddaughter's pain. In Angela's words, "She transmits to me whatever she's feeling. . . . It's that I'm living what she's living

[Me transmite lo que está sintiendo. . . . Es que estoy viviendo lo que ella está viviendo]." This is a vivid example of the way grandmothers mediate the troubled emotional lives of children of parent migrants and also how the emotional experience of parent migration is a shared, intersubjective experience.[10] Angela fills the space of absence left by mother migration with her care for Laleska as another mother, *una otra mamá*. The emotional experience of mother migration is compounded for grandmothers like Angela, who often experience the absence of their migrant daughters through the prism of past pain and loss and share the emotional experiences of the children in their care.

Angela's family history of migration contains striking intergenerational parallels. Angela portrays her concerns about Laleska's experience of her mother's migration in a way that echoes her own problematic experience of her husband's migration. Angela's concerns about the effect of Karla's migration on Laleska reflect Angela's personal, prior experience of her husband's migration. As mentioned above, Angela still resents her husband's reneging on his promise to support Jonathan and Karla while they finished their educations in the United States. Angela is concerned that this history of unrealized ambitions will repeat itself if Laleska leaves to join Karla in the United States. Angela rhetorically asks, "If she is going to take her there, what would happen if she's not going to send her to school?" Angela contemplates her own investment in ensuring Laleska's educational success after Karla migrated—supporting her attendance in private school and overseeing her getting good grades over the past ten years. Beyond education, Angela considers Laleska's potential future migration in terms of the family unity Angela so fervently desires. Just as Carlo's encouragement of Jonathan's and Karla's migrations undermined Angela's "right" to be physically and emotionally close to her children, Angela is concerned that Karla's ongoing absence is undermining Laleska's "right" to her mother's physical and emotional proximity.

Angela ultimately feels that her husband abandoned her, and she works hard to mediate Karla's relationship with Laleska to avoid a similar sentiment in her granddaughter. Still, Angela told me on many occasions that Karla's relationship with Laleska is slowly deteriorating. For example, Angela said,

I feel that Karlita now is more distant from the girl. So it's like with time, she is growing accustomed to the distance from the girl. And Laleska, sometimes I tell her, "Come, talk to your mom," and she tells me no. She says, "If my mom doesn't ask to talk to me, don't pass me the phone." So I tell Karla, "Are you going to talk with your daughter?" She doesn't tell me to pass the phone to her. She doesn't ask, "How is my girl doing?" And she—before, she wasn't like that. Before, she was like, "My little girl, my little girl." She sent her little cards; there was this dedication that she had to her daughter. For my part, I understand that now, with her three [U.S.-born] children, one of whom is just an infant, and the problems she has and over time—it's just like she can't [relate to her] anymore. But of course I understand this, but with Laleska I'm feeling and I'm living this distancing; I see Laleska notice that her mom doesn't want to talk to her. And it's like, "If she wants to talk with me, fine; if not, fine." So time is separating them more and more. So because I have felt this myself [with my husband's migration], I tell this girl here, I'm going to pass you the phone; talk to your mom.

Fascinating in this description is how Angela experiences Karla's distancing from Laleska as if it were a sort of reliving of her experience with Carlo's migration. Recall how Angela described her depression in response to Carlo's migration as gathering over time, until finally she could not bear it and physically collapsed under the weight of her feelings. In Angela's description of Laleska's relationship with Karla, there is a similar sense of the looming threat that the emotional tie between mother and daughter (in both generations—between Angela and Karla, and between Karla and Laleska) will wear thin with time and distance. Angela is troubled by the growing distance between mother and child, not in small measure because she witnessed a similar dynamic between her husband and *his* children. In response, Angela's caregiving is oriented toward repairing the mother-daughter relationship by encouraging Karla to talk to Laleska more frequently and to come home and visit. Furthermore, by working to uphold the tie between a transnational mother and the granddaughter in her care, Angela is investing in family solidarity and continuity across the generations.

A Granddaughter's Experience of Migration

Laleska was a reserved, insightful girl of eleven at the time I met her. Although she was always willing to talk with me, I was never certain how much of the complexity of her experience she was revealing to me. After our conversations, I often was left feeling as though I was barely penetrating her outer layers and struggling to understand what it was really like to be living her situation of mother migration and transnational life. Laleska did open up on social media, however; she could spend hours sending text messages to her schoolmates on her cell phone, and she insisted on setting up a Facebook account for me (which we have used to stay in touch ever since). One thing about her mother's absence about which Laleska always expressed clarity was that Karla's migration was intended to provide Laleska with a better future. Laleska said, "[My mother is] working hard over there so that I do well here," iterating the same narrative framing of migration as sacrifice that Angela did and that we see reflected in generational relations of care throughout this book. Laleska is also aware of the amount in remittances Karla sends home and how *remesas* are shared by Angela with her two cousins for school fees, food, and other costs. Remittances have an affective dimension, for Laleska feels partly connected to her mother through the money she sends home. However, despite her awareness of the economic determinants and the benefits of her mother's migration, Laleska's experience of her mother's absence is intensely ambivalent.[11] Children like Laleska are keenly aware of the economic realities pushing their mothers to migrate and appreciate the sacrifice embodied by remittances, and yet they still long for their mothers to return home and are uncertain about the prospect of their own migration to reunite with mothers abroad. For instance, Laleska remembers fondly and in detail her mother's two visits to Nicaragua since migrating, the most recent of which took place around Laleska's eighth birthday. Laleska still keeps a card her mother gave her on that occasion and recounts how they spent their time together: visiting a lake, eating out at the mall, going to the market, spending time with extended family. The fondness of these memories is countered by Laleska's lack of certainty about whether her mother will be able to visit again; Laleska is unsure what the future holds for her family's transnational ties.

As Laleska and Karla's relationship deteriorated, transnational communication felt futile, since, in Laleska's words, "How am I going to tell her things if she can't do anything for me from over there? Because of the distance, she can't do anything for me, over the phone she can't solve my problems." The distance and the duration of migration were deepening the emotional separation between daughter and mother. Further contributing to Laleska's sense of distance was that her mother has three U.S.-born children with whom Laleska felt little connection. When Karla talks to Laleska about her half-siblings, about the outings she takes them on and the things they do together, Laleska feels slighted, reminded that *she* is unable to spend time with her mother in those ways. For her part, Angela responded to these tensions by increasing her investments in care, trying to repair the mother-daughter tie through assertions of the importance of parity and solidarity. For instance, Angela told Karla not to talk about the excursions she takes with her children unless she also sends money for Laleska to have similar experiences in Managua; otherwise, she risks fostering even greater resentment in Laleska. As Laleska grew estranged from her mother, she was growing closer to her "mamá Angela," who attended to her everyday needs with physical care and emotional proximity.

One of the most striking tensions in the transnational relationship between Angela, Karla, and Laleska surrounded the uncertain possibility that Karla would send for Laleska to join her in the United States. Part of this uncertainty comes from the family's experiences of Karla's two visits to Nicaragua, which have been happy encounters but have left uncertainty in their wake. For instance, Angela recalls how Laleska responded to her mother's leaving after one visit: "I saw her cry, and I felt it too because I didn't want my daughter to leave again, to see her again in two years. I said, 'Now until when?'" Angela felt sad as a grandmother but also as a mother, uncertain when her daughter would be able to visit again. (Part of the reason Karla limited her visits home was that while her legal residency petition was being processed, she was prohibited from leaving the United States.)[12] This is emblematic of the ways migrant visits home become part of the "herida resangriente" (the reopening wound) of migration.[13]

Karla's two visits had not only reminded Angela and Laleska of her continuing absence but also raised unavoidable questions about Karla's future plans regarding reunification with her daughter. As we have seen throughout this book, mother-children reunification is problematic from grandmothers' perspective because it separates them from children with whom they have grown emotionally close through their caregiving. For families who remain behind, like Angela and Laleska, reunification is also a troublesome temporality of waiting, because the complex immigration bureaucracy that migrants like Karla must negotiate to bring children legally to the United States further entrenches the uncertainty shrouding the future.

For her part, Angela tried to make sense of the possibility of reunification, despite the length, uncertainty, and confusion surrounding the legal processes involved. At one point, in October 2009, Angela thought that the approval of Laleska's residency petition was imminent, and she was mentally and emotionally preparing herself and her granddaughter for Laleska's departure. Foremost among Angela's concerns was how Laleska and Karla would get along, given the recent troubles in their relationship. Nonetheless, time continued to pass, suspending Angela and her granddaughter in the ambivalent temporality of immigration proceedings—unsure whether Karla had submitted the visa petition or whether it would be approved. Several months later, in February 2010, it seemed that Karla was planning a visit home to complete bureaucratic *trámites* (procedures) needed for Laleska's visa. However, this visit never materialized, the months continued to pass, and Angela and Laleska remained in the liminal space between here and there, uncertain of whether Laleska would stay in Nicaragua or whether Karla would inform them that the visa had been approved.

As time passed and it remained unclear whether Laleska would stay or go, she and her grandmother expressed deeper doubts about leaving for the United States. In December 2009, when the possibility of her emigration seemed imminent, Laleska was ambivalent about the prospect. About migrating to join her mother in the United States, she said, "I want to go, and I don't want to go [Quiero ir, y no quiero ir]." Among the reasons Laleska gave for going to the United States were that she wanted, she said, "to stay for a while," "to see how it is over there," "to meet my younger brothers and sisters," and "to see my mom; to be with her." On the other hand, Laleska felt that migrating was undesirable because she did not want to leave her school, her friends, her mamá Angela, or her hermanas, Alexa and Reyna. What struck me most in my conversations with Laleska was how this uncertain future of migration threw her into a limbo between her everyday life in Nicaragua and the uncertainty of a future in the United States.[14]

For Angela, the possibility of her granddaughter's departure recalled two previous generations of migration, and she responded to the uncertainty of Laleska's departure through the prism of past experience. Angela feared abandonment for a third time and losing the emotional closeness she and Laleska had developed, as she had experienced the fraying of her ties with her husband and migrant children before. Angela's emphasis on family unity was complicated, however, since she simultaneously felt drawn to support reunification between Karla and Laleska. Ultimately, Angela viewed the possibility of reunification in terms of her past experiences: just as she had not wanted to be separated from her husband or children, she would not deny her daughter the chance to reunite with her child. As a grandmother caregiver, she again was called to sacrifice her individual desire (to have her granddaughter remain in her care) to her family's solidarity (which meant supporting Laleska's departure and reunification with her mother). Indeed, nearly a year later, when Karla informed her mother that she had finally secured Laleska's visa, Angela sacrificed her personal tie to her granddaughter and supported reunification; Laleska boarded a plane to Miami soon thereafter.

Transnational Troubles at the Cyber Café

Months into my developing relationship with Angela's family, she invited me to her home to discuss a troubling experience granddaughter Laleska had had the previous weekend. Angela and Karla had scheduled a time to talk using a computer equipped with a camera; this was to be the first time they would converse in this way, and Angela took Laleska to the neighborhood cyber café at the arranged time. Angela herself was excited to experiment with this form of communication; she was eager to see Karla and her other grandchildren in the United States and talk to them. For Laleska, however, the experience was deeply unsettling. Laleska declined to go to the computer where Angela was talking with Karla, instead burying herself in her Hotmail account and e-mailing with school friends. Laleska refused Angela's multiple entreaties to talk with her mother, leaving Angela suspended in the awkward virtual distance—a gap at once emotional, temporal, and spatial—between her daughter and granddaughter. Ever the mediator of these transnational tensions, Angela used the moment to remind Karla that Laleska's behavior was evidence of a void that would only be bridged (in Angela's view) if Karla came to visit, soon.

On the afternoon that Angela recounted the above scene to me, she asked me to speak to Laleska about her feelings. I remember the moment, seated in Angela's patio, sipping the cool fruit agua fresca drink that she had prepared for me, as one wherein I was extraordinarily attuned to the plural positionalities of the ethnographer. With Angela asking me to reach out to her troubled granddaughter, any semblance of boundaries between researcher and counselor, observer and friend, had become nearly indistinguishable. I was being sought out to provide a listening ear, counsel, and encouragement to a girl undergoing a troubling emotional experience. As on the day when I was sick and she attended to my illness, Angela was leading me yet again outside my researcher role, this time to the role not of care recipient but of a provider of care and emotional support for her granddaughter. As Laleska approached me and sat down in the white plastic chair Angela had set out, I reminded her she did not have to talk if she did not want to. Laleska nodded, indicating that she did want to talk with me. I wondered how I had managed to gain her confidence, remembering our first interview months earlier, at the conclusion of which Laleska asserted, "I haven't told you how I *really* feel," emphasizing that there was something she was holding back, which she did not yet trust me enough to tell. Now, after I had spent time with her and her family over several months, Laleska decided that I was worth her confidence.

Laleska went on to recount her version of the cyber café episode, telling me she was reluctant to talk with her mother because of the physical distance separating them, as she felt this gap made it impossible for her mother to assist and care for her—to be there for her—in the way Laleska desired. This breach of communication embodied all the challenges Laleska felt in her relationship with her mother, especially the uncertainty that shrouded her future as she wondered whether one day she would move to Miami and become an immigrant Latina in the United States. These were uncertainties I could not imagine facing at eleven years old, and I still ponder the immensity of the circumstances shaping the lives of Laleska and other children in transnational families: the political economic circumstances pushing their mothers to emigrate, years or even decades passing during which families negotiate the emotional complexities of mother absence and children form strong ties with grandmother caregivers, and a future that becomes suspended in space and time between *allá* (over there, in destination countries) and *acá* (here, home in Nicaragua).

As much as I was attuned to Laleska's emotional pain that late afternoon in her patio, these are uncertainties that exceed the boundaries of empathetic understanding. After Laleska's emotional disclosure, I felt challenged to come up with an effective, or at least adequate, response—something that would illustrate the sort of solidarity and alignment that I had observed in Angela and other grandmother caregivers. I attempted to align with Laleska emotionally, I listened to her, and I offered her my moral support. Admittedly clumsy, this response reflected my humanity, not my ethnographic training, and was perhaps also an extension of my past professional training in community mental health. And yet these encounters were made possible by anthropological engagement and would not have happened if I had not been working with families in a research capacity. These encounters also become, in the process of analyzing and writing about them, a sort of evidence, useful for enriching my understanding of transnational family life in all its complexity, uncertainty, and precarity.

I show throughout this book how *solidaridad* is a form of empathetic alignment with others—one that embodies practical action. Empathy is a complex sentiment in ethnographic encounters and one subject to much debate. A simple definition of empathy may be "to understand another's experience through feeling or thinking something similar oneself" (Kirmayer 2008: 458). For instance, in the encounter described above, my response to Laleska was an attempt, however feeble, to connect with a struggling young girl by drawing on our shared human experience. However, I felt immediately that my attempt fell short, as I saw in Laleska's eyes a semblance of recognition tempered by the social distance separating us. Of course, I am aware that these differences—in citizenship, age, class, nationality, and culture—are irreducible. Certainly, I believe my engagements with grandmothers, children, and other members of families during fieldwork were shaped as much by their willingness to let me into their lives (or not) as by my ability to be drawn in. And yet I attempted to connect with Laleska, Angela, Olga, Manuela, and others I encountered during fieldwork to share what I had (knowledge, resources, a listening ear, possibly even solidarity). It has also been suggested that "empathy must be coupled with moral commitments and translated into action" (Kirmayer 2008: 461). Casting empathy as more than emotional alignment, as a form of moral action, is consistent with the rendering of solidarity I have pursued throughout this book. I learned about *solidaridad* as an enacted, embodied practice from spending time with Nicaraguan families, and this knowledge forever changed me as a researcher, advocate, friend, and family member.

Of course, these engagements also raise difficult questions for ethnographic connection well beyond fieldwork. I struggle to maintain my commitments to keeping in touch with families over time. This is the case particularly for several families, including that of Angela, with whom I grew especially close. I remember specifically Laleska's matter-of-fact tone of voice when she told me, after our conversation about the cyber café episode, which took place near the end of my fieldwork, "Soon you too will leave [Pronto vos también vas a ir]." It was impossible for me to respond to this declaration, for my departure *was* imminent. More troubling to me is that, over time, I have found myself falling into the patterns of care from a distance that unsettle moral economies of migration and care: sending money or gifts for birthdays and *quinceñeras* (fifteenth birthday celebrations) because being there, physically present in Nicaragua, has become difficult given professional and other demands of life in the United States. While I do not mean to suggest that my absence from family life is anywhere near as significant as that of mothers who migrate, these troubling engagements and competing commitments do give me a glimpse of the challenges involved in maintaining relatedness and care across borders and over time in transnational families.

Migration and Care Across Generations

Angela's family portrait of migration illustrates the importance of an inter-generational perspective for understanding the value of caregiving in trans-national families. Angela's first abandonment, the migration of her husband, shaped the ways she responded to the migration of her children and the poten-tial migration of her granddaughter in subsequent decades. Angela attributes much of the disruption in her family to her husband's original departure: "If he had never left, all of this would not have happened [Si él nunca hubiera salido, todas estas cosas no hubieran pasado]." Over time, Angela responded to the disruption and uncertainty of transnational family life by reaffirming her commitment to family unity, using her care as a form of sacrifice for family solidarity.

This portrait shows that, although Angela has never herself migrated, she has nonetheless experienced migration in a profound and personal way—as a spouse, mother, and grandmother. The dynamics shaping relations of care and kinship in this one transnational family—profound feelings of ambivalence, tensions around monetary remittances, challenges associated with transna-tional communication, and the uncertainties surrounding the future—are also central to the experiences of other Nicaraguan families of migrants discussed in this book and for transnational families elsewhere around the globe.[15] The personal and interpersonal tensions within families of migrants reflect broader geopolitics of migration, which structure departures, visits, remittances, and the possibility of returns or reunifications. Through Angela's family story, we see how U.S. immigration policy has shaped migration trajectories, reconfigu-rations of care, and the emotional experiences of family members by magnify-ing distance, separation, and uncertainty. In the conclusion, I consider possible responses to these troublesome immigration policies, responses that acknowl-edge the importance of care and of solidarity, as embodied in grandmothers' intergenerational care.

In the introduction to a volume on phenomenology in anthropology, Michael Jackson describes the importance of ethnographic fieldwork:

> For anthropology, ethnography remains vital, not because ethnographic meth-ods guarantee certain knowledge of others but because ethnographic fieldwork brings us into direct dialogue with others, affording us opportunities to explore knowledge not as something that grasps inherent and hidden truths, but as an

intersubjective process of sharing experience, comparing notes, exchanging ideas, and finding common ground. In this process, our social gumption and social skills, as much as our scientific methodology, become measures of the limits and value of our understanding. (1996: 8)

The "direct dialogue with others" that Jackson highlights as a hallmark of ethnography leads to complicated human relations such as those I describe here. Extending his phenomenological approach into contemporary studies of migration and well-being, Jackson asserts that the ethical dilemmas raised by migration—within families, between researchers and participants, and between communities and policy makers—"are never resolved simply by laying down the law. . . . [T]he dilemmas require collective *discussion*, in which people attempt to come up with the best solution possible, given the complex circumstances" (Jackson 2013: 12). Certainly, my complicated ethnographic entanglements were not planned; they were not included in my research design or part of my proposed methodology. Instead, they emerged out of the human relationships I formed over time with families, shared connections that continue to the present. Such emotional connections and the "limits and value of our understanding" that Jackson refers to inevitably unsettle naïve assumptions of empathy or straightforward portrayals of the research endeavor.

Ethnographic entanglements also challenge the anthropological tendency to produce "texts that convey another's world in a seamless and evocative way" (Kirmayer 2008: 458). So rather than presenting a seamless analysis of transnational family life, I am situating my interpretation in this confusing messiness of ethnographic engagement. There is no facile resolution or convenient denouement to Angela's story because it contains all the unexpected uncertainties of transnational family life. Even as I have stayed in touch with Angela's family (and other families in this book) during return visits to Nicaragua and through the use of social media and phone communication, I continue to have nagging feelings of failing to live up to families' expectations to stay in touch or, in their words, to be "sufficiently in solidarity" with families over time. While I am certainly not transposing my experience of longing and inadequacy onto that of the families in this book, I do believe that my unsettled sense of inadequacy, failed responsibility, and uncertainty about the future does offer insight into the troubles of transnational family relationships. Nonetheless, grandmothers continue to respond to these threats to ties of relatedness through their very acts of caregiving. On every one of my return visits to Nicaragua, grandmothers like Angela continue to open their homes to me, without asking questions about what took me so long to return, instead offering me a cool drink and a place to sit in the shade and engaging me in conversations and other acts of care that momentarily seem to bridge time and distance.

Conclusion

Valuing Care Across Borders and Generations

Las migraciones nos conectan con el mundo. . . . ¿Los empezaremos a ver como reto, amenaza u oportunidad de enriquecimiento cultural y ejercicio de solidaridad? Nos muestran los alcances, pero tambien los límites de la globalización. (Migrations connect us to the world. . . . Will we begin to see them as a challenge, a threat, or an opportunity for cultural enrichment and the exercise of solidarity? They show us the progress, but also the limits, of globalization.)

—**Migrant Rights Forum Agenda, Managua, 2009**

The Value of Intergenerational Care

Migration is a central feature of contemporary globalization, reshaping social and cultural life in migrant-sending and migrant-receiving countries. As women have increasingly joined global migratory flows, transnational families are becoming more common, highlighting the need to understand the effect of mother migration on children and their caregivers in care networks extended across borders and over generations. Migration and the reconfigurations of care in its wake are shaped by the political and economic dynamics of globalization, as migrants move from sites of relative deprivation to locations of greater economic opportunity. As the stories presented here remind us, these global flows are not always south to north but follow lines of relative inequality, wherever they may lead. As they care for children of mothers living and working in service sector economies in Costa Rica, Panama, Spain, and the United States, grandmothers in Nicaragua participate in global care circulations (Baldassar and Merla 2014), supporting their migrant daughters' ambitions to achieve a better life for themselves and their families through their caregiving. For Nicaraguan grandmothers, these care reconfigurations are not just about the important work of caring for children but also about the deeply valued activity of regenerating cultural values (Cole and Durham 2007) of solidarity and sacrifice.

This analysis has situated grandmother care in transnational families within structures of inequality—political-economic and gendered—but has emphasized the social, cultural, relational, and moral significance of grandmother caregiving as a source of solidarity and sacrifice in Nicaraguan families. In drawing attention to grandmother care, *Care Across Generations* frames it as an embodied moral practice that contributes to social reproduction and cultural regeneration. For grandmothers, care embodies their sense of what is most at stake in the local moral world of Nicaraguan families (Kleinman 2006): solidarity and sacrifice—being there for their daughters, grandchildren, and families by giving of themselves to foster collective well-being. Intergenerational care is therefore not only about raising children but also about fostering family relationships and sustaining family values of unity and solidarity across time and space. In this way, care is experienced by grandmothers as partly burdensome, as it is the physical labor of caregiving, and partly pleasurable, as care becomes a source of purpose and meaning for caregivers, which helps them manage the uncertainties of transnational family life.

The values of sacrifice and solidarity shape intergenerational care in Nicaraguan transnational families over time and across generations. These values motivate grandmothers' assumption of their grandchildren's care and assist them in coping with the vulnerabilities of their roles as mothers again in transnational families. Understanding their daughters' migrations as necessary sacrifices for the sake of family economic well-being, grandmothers situate their caregiving as a parallel sacrifice, which supports children's welfare and families' togetherness over time and across distance. Nicaraguan grandmothers draw on the value of sacrifice to help explain mother migration to children, motivate intergenerational care, and relinquish care when children reunite with mothers abroad. Thus, grandmothers' sacrifices extend backward and forward into and over time, one indication of the temporality of transnational family life. Despite the importance of grandmother care to children and families, grandmothers may be viewed as surrogate, temporary mothers. This despite the close emotional ties grandmothers forge with children, over years or even decades of mother absence. These ties complicate a straightforward view of reunification between children and mothers abroad, because "reunification" implies another separation for grandmothers back home; this time, grandmothers suspend their care for grandchildren, losing the everyday companionship and sense of purpose they received from providing care. And yet grandmothers relinquish care precisely as an expression of solidarity with their migrant daughters and as an instantiation (yet again) of sacrifice for the sake of their families.

Tensions and Uncertainties in Grandmother Care

Focusing attention on grandmother caregivers' experiences of the uncertainties of transnational family life calls on us to think more broadly about migration's effects on extended families across national borders, in host and home countries, and across generations, beyond mothers and children and into the networks of extended kin who assume essential caregiving roles in migrant-sending countries. Grandmothers in Nicaraguan families assume responsibilities for children of parent migrants through an informal reconfiguration of caregiving and kinship obligations, one that is not given social or legal support. Grandmothers are motivated to assume care for grandchildren not because of the promise of material gain from remittances but because of their moral commitment to uphold the ideals of sacrifice and solidarity that are culturally expected of mothers and, by extension, grandmothers. However, just as mothers face vulnerabilities as migrants in destination countries, grandmothers face vulnerabilities back home in Nicaragua in their positions as mothers again in transnational families. First, grandmothers do not enjoy legal protections as caregivers given the difficulty of transferring children's custody to them, as we saw most particularly in the case of Olga. Without legal protection, grandmothers are less able to ward off threats from children's fathers, who may seek to claim portions of the remittances sent home by mothers. Nor does the Nicaraguan state provide any type of pension for caregivers in families of migrant parents. In fact, on several occasions in the past decade, the Nicaraguan government has sought to levy higher taxes on migrant remittances, only to be met with solid opposition from families of migrants.

Remittances in families of migrant mothers are managed by grandmothers and invested in children's care. In Chapter 2 grandmothers describe how remittances "don't measure up" (*no se ajustan*), which is an expression not only of the economic inadequacy of remittances but also of the threats to moral values for unity and solidarity in Nicaraguan families from transnational migration. Grandmothers' relationship to remittances thus indexes the tensions surrounding love and money in transnational families, showing that they acknowledge the importance of remittances to household economies but feel money sent by migrants from abroad fails to compensate adequately for mothers' ongoing absence from family life. I also suggest that grandmothers' insistence that remittances *no se ajustan* reflects a broader critique they have about the political economy of global migration, which pushes mothers to migrate and forces families to separate to secure a better life for children and future generations.

All the women in this study, without exception, were emphatic that, if they could choose, they would have their daughters return to Nicaragua. Grandmothers desire to have their families all together, in copresence in Nicaragua, but over time this becomes an ever-more uncertain prospect for transnational families. In lieu of their daughters' physical presence, grandmothers feel a longing or nostalgia, which they attempt to fill through caregiving itself.

While intergenerational care is a vital resource for family well-being and cultural continuity, grandmothers experience tensions and ambivalences as they reconfigure cultural expectations for care across generations. While grandmothers may also be caregivers for grandchildren in Nicaragua in non-migrant families, the women profiled in this book are clear that taking on care responsibilities following mothers' migration is a distinct experience, given the absence, distance, and uncertainty migration implies. The tensions grandmothers face as they encounter the "care slot" (Leinaweaver 2010: 69) are revealed in an examination of their embodied, emotional distress. Through the culturally significant idiom of distress *pensando mucho*, women call attention to their sacrifice as members of transnational families. This effort to seek recognition occurs because, like migration scholarship itself, cultural discourse in Nicaragua and other Latin American–sending countries has largely sidelined the roles of women of the grandmother generation (*la tercera edad*). The women whose stories fill this book, from Marbeya to Olga, Aurora to Angela, desire recognition for the social and cultural value of their caregiving labor.

Care in Migration Policy

There are social and political implications to focusing on the value of intergenerational care in transnational families. Feminist care ethics insists on advocating for social policies and arranging social relations in ways that value care and support caregivers (Tronto 1993; Held 2006). To date, migration policies, whether in sending or receiving countries, have failed to squarely address migration's effects on families and communities in migrant-sending countries. Given the increasing feminization of global migrations, the phenomenon of children left behind in the care of grandmothers and other women in extended kin networks will expand as transnational families become ever-more common. One important implication this discussion reveals is the need to destigmatize such family forms by valuing intergenerational care and normalizing the experiences of children of migrant parents and their caregivers.

An important insight from the literature on global care chains is that women's migration to work, especially, as *domésticas* and child and elder care-givers in host countries implies a transfer of social and economic resources from home to host countries. For instance, when working-age women and men migrate, the Nicaraguan economy loses the investment to social service and pension systems that otherwise would be made. At the same time, when migrants work as undocumented workers abroad, their tax payments support social service and benefit systems from which they will not be likely to benefit. Just as migrant women's work is undercompensated in host countries, grandmothers' caregiving in home countries goes undervalued; at both ends of this global chain, women's care work is undervalued (Yeates 2005). As feminist economist Nancy Folbre has argued, "The costs of providing care need to be explicitly confronted and fairly distributed" (2001: 230). Extending Folbre's claim to the transnationalization of care work, we might argue that the costs of social reproduction must be shared across national borders. In other words, imagine a world in which caregiving for children in home countries would be compensated for in part through payments made to migrant women workers by employers in host countries—a sort of care levy or investment in care shared across borders. While this may seem like a far-fetched ideal, in fact, recent successes organizing domestic workers in California, New York, and other U.S. states suggest that obtaining fairer compensation for migrant women's care work is politically achievable.[1]

What are the implications of an intergenerational perspective on care in migrant-sending countries for our thinking about immigration policies in particular? First, as the stories of the families presented here make clear, restrictive immigration policies that make it difficult to obtain "legal" residency and to process residency visas for children of immigrants have a constellation of impacts on families back home. Without legal status, migrants have difficulty establishing themselves economically, and remittances may falter in the first months or years of migration. Worse, from the point of view of the grandmothers in this study, is that their migrant daughters' undocumented status makes it risky or even impossible for the daughters to visit home, given the dangers of illicit border crossing. This prolongs periods between visits and allows a sense of disconnection and distance to fester (as we see in Chapter 4 with Laleska) despite migrants' attempts to remain *pendiente* (responsible) for families back home through regular communication and remittances. Furthermore, existing migration policies in destination countries like the United States and Costa Rica make obtaining legal residency or citizenship a time-consuming, expensive process that is prohibitive for most immigrants. This burdensome immigration bureaucracy heightens uncertainty about the future for children and their caregivers, who are unsure whether and when children might rejoin their mothers abroad.[2]

My collaborations with migrant-rights-serving NGOs in Nicaragua, La Red and Servicio Jesuita para Migrantes (SJM), offer additional insights into the policy implications of this work. The basis for SJM's advocacy work is documenting human rights violations suffered by Nicaraguan migrants abroad. In 2010, SJM coordinated a major public education campaign (La Campaña para la Defensa y Protección de la Población Migrante) to pressure the Nicaraguan government to improve and expand consular attention in countries of transit (Mexico) and destination (Costa Rica and the United States). I joined La Campaña as a volunteer and worked alongside SJM staff, traveling to migrant-sending communities and collecting testimonies of returned or deported migrants and their family members to document human rights violations suffered by migrants in transit or living undocumented abroad. The campaign used such testimony to encourage the Nicaraguan government to invest in consular services abroad, affording greater protection for migrants traveling through or living in Mexico, Costa Rica, or the United States. Such consular services—for instance, the ability to process visa paperwork or obtain a missing passport—would aid migrants in regularizing their legal status and decrease the worry and uncertainty for family members back home.

In this *trabajo de campo* (fieldwork), I heard harrowing tales of migrants traveling to the United States through Mexico, where attacks by armed gangs affiliated with organized crime or paramilitary groups such as the infamous Zetas are unfortunately all too common.[3] SJM was concerned that many Nicaraguan (and other Central American) migrants had little to no legal protection in Mexico, increasing their vulnerability to such attacks.[4] These stories of danger, extortion, kidnapping, and murder impressed me with the desperation that pushes migrants to risk such treacherous passage to leave Nicaragua in search of a better life. It is this sense of a lack of opportunities and alternatives in Nicaragua that grandmothers allude to when they describe the sacrifice their daughters make through migration, a desperation that in part also motivates grandmothers to assume care for grandchildren, because, they say, "Tenemos que hacerlo" (We have to do it).

My work with NGOs increased my awareness of the broader issues related to human rights and social justice for Nicaraguan migrants, but it also highlighted that relatively little attention was being paid (within advocacy and human rights circles) to the experiences of family members of migrants in Nicaragua. As one effort to rectify this imbalance, through my collaborations with SJM and La Campaña, I invited family members participating in my study to share their stories publicly, as part of SJM's radio program *La mochila viajera* (The traveling backpack). These recorded testimonies were used by SJM as part of a public education effort to increase awareness about the realities of families living with mother migration, their struggles and the sacrifices they make to hold their families together.

This was the radio program on which grandmothers Angela and Marbeya gave their testimonies, in the vignette with which I open this book. Thus, Marbeya's and Angela's stories were heard throughout Nicaragua in radio public service announcements over the course of several weeks. When I asked the women how they felt about having their testimonies out in the public, their response was that while their radio interview was an emotional experience for them, they were happy to share their stories as a means of sensitizing other Nicaraguans to the struggles of grandmother caregivers in transnational families and encouraging greater social support for these families. In this way, caregivers like Angela and Marbeya claim social recognition, and such recognition itself represents a form of both solidarity and care.

In the radio program, Angela and Marbeya described their experiences as intergenerational caregivers in families of migrant mothers, emphasizing their shared sacrifice to support children and grandchildren. This sacrifice is connected through women, across generations and over borders, as grandmothers parallel the sacrifice of their migrant daughters with their own caregiving. Further, grandmothers extend this value of sacrifice out into the future, by reminding children, in Marbeya's words, "Su mamá está allá trabajando duro para que puedan estar mejor aquí" (Your mom is over there working hard so that you can be better off here). In other words, grandmothers narrate the significance of mother migration to children in terms of their own well-being and use sacrifice to connect family members divided by borders and to motivate children to behave well and work hard in school so that they too can embody the shared, intergenerational sacrifice of migration.

Like other grandmothers in this study, Angela and Marbeya assert their claims to a moral economy of care grounded in Nicaraguan cultural values for solidarity and sacrifice. Grandmothers perceive these values to be threatened by the absence and distance that characterize transnational family life, and their care offsets these threats. In this way, the care provided by grandmothers exists suspended across time and over generations, connecting caregivers and families to past experiences, seeking to strengthen the emotional ties between grand-mothers, mothers, and children in the present and calling on values of sacrifice and solidarity to hold families together into the future. This moral economy of care through embodied sacrifice stands in opposition to the logics of a global economic system that perpetuates the very inequalities that push migration and divide families across borders in the first place. Grandmothers respond to transnational migration by reconfiguring care, embodying sacrifice for the sake of children and grandchildren and thus regenerating cultural values of soli-darity over time and across generations in Nicaraguan families. Grandmother care constitutes not a barren form of labor exploitation, care extraction, or so-cial reproduction but a deeply moral relationship of sacrifice and solidarity—being there for others—that is embedded in Nicaragua's cultural history and that makes transnational family life possible now and into the future.

Appendix

Interviews and Spending Time:
Ethnographic Methods with Families

Overview and Aims of Research

This book is based on ethnographic field research conducted with families of migrants in Nicaragua during eleven consecutive months (2009–2010) and three weeklong visits (in December 2010, 2011, and 2013). During fieldwork, I lived in a family home in Managua, Nicaragua's capital city, and conducted research with families living in Managua and in three rural communities in surrounding *departamentos* (states). To visit those families in the states of Chinandega, Rivas, and Matagalpa, I would usually make day trips by bus, sometimes accompanied by a colleague from one of the NGOs I collaborated with. Since 2010, I have maintained contact with several families in the study via e-mail, phone calls, WhatsApp, and Facebook.

Because my main research aim was to understand migration's effects on grandmothers raising children of parent migrants, I developed three specific inclusion criteria for families to participate in this study: (1) the family currently had a mother (or father, for comparison purposes) absent from the household who was an international migrant; (2) the migrant mother (or father) had left at least one child (age seven to thirteen) in Nicaragua; and (3) a grandmother (maternal or paternal) was the primary caregiver for this child. I chose this age range for children because the experiences of older teens differ from those of younger children for developmental reasons. In total, twenty-four families participated in the study; fifteen were families in which mothers had emigrated and nine were families of father migrants, which are used in this analysis only for comparison purposes.

Data Collection and Interviews

With each family participating in the study, I conducted a series of interviews, participant observation, and home visits. I obtained oral informed consent from all participating adults; from children, I obtained oral assent. (Institutional Review Board approval for this study was obtained from the UCLA IRB. Colleagues at the Universidad Centroamericana, Managua, also provided feedback on the research design, methods, and analyses, although I am ultimately responsible for the study design and procedures.) While the focus of this book is on grandmothers' experiences, I draw on information obtained through interviews and conversations with children and other family members to enrich my analysis of relations of care and transnational family life. In total, across a year of fieldwork, I completed fifty-four interviews with grandmothers, twenty-three interviews with children, six interviews with mother migrants (either during their visits home to Nicaragua, over the phone, or—on one occasion—during a visit I made to Panama), and sixteen interviews with extended family members (e.g., aunts, uncles, siblings, and spouses). Nearly all interviews were completed in family homes; however, time spent with families occurred at homes and in the community (e.g., at schools, churches, and shopping malls). The interviews I completed with grandmothers were conducted sequentially using predeveloped, semistructured interview guides.

Abuela Interview 1   The first interview I conducted with all grandmothers in the study, abuela interview 1, collected general information about the family's migration experience—destination, duration, remittance patterns, and other general characteristics of migration. This was a semistructured interview containing a total of thirty-nine open-ended questions that focused on gathering basic household sociodemographic information, the history of mother migration, and any other migration experiences in the immediate or extended family. Questions asked grandmothers to reflect on both their personal experience of their child's migration and their experience of assuming caregiving for grandchildren. I always conducted this interview in family homes. The interview lasted between one and four hours, depending on participants' responses, and thus sometimes took multiple sittings. While I attempted to make this interview a private conversation with grandmothers, sometimes this was impossible (because of household size and space constraints); therefore, on occasion other family members would overhear the interview and offer their opinions as responses to my questions. Data from the abuela interview 1 inform this book in its entirety.

Abuela Interview 2   The second interview, abuela interview 2, that I conducted with all grandmothers was a health interview, which consisted of thirteen open-ended questions designed to elicit the women's perceptions, concerns, and values related to family health and well-being. The interview guide was modeled after a health and well-being interview implemented in a study of an ethnically diverse sample of Los Angeles families (Garro and Izquierdo 2003). The questions I asked in this interview included "What does health mean to you?" "What does well-being mean to you?" and "How has migration affected your personal health, the health of your family, or the health of your grandchildren?" I elicited grandmothers' beliefs and opinions about the consequences of migration for family health, both positive and negative. This interview took between thirty minutes and two hours to complete, depending on responses.

During the same sitting as the health interview, I administered three standardized psychometric measures of physical and mental health: (1) the Self-Rated Health tool (SRH; which I translated into Nicaraguan Spanish), (2) the Center for Epidemiological Studies of Depression (CESD) scale of depression symptomatology, and (3) the Perceived Stress Scale (PSS). The SRH question asks, "How would you rate your health?" and respondents select an answer from 1 (excellent) to 4 (poor). This question has been used internationally in health research and, while controversial, is a predictor of physical health outcomes (Benyamini and Idler 1999). The CESD depression symptomatology scale was developed by the Stanford Patient Education Center. Its short version consists of ten items asking about the frequency of symptoms such as fear, anxiety, depression, inability to concentrate, or sleeplessness, to which respondents answer using a Likert scale on which 0 indicates not at all and 3 means all the time. I used a version of the depression symptomatology scale that had previously been translated into Spanish but retranslated some of the questions to help women understand them. The PSS measures the degree to which respondents perceive events in their lives as stressful and is a useful indicator of emotional well-being (Cohen, Kamarck, and Mermelstein 1983). The PSS asks respondents to rank from 1 to 4 the degree to which in the past month they have felt "nervous and tense" or that "things were outside [their] control," to give two examples. In this book, I make use of data from the health interview as background information, particularly in my analysis of the effects of migration on grandmother and family health and well-being. (For a preliminary discussion of my CESD findings, see Mendenhall, Yarris, and Kohrt 2016.)

Abuela Interview 3   The third semistructured interview I conducted with grandmothers, abuela interview 3, was one that I developed while in the field to explore themes that had emerged in the health interviews and other conversations with women about their physical health and emotional distress. Abuela interview 3 was conducted with a subsample of seven grandmothers, selected purposively from the larger sample of twenty-four women because they had mentioned specific complaints related to three idioms of distress: *pensando mucho* (thinking too much), *depresión* (depression), and *presión* (blood pressure). Questions asked grandmothers to reflect on the meanings of these three embodied complaints and the perceived associations between them, essentially using an explanatory model framework. I was specifically interested in how women viewed these forms of distress in relation to migration, caregiving, and transnational family life. This interview took between one and two hours to complete, depending on responses. Data from this interview form the basis of Chapter 3.

Child Interviews   I also conducted a semistructured child interview with target children in participating families. A "target child" was a migrant's child, age seven to thirteen; on occasion, I would interview younger children when their grandmothers encouraged me to do so (this was the case for grandmothers Viviana and Ismelda). In other families, I conducted interviews with more than one child (those of Angela, Marbeya, and Teresa) because there were additional children who wanted to participate (Marbeya and Teresa's grandchildren) or because a grandmother (Angela) asked me to interview another child in the household because she felt the interview would be beneficial to the child. In two families (those of Aurora and Juana), I did not interview children because they left Nicaragua to join their mothers abroad before I scheduled the child interview. For the most part, data from child interviews describe grandmothers' relationships with children and experiences of care across generations, even though a focused discussion of children's experiences of mother migration is not incorporated into this book. I have published findings from my research on children's experiences of mother migration elsewhere (Yarris 2014a).

Mother Migrant Interviews   Before my fieldwork I had not anticipated interviewing mother migrants, but the opportunity emerged when mothers returned to visit Nicaragua or, in one case, when I visited a mother abroad (in Panama). In total, I conducted six interviews with five migrant mothers (daughters of Marbeya, Norma, Beatriz, Teresa, and Olga). I developed a guide for these interviews with twenty-two open-ended questions, which took anywhere from one to three hours to complete. I assured mothers that their responses would remain anonymous, since all but one of these women were living abroad without legal documents. The information I gained from these conversations is used in this book to provide deeper insights into inter-generational relations of care: the sacrifices women make as migrants, their perspectives on their mothers' caregiving, and their experiences as transnational mothers.

Other Family Member Interviews   In addition to the interviews mentioned above, I conducted informal interviews with other members of participating families: aunts, uncles, grandfathers, and fathers of participating children. These interviews occurred either when family members expressed an interest in telling me their stories, when I considered obtaining their perspective and experience central to understanding the family's experience of migration, or when I formed a strong rapport with the family and someone requested we sit down for a more focused conversation about his or her role in the transnational family experience. I interviewed Angela's daughter Noelia; Beatriz's daughter Jimena; Isabel's son René; Ismelda's son Emilio; Juana's husband, Pedro; Marbeya's daughters Jessica and Lesbia; Norma's son Norman; and Olga's daughter Ana María. In these interviews, I solicited family members' experiences of their sisters', children's, or spouses' migrations; their views on how migration had affected their families; and specifically, their views on grandmothers' roles in transnational families. Interviews lasted between one and five hours and took place in family homes, sometimes over multiple sittings.

While this book focuses on grandmothers as primary caregivers and heads of transnational households, I draw on conversations with children, mothers, and other family members throughout to paint a fuller picture of intergenerational care and transnational family life.

Spending Time with Families

In addition to interviews, I spent a lot of time during fieldwork hanging out with families. I accompanied families on outings (for instance, to the mall or market), and I participated in family life by helping children with homework, joining in celebrations of birthdays and other special occasions, and engaging in other activities. In total, I conducted 104 home visits over a year of field-work, with visits lasting an average of one and a half hours but sometimes con-tinuing over an entire day. An essential part of my fieldwork, home visits were particularly useful in grounding my understanding of grandmother caregiving within the realities, routines, and everyday challenges of family life. Through these visits, I became especially close to five families, spending a great deal of time with them during fieldwork and staying in touch ever since. This sort of ethnographic engagement leads to emotional investments that extend beyond the boundaries of researcher and subject, and I draw attention to such engage-ments throughout this book. Complicated emotional entanglements are a hall-mark of ethnographic research and sociocultural anthropology and a source of rich insight, but they are also relationships we anthropologists carry with us well beyond the completion of fieldwork.

Kinship Migration Mapping

As I describe throughout this book, relations of kinship and care in the transna-tional families in this study are complex. In Nicaragua's matrilocal kinship pat-terns, most families live in intergenerational households shared with extended kin; this is indicated by the right-hand column in Table A.1, which shows that many adult children live in the same household as their mothers (the grand-mothers). The data presented in Table A.1 are a summary snapshot of the extended-family relations and the migration patterns that surround grand-mothers. To make sense of these complicated kinship relations and migration networks, I created visual diagrams drawn from demographic information I gathered during interviews and household visits. I developed these diagrams, which I call kinship migration maps, using a modified version of classic an-thropological kinship charts, and I used symbols to visually indicate gender, marriage, death, parentage, and other relationships (El Guindi 2004: 77). But I added symbols to indicate shared household residence, caregiving relations, and out-migration situations. Ultimately, these kinship migration maps orga-nized my understanding of each family in my study, using the grandmother head of household as the "ego," or point of reference (Murchison 2010: 148). Indeed, I built these diagrams outward from women's own renderings of their relations of kin and care in response to my questions about who shared their households, where their children lived, and which children were in their care. I also asked grandmothers which of their adult children were sources of support or care for them. Ultimately, these kinship migration maps are less dynamic

Table A.1 Family descriptive information

Grandmother	Age	Residence	Grandchildren in care (age)	Mother, duration of migration	Mother's destination/ residence	No. of other migrant adult children (residence)	No. of nonmigrant adult children (residence)
Angela	53	Managua	Laleska (11)	Karla, 10 yrs	U.S.	3 (U.S.; 1 returned after deportation)	2 (Managua)
Aurora	63	Managua	Salensca (7) Daniela (5)	Elizabeth, 2 yrs	Spain	0	1 (Managua)
Beatriz	63	Managua	Alejandra (10)	Jimena, 6 mos	U.S.	0	3 (same HH)
Concepción	57	Chinandega	Kevin (7)	Claudia, 5 yrs	Mexico	1 (Mexico)	4 (3 Chinandega; 1 in same HH)
			Marelly (7), Francis (11)	Yamileth, 3 yrs	Guatemala		
			Ruby (12), Alexa (14), Elvin (15)	Melba, 7 yrs	Costa Rica		
Isabel	54	Managua	Robin (6)	Katherine, 2 yrs	Spain	0	3 (same HH)
Ismelda	55	Chinandega	Caterin (2), Miguel (2 mos)	Cristel, 8 mos	Panama	2 (U.S.; both returned after deportation)	3 (same HH)
Juana	47	Rivas	Marelis (9), Lucy (5)	Juanita, 1 yr	Costa Rica	1 (Costa Rica)	2 (Rivas)
			Loryi (3)	Rosa, 6 mos	Costa Rica		

(continued)

Table A.1 (continued)

Grandmother	Age	Residence	Grandchildren in care (age)	Mother, duration of migration	Mother's destination/ residence	No. of other migrant adult children (residence)	No. of nonmigrant adult children (residence)
Luisa María	55	Chinandega	Ingrid (12), Carlos (9), Jefrey (7), Natalie (5)	Salvarita, 3 yrs	Costa Rica	1 (Costa Rica)	4 (same HH)
Marbeya	52	Managua	Vanessa (14), Selso (9)	Azucena, 12 yrs	Costa Rica	0	4 (same HH)
María Auxiliadora	68	Managua	Alexandra (10)	Reyna, 6 mos	Panama	0	1 (same HH)
María Luisa	50s	Chinandega	Yaritza (13), Denis (15), Emerson (18)	Denia, 3 yrs	Spain	3 (1 U.S.; 2 El Salvador)	1 (same HH)
Norma	57	Managua	Jeremy (11)	María José, 10 yrs	U.S.	1 (U.S.)	2 (1 Managua; 1 same HH)
Olga	72	Managua	Juliana (9), Dayton (17)	Manuela, 2 yrs	Panama	0	3 (Managua)
Teresa	56	Managua	Maykeling (10), Katerin (14)	Lisdamur, 2.5 yrs	Costa Rica	1 (U.S.)	3 (Managua)
Viviana	75	Matagalpa	Escarly (6), Jocelyn (3)	Juana, 14 mos	Costa Rica	1 (Costa Rica)	3 (same HH)

Note: Names are either first or second names or pseudonyms. HH = household.

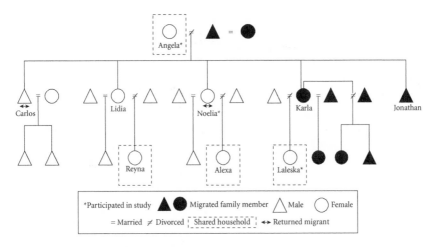

Figure A.1 Angela's kinship migration map

than the actual relations of intergenerational care in which grandmothers are embedded, but they do offer a visual representation of the complexities of migration and relatedness in these transnational families, moving our gaze beyond the mother migrant–child relationship into the webs of interrelatedness that form family relations.

One example of such a kinship migration map is Figure A.1, an illustration of Angela's transnational family relations, which are discussed in detail in Chapter 4. Figure A.2 is a kinship migration map for Olga, whose family migration story is presented in Chapter 1. Olga has four adult children in addition to her migrant daughter, Manuela. One of her daughters, Ana María, lives in Managua and is a source of limited social support for Olga (e.g., Olga turns to her for advice on occasion). Olga has one son who died in adulthood and two adult sons who live in Managua, one of whom provides her with a limited amount of support (e.g., visits on occasion). Ana María has three sons who have migrated to Guatemala, so Olga's migratory map extends across generations, space, and time.

Data Analysis

In nearly all cases (except when participants requested otherwise or when there was a technical problem), interviews were audio recorded, transcribed (by me and by two Nicaraguan research assistants), and translated into English (by me). I took copious field notes throughout my research, recording interactions, conversations, observations, questions, and my feelings associated with my

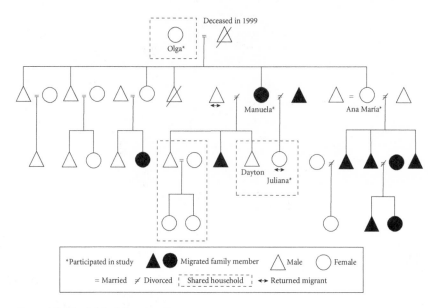

Figure A.2 Olga's kinship migration map

research. I made a practice of making notes of every interview or home visit within twenty-four hours, recording thoughts, reflections, and questions for further examination. My process of data analysis was iterative and began while I was in the field; I would identify themes while writing field notes or transcribing or listening to interview recordings, and I developed a theme document, which I continually expanded, modified, and amended throughout fieldwork. I continued to analyze data after returning from the field, eventually developing a list of about ten themes that seemed significant enough to begin to structure my writing around them. As I wrote drafts of each chapter of this book, I returned repeatedly to my data, checking and double-checking my analyses and strengthening them with additional evidence. I also checked my interpretations while I was in the field through conversations with NGO and university colleagues. For instance, I gave a presentation of my preliminary findings to an audience of academics, students, and NGO practitioners at the Universidad Centroamericana, and questions from and discussion with that audience helped me refine my arguments and discern more clearly the contributions of this book. While all the interpretations and arguments in this book are my own, they have emerged from my ethnographic engagements in Nicaragua, many conversations with my Nicaraguan colleagues, and insights gained from spending time with members of the families participating in this study.

Notes

Introduction

1. Throughout this book, I use first names to refer to study participants. It is customary in Nicaragua to have two first names. Here, I use one first name, with participants' permission; otherwise, I have assigned pseudonyms. While participants wanted me to tell their stories in this book and gave me permission to do so, I have changed names to protect identities in some cases in which a lack of legal documentation may pose a risk to migrants or their families.

2. While I use "transnational families" to describe families with members living in more than one nation-state (Fog Olwig 2003, 2007; Levitt and Glick Schiller 2004), I am wary that this phrase may leave an impression of connectedness that would falsely portray the realities of the families in this book, who emphasize that distance, time, and separation matter in their experiences of caregiving and family life. A better phrasing might be "families divided by national borders" (Joanna Dreby uses a similar phrase in her 2010 *Divided by Borders*), for it captures the materiality of division that comes from state immigration policies that separate families based on nationality, citizenship, and documentation status. Nonetheless, despite the separation of geographic space, political borders, and generational time, the families in this book *do* manage to remain connected and retain a strong sense of family. Thus, I use the term "transnational families" while cognizant of its limitations and yet finding it conveys part of the complicated realities of connection and distance, closeness and separation, that characterize the lives of the families in this book.

3. Tatjana Thelen argues that anthropologists have "exported a self-understanding" of the essential value of care within nuclear families, thereby reinforcing what are construed to be "natural" (and gendered) hierarchies of care (Thelen 2015: 503).

4. Most studies of transnational families have taken the biological-parent, nuclear family as the model for understanding migration and family life. This is particularly true for studies of Mexican transnational families (Dreby 2010; Boehm 2012) but also for the few studies of Central American transnational families (Abrego 2014; Moran-Taylor 2008). Scholars of Caribbean transnational families, on the other hand, have been more willing to analyze extended family networks of migration and care (Fog Olwig 2007).

5. Some migrants fled in anticipation of a Sandinista expropriation of land and property (Baumeister 2006). Sorting out land claims after the revolution has been a complicated legal problem involving national and international negotiations in the decades since.

6. This situation is unlike that of other Central Americans fleeing to the United States in the 1980s to escape political violence, such as Salvadorans and Guatemalans. Those countries were under U.S.-friendly regimes, and migrants struggled to obtain refugee status. See Bibler Coutin 2005 for a fuller discussion of the different processes of incorporation for Central American migrants to the United States.

7. I outline my argument about the problematic dichotomy between voluntary, economic migration and forced migration and between migrants and refugees in Yarris and Castañeda 2015. Other anthropologists have similarly argued that this dichotomy is problematic for delimiting political and social rights for migrants who are not deemed to have sufficient grounds for leaving home countries, while refugees are viewed as deserving of social and political support precisely because of the "involuntary" nature of their suffering (also see Holmes and Castañeda 2016).

8. I place "legally" in quotation marks to reflect the view that all migrants are "legal" from a human rights standpoint, even though states create categories of illegality. As anthropologists have argued, illegality is a sociopolitical process whereby national laws and economic interests structure the delineation between those lives deemed "legal," authorized, and therefore worthy of political recognition and social support and other lives deemed "illegal," unauthorized by the state, and therefore not deserving of assistance (Yarris and Castañeda 2015; Andersson 2014; Willen 2007, 2012; De Genova 2002).

9. One highly visible and tragic case of the discrimination of Nicaraguans in Costa Rica is that of twenty-five-year-old Nicaraguan migrant Natividad Canda, who in November 2005 was attacked and killed by two Rottweiler dogs in a town outside San José, Costa Rica's capital, while residents and the police stood by. The nonintervention of civilians and authorities in this brutal mauling was met with horror and consternation in Nicaragua as video of the incident spread rapidly over the Internet. Soon thereafter the Nicaraguan government charged Costa Rican authorities in the Inter-American Court of Human Rights of human rights abuses. The court, based in Costa Rica, astonished many observers by refusing to hear the case, effectively letting

the Costa Rican government off the hook for institutional racism and discrimination against Nicaraguans. This case continues to reverberate in Nicaraguan public sentiment as evidence of Costa Rican hostility and injustice toward migrants and reminds families of the very real vulnerability of their migrant members in Costa Rica. Nicaragua's daily newspaper, *El Nuevo Diario*, covered the Natividad Canda case at length; for example, see Sirias 2008.

10. While the legislation was couched in human rights language—for example, promising Costa Rica would uphold its adherence to international conventions on the rights of migrants and migrant children—for advocates with whom I work in Nicaragua the law was unquestionably restrictive, preventing Nicaraguans from accessing legal residency and services in Costa Rica.

11. One poignant illustration is the song "Diakachimba," played repeatedly on Nicaraguan radio stations in 2008–2010 and originally recorded by Punto 5, a punk band from León. The song's chorus calls on youth to reflect critically on the allure of migration:

No se vayan, somos Nicas, no nos quieren en Costa Rica.
Ya no digan "pura vida," aquí somos de a cachimba.
(Don't leave, we're Nicaraguan, they don't want us in Costa Rica.
Stop saying "pure life," here we are made of cachimba.)

In these lyrics, Costa Rica is emblematized by the popular expression "pura vida" (pure life), which the song counters through the oppositional refrain of "de a cachimba," a Nicaraguan saying referring to a particularly resolute and independent quality of character.

12. I heard several stories of women calling on family members in Nicaragua to help them pay off agencies' service fees. For families unable to do so, migrants can end up in bondage labor, as reported in Aguilara 2010.

13. One exception is an edited collection of transnational family stories published in Spanish, in which "solidarity" appears in the title but still does not receive explicit analytical attention. The authors use "solidarity" to refer to the maintenance of affective and relational ties in families stretched across national borders (Soronellas Masdeu 2010).

14. All translations are mine unless otherwise noted.

15. U.S. imperialism is central to Nicaragua's political and cultural history. One of the first stories anyone from the United States living in Nicaragua will hear is the incredible tale of William Walker. In a bizarre episode characterizing mid-nineteenth-century expansionist fervor, Walker, a mercenary with grandiose ambitions, arrived in Nicaragua, declared it part of U.S. territory, and named himself governor. While his tenure lasted only a few years, Walker established a legacy of U.S. imperialist intervention. In political events, national holidays, and folk music, the

story of Walker is invoked as a potent reminder of the threat posed by *Los Yanquis*. While the out-migration of Nicaraguan mothers in the twenty-first century might seem far removed from stories of imperial plunder, the tales are connected through a history of expropriation of Nicaraguan resources (land and labor) and political and economic marginalization, to which Nicaraguans have consistently responded with a strong ethos of resistance, resilience, and self-sacrifice for a collective good—a set of values that correspond with solidaridad.

16. Several U.S.-based NGOs formed in solidaridad with the Nicaraguan Revolution and people during this period, including Witness for Peace and the Nicaragua Network; these groups continue to monitor U.S. policy and support human-centered development in Nicaragua.

17. Readers interested in Nicaragua's history of liberation theology and the occasionally fraught relationship between local priests and the Catholic hierarchy are referred to Fernando Cardenal's autobiography of the Sandinista revolutionary period, *Faith and Joy: Memoirs of a Revolutionary Priest* (Cardenal 2015).

18. I was in Matagalpa in 2006 when the presidential campaign was in full swing and witnessed intensive campaigning by both major political parties: the right-wing Liberal Alliance (with candidate Eduardo Montealegre), and the left-leaning FSLN (with Daniel Ortega). Ortega is a former political prisoner who had previously served as president during the revolutionary period (1984–1990). After sixteen years of successive neoliberal administrations, Nicaraguans wanted change but were fearful of what an FSLN victory might bring. Sandinista supporters were hesitant to vote for Ortega because they thought his victory would prompt another U.S. invasion; in 2006, I often heard people say that if the FSLN won, "van a venir los Contras" (the Contras are going to come). This shows the imprint of political violence on collective memory. For more on political trauma and memory in Central America, see Seider 2001.

19. For more on ALBA, see Hirst, n.d.

20. For example, Pope John Paul II declared, "It is incumbent on all of us to question the extreme poverty in which the majority of families in our continent live. Savage capitalism and the dictatorship of the market provoke ever-greater inequality between men and the growth of unemployment. We share the suffering of so many families who must emigrate because of the lack of work in many regions." Quoted in Martínez Ramírez 2009.

21. Opposition to Ortega from the Nicaraguan left criticizes what is viewed as Ortega's co-optation of the popular mobilization of the Sandinista revolutionary period into a form of electoral clientelism. Opposition from the left and environmentalists has crystalized around the development of a transoceanic canal through Nicaragua using Chinese capital. See Simpson 2010; Kinzer 2015.

22. The U.S. State Department and its ambassadors have been unabashedly critical of the Ortega administration, funding opposition parties through the National

Endowment for Democracy (NED). While public information on the NED is not readily available, see NicaNet 2009 for one critique of the bias in State Department policy.

23. For example, in Nicaragua, I was often told by family members, friends, and colleagues, "Thank you for being in solidarity with Nicaraguan families [Gracias por ser solidaria con las familias nicaragüenses]." This phrase illustrates the active dimension of solidaridad, implying not just interpersonal alignment but also action in the social world. This attribution pushed me to reflect on whether I was being *bastante solidaria* (sufficiently in solidarity), because as an ethnographer I often felt incapable of adequate responses to the social and economic struggles of the families with whom I worked. Motivated by this cultural value of solidaridad, on multiple occasions I stepped outside the role of anthropological observer and actively engaged with families, engagements I describe throughout this book.

24. In her compelling ethnographic study of Peruvian migration to Spain and Spanish adoption of Peruvian children, Jessaca Leinaweaver (2013) shows that solidarity is a primary motivation of many Spanish parents seeking to adopt children from Peru, and they frame their intentions in terms of a humanitarian desire to assist Peruvian children (not without resistance from adoption professionals, who want the focus to be on parents and families, rather than political solidarity). Leinaweaver's discussion suggests that solidarity has broader relevance for understanding kinship practices and migration patterns in the Latin American context.

25. Decades old, Roger Lancaster's excellent *Life Is Hard* (1992) remains one of the only book-length ethnographic studies of gender and family life in postwar, urban Nicaragua. A study of gender and ethnicity among indigenous groups of Nicaragua's Atlantic coast region is found in Bourgois 1989.

26. A growing minority of Nicaraguans identify as evangelical, or non-Catholic Christian, and there are also small Jewish and Islamic communities.

27. For a fuller description of this narrative trope in Nicaragua's literary history, see Orr, n.d. I thank Iván Sandoval-Cervantes for pointing me to Orr's article.

28. The Sandinista period was also one of revolutionary feminism, with women fighting on the battlefields and in popular consciousness-raising groups to struggle for women's rights and social justice. Margaret Randall's *Sandino's Daughters* (1995) provides a compelling account of this period, using interviews with women active in the 1979 revolution to tell stories of the successes and failures of their struggles. While influenced by the international women's movement, Nicaraguan feminists have sought to envision and realize a unique, culturally and historically grounded feminism. For an excellent review of the complicated and often-antagonistic relationship between Sandinismo and feminism, see Heumann 2014.

29. Anthropologists of aging have critically scrutinized the "third age," situating social processes of aging in cross-cultural perspective (for example, see Lamb

2014; Robbins-Ruszkowski 2013). In Nicaragua, *la tercera edad* maps onto cultural expectations around biological reproduction, where the third age is situated within a reproductive life course as one moves from the parent to grandparent generation. As I argue here, however, members of the third age remain active participants in social reproduction and regeneration.

30. Considering morality as an embodied practice is distinct from conceptualizing morality as an abstract categorization of right versus wrong. Throughout this book, I consider the *moral* as practical action that reflects and extends what is most at stake (Kleinman 2006) for caregivers in Nicaraguan transnational families. Recognizing morality in its local, cultural inflections is central to my analyses. For instance, caregiving for elder adults and ill relatives in the United States may be oriented toward upholding independence of personhood, reflecting the moral imperative of individualism in U.S. culture (for example, see Buch 2014; Kleinman 2006). Reflecting a different local instantiation of moral personhood, in Nicaragua the commitments of grandmother caregivers are to individual sacrifice for family solidarity and well-being.

31. La Red was funded by a Costa Rican–based NGO working with Nicaraguan women migrants in Costa Rica. This NGO was financed by the Spanish Basque government and other Western European organizations, but its financing was discontinued in March 2010, and La Red largely went dormant. However, in 2014, the coordinator of La Red reactivated the group and has since applied for NGO status in Nicaragua. SJM is a Nicaraguan-based project of the Central American branch of the Company of Jesus (the Jesuit order).

32. Average life expectancy for women in Nicaragua is seventy-eight years. See Pan American Health Organization 2017.

Chapter 1

1. National statistics provide prevalence data for households with international migrants at the municipal level. However, data on caregiving configurations within migrant-sending households is not collected, making it impossible to know the precise number of grandmother heads of household in transnational families. See Gobierno de Reconciliación y Unidad Nacional 2007.

2. In Nicaragua, women over thirty-five are culturally viewed as past both their employment-productive and social-reproductive prime. For example, job announcements in Managua commonly and unabashedly state, "Buscando muchachas entre 18–24 años" (Seeking girls between 18 and 24). The grandmothers in my study who had been employed in sales or domestic service earlier in life recounted employers firing them when they reached forty for no other reason than age. There are very few opportunities in Nicaragua's formal labor market for women in their fifties and sixties.

3. For transnational mothers, gendered cultural expectations for physical and emotional proximity between themselves and their children exacerbate feelings of guilt and stigma related to migration (Hondagneu-Sotelo 2001; Parreñas 2001; Abrego 2014). These are among the consequences of migration for women who mother from a distance (Horton 2009; Bryceson and Vuorela 2002). For mother migrants, this can result in the liminal feeling of being "here but really there"—working in destination countries but emotionally tied to children and families back home (Hondagneu-Sotelo and Avila 1997: 548). For families of migrants in Nicaragua, there is a similar feeling of lives transformed across transnational space and time, as grandmothers and children feel their emotional lives extended transnationally, even though they themselves have not migrated.

4. The LGBT community in Nicaragua is increasingly visible, winning some recognition in recent years (such as the overturning, in 2008, of a national law criminalizing homosexual relations and winning the right to nondiscrimination in public health services), but struggles for marriage equality and full social inclusion continue. For more, see Howe 2013 and Babb 2003.

5. Ligia Arana (director of Program on Gender and Development, University of Central America, Managua), personal communication, May 13, 2010. During my fieldwork, I often heard women discursively frame male infidelity as "It's that he's a man, and men have needs [Es que es hombre, y los hombres tienen necesidades]," which I interpret as a deeply ingrained sexism perpetuating women's inequality in heterosexual conjugal relationships.

6. For an example of this pervasive, rational-actor model of household migration, see Cohen 2011 and Donato 1993. A limitation of this economically determined view is that although economic opportunity is a common motivation for migration, the actual decision about who should migrate and where is not the result of careful calculation but rather fleeting and seemingly random opportunities presented through, for instance, social networks (e.g., friends who line up housing or employment for a migrant abroad).

7. Other scholars have suggested that grandmother caretakers may be motivated by a future expectation of return (for example, see Dreby 2010; Moran-Taylor 2008). That is, grandmothers' care for grandchildren in the present is motivated by the desire that their support will be reciprocated in the future—for example, when grandchildren take over their grandparents' care. This sentiment was not explicitly expressed by the grandmothers in my study. While it is possible that an expectation of intergenerational return forms part of the implicit motive for grandmother caregiving, the pervasive lack of certainty about the future of family life in the context of transnational migration complicates this interpretation.

8. Heather Rae-Espinoza found that children of Ecuadoran parent migrants actively seek continuity in cultural models of family caregiving, trying to fit

grandmothers and other surrogate caregivers into the social role of mother and yet struggling to do this while maintaining connections to migrant mothers abroad (2011: 131). Somewhat differently from Rae-Espinoza's study, my research found that grandmothers uphold the mother-child transnational tie while simultaneously forming strong emotional ties with children in their care, making the prospect of mother-child reunification that much more complicated.

9. Cándida Gómez Suarez (program director of Servicio Jesuita para Migrantes), personal communication, October 19, 2009.

10. Evelyn Nakano Glenn (2010) has outlined how laws and social policies in the United States reinforce women's responsibilities for child and household care.

11. Aurora did the emotional work of convincing the children's father to assent to their migration. This type of negotiation is no small feat, and much is at stake, since a father's permission is needed for children to legally leave Nicaragua.

12. Elizabeth had purchased a computer for her daughters to use to communicate with her during their two-year separation; after her granddaughters left, Aurora used it to stay in touch with all three of them in Spain. For Aurora, seeing her granddaughters online and hearing them tell her they love her, even virtually, helped her cope with their absence.

Chapter 2

1. In an interview I conducted with the director of the Nicaraguan Ministry of Family's Programa Amor, which works to protect vulnerable and exploited children nationwide, she echoed the idea that grandmothers raising children of parent migrants are primarily motivated by the promise of personal financial reward. This was used to justify Programa Amor's reluctance to provide legal assistance to grandmothers seeking custodianship of children of parent migrants, a programmatic decision that further reinforces grandmothers' precarious sociolegal position vis-à-vis the children in their care.

2. For other examples of events leading to irregular remittance flows, see Michelle Moran-Taylor's (2008) discussion of Honduran transnational households and Joanna Dreby's (2010) discussion of Mexican families divided by borders.

3. The high surcharge (up to 15 percent per transaction) levied by these companies has been strongly critiqued by migrant rights groups and led to a 2007 campaign urging Western Union to reduce transfer fees and support community reinvestment. (See "Grupos de inmigrantes" 2007.) The campaign has so far been unsuccessful in changing Western Union's practices.

4. Throughout this chapter, when referring to the dollar value of remittances, I use estimates of value in U.S. dollars at the time of the study (2009–2010).

5. Semiprivate schools in Nicaragua are usually run by religious institutions, such as associations of Catholic nuns, and financed through student tuition and private

donations (church resources) but also may receive some government funding via the Ministry of Education. In my study, children in eight of the twenty-four families attended private parochial schools (all these lived in Managua; outside the city, public school is usually the only option).

6. Costa Rica allows for birthright, or jus soli, citizenship. For information on Costa Rican naturalization policies and procedures, see Dirección General de Migración y Extranjería, n.d.

7. For discussion of the shifting meanings of "home" in Filipina families of migrant mothers, see Constable 1999.

8. Heather Rae-Espinoza (2011) makes a similar argument about children in Ecuadoran transnational families, showing how children's emotional well-being may be protected to the extent that they view their mothers as remaining responsible for their care.

9. Jason Pribilsky (2012) provides an ethnographic description of how Ecuadoran men living as migrants in New York manage contradictory gendered cultural expectations of fathers, confronting social pressures to spend money on alcohol consumption while simultaneously managing expectations of families back home that they will regularly send remittances.

10. The exception to academic success was eight-year-old Selso, who had failed to advance to first grade, causing Marbeya and Azucena a good deal of despair. When children fail to uphold their sacrifice of doing well in school, the value of the intergenerational sacrifice of transnational families is threatened.

11. I discuss grandmothers' narrative framing of migration across generations as a form of kin work in transnational families further in Yarris (2017).

12. *Idiay* is an idiomatic expression that is difficult to translate. It means something like "You know, what's going on over there . . ."

13. In her work with Australian transnational families, Loretta Baldassar (2007) similarly found that monetary remittances and social ties (e.g., communication using the Internet and text messaging) failed to satisfy sending families' desires to have migrant members physically present.

14. Leslie Rebhun illustrates these complicated realities surrounding intimate relations through her ethnographic work in northeast Brazil, where she finds that love is always tied to "interests," or expectations for social, emotional, and economic support (Rebhun 2007: 117).

15. This is similar to what João Biehl has referred to as "local economies of salvation" (Biehl 2007: 1086) or what Angela Garcia has called "necessary measures" (Garcia 2010: 191)—forms of care that are necessary to sustain life but terribly insufficient to meet macrostructural changes in politics, economics, and institutions of care. Although the stakes for families in my study might not seem as high as they are in the epidemics of HIV/AIDS in Brazil or heroin use in New Mexico's Española Valley, the

intergenerational care provided by grandmothers sustains cultural values of sacrifice and solidarity across generations in Nicaraguan families in which these values are threatened and disrupted by global migration.

Chapter 3

1. The incorporation of the "cultural concepts of distress" framework into *DSM-V* is a product of decades of research and advocacy by psychiatric anthropologists and transcultural psychiatrists, who pushed for revisions of outdated, overly generalizing, and exoticizing formulations of culture such as culture-bound syndromes. For more on this history, see Mezzich et al. 1996.

2. For a systematic review of "thinking too much" idioms of distress in cross-cultural psychiatric literature, see Kaiser et al. 2015.

3. While I appreciate the effort of many in this field to expand access to early diagnosis and treatment for mental illness in settings where mental health services are limited, I am also wary of collapsing cultural concepts of distress into *DSM* categories, because such an interpretation risks losing the sociocultural significance of particular expressions of distress and, by extension, reducing the response to clinical intervention rather than broader social intervention. Instead, my aim here is to take seriously the social dislocation and cultural disruption in kinship and care that provoke pensando mucho for grandmother caregivers in transnational families.

4. The two grandmothers whose sons had migrated also associated pensando mucho with the uncertain future of their family life. However, paternal grandmothers do not lose the culturally expected support of adult daughters and do not have to fill the "care slot" in the same way that mothers of migrant daughters do.

5. The data presented in this chapter come primarily from one structured interview guide, the abuela interview 3 (see the appendix), which I used to interview a subset of grandmothers who had mentioned pensando mucho in earlier interviews and conversations.

6. These initial bouts of physical sickness would be most acute during the first days after migrants' departures; once migrants had arrived at their destinations and telephoned home, grandmothers' symptoms would begin to lessen.

7. According to one of my Servicio Jesuita para Migrantes colleagues, "affliction" is a common term for Nicaraguan women of lower socioeconomic classes (such as those participating in this study) to express feelings of depression; *aflicción* may be a sign or even a synonym for *depresión*. Olga also told me, "Well, at first I felt grief-stricken [afligida]. I think that's what it was, grief [aflicción]."

8. This idea of a "wearing out" of the brain or a tiredness (*cansancio*) in the brain from thinking too much recalls an earlier study of Puerto Rican mental health patients in the United States, in which dolor de cerebro was cited as a specific pain associated with "un desgaste cerebral" (a wearing out or tiring out of the brain) (Abad

and Boyce 1979: 34). These findings reveal the possibility of an emergent explanatory model that may have cross-cultural significance in different Latin American contexts.

9. This sort of information management was common in the families in my study. For instance, in my interviews with migrant mothers, I learned that these women often avoided telling me details of their lives abroad that they thought might upset their mothers back home in Nicaragua (e.g., exploitation by employers, job loss, or plans to marry men—and therefore likely stay—abroad). Grandmothers similarly manage their transnational communications, avoiding telling migrant daughters about troubles at home with children or money so as not to worry them. These sorts of avoidances and omissions can be considered transnational emotional labor (Hochschild 1983, 2000) that accompanies global care chains. Jennifer Cole (2014) has shown how Malagasy marriage migrants in France also carefully manage their transnational communications, engaging in gossip and other forms of communicative work to shape how relatives in Madagascar view them, through the *télèphone malagache*.

10. Pierrette Hondagneu-Sotelo and Ernestine Avila (1997) first used "here" and "there" to aptly describe how transnational mothers working as domésticas in Los Angeles feel torn between the children they have left in origin countries and the demands of their lives in Los Angeles. For a discussion of this sentiment as it is experienced by children in Nicaraguan transnational families, see Yarris 2014a.

11. Cati Coe (2015) argues that care reconfigurations in Ghanaian transnational families follow lines of gender and generational inequalities and that notions of time often diverge between migrant parents and families back home. Coe argues for an anthropological attunement to the temporalities (not just spatialities) of transnational migration.

12. For more on the "larger temporal surround" of illness narratives, see Garro 2005: 52.

13. Juana used the phrase "entre la espada y la pared," which literally translates as "between the sword and the wall" but can be idiomatically translated as "between the devil and the deep blue sea" or "between a rock and a hard place."

14. See Arthur Kleinman for a discussion of the relationship between resistance—as disruption in the "lived flow of experience in local moral worlds"—and pain (Kleinman 1992: 174). Michael Jackson (2011) also movingly engages with the existential dimensions of global migration for migrants' sense of self and hopes for the future and the disjunctures that often exist between migrants and their kin back home in sending countries.

Chapter 4

1. Cati Coe argues for the importance of a "transtemporal" perspective on transnational caregiving, showing how care responsibilities in Ghanaian migrant families

are structured by gender, generation, and cultural understandings of time in sending and receiving contexts (Coe 2015).

2. Interestingly, Carlos earned a scholarship to obtain his bachelor's degree in the United States, where he studied business before returning to Nicaragua in the late 1990s. He has held a professional sales position ever since and lives with his wife and two children in the same barrio as Angela.

3. That Carlo was able to remarry in the United States hinged on his denial of his Nicaraguan marriage and family ties and points to another loophole in the U.S. immigration system. When Carlo registered in the United States under the Nicaraguan Adjustment and Central American Relief Act (NACARA), he declared himself unmarried and without children. This left Angela and her children in a legal limbo. Once she found out about Carlo's second marriage, Angela considered filing for divorce in Nicaragua but was concerned that doing so would make it more difficult for her children to file residency petitions in the United States using their paternity connection. Because they lacked the legal resources to prove they were children of a U.S. resident, Jonathan and Karla had to petition separately for their green cards (which they eventually received). U.S. immigration law has no way of accounting for these types of relational complexities. See U.S. Citizenship and Immigration Services 2016.

4. Karla's ex-boyfriend filed a custody suit for their twins, one of whom has a disability and requires special care and services. This case was long and drawn out and—for legal and economic reasons—made it impossible for Karla to file for Laleska's residency petition until the custody over her twins was settled.

5. Throughout the decade since her mother left, Laleska saw her father infrequently, even though he lived (in his mother's home) in the same barrio as Angela. Angela preferred for his visits to take place in her home, where she would offer him lunch and supervise his encounter with Laleska. Angela never fully trusted him to be alone with his daughter. Laleska's father has never provided economic support to his daughter or to Angela for the household.

6. Noelia recounted this experience during an interview, telling me she received a phone call at five o'clock one morning from Laleska, who was in a state of mild panic because she had woken up bleeding and did not understand what was happening. Laleska asked her aunt to show her what to do. Noelia went to Angela's house, where she proceeded to show Laleska how to use sanitary pads and maintain menstrual hygiene. Noelia spent the entire next day with Laleska. Laleska and Noelia left messages for Karla to call them back about something "important," but Karla did not call back that day. For Noelia and Laleska, this episode was a hurtful reminder of Karla's absence at a critical point in her daughter's life.

7. Many evangelical sects exist, along with Catholicism and other religions, in what has been described as the plural religious marketplace (Selka 2010) of contemporary Managua. There can be quite a large amount of tension—at least discursively, for

example, on popular radio stations—between those who identify as *Cristiana* (meaning *evangélica*, or one who follows any number of Protestant sects) and those who are *Católica* (Catholic).

8. While this type of control might be motivated by religious beliefs, it is also a reaction to the real threat of sexual violence. While I do not have statistical data on the prevalence of incest in Nicaragua, during my fieldwork a number of prominent cases of child sexual abuse were in the news and public debate, including the high-profile case of President Ortega, whose young adult stepdaughter accused him of incest.

9. This transnational moral bargain seems to have paid off for the present generation: Angela's granddaughter Reyna passed the entrance exams to attend a major public university, where she began her college career studying accounting.

10. Sarah Horton (2008) shows how the emotional experience of transnational life is shared across borders between Salvadoran migrant mothers in the United States and their children in El Salvador; here I extend this analysis of intersubjective emotional distress across a third generation.

11. Migration scholars have suggested that remittances help children of migrant parents feel an emotional connection (see, for example, Dreby 2010; Fog Olwig 2007; Parreñas 2005). While I have found similarly that children whose mothers regularly send money feel as though their mothers remain *pendiente*, or responsible, for family back home in Nicaragua, this does not resolve children's emotional ambivalence about migration (see Yarris 2014a).

12. Patterns of migrant visits and returns are shaped in large part by immigration policies in destination countries such as the United States (see Dreby 2010; Menjívar 2006; Parreñas 2005). Although family reunification is ostensibly one of the pillars of U.S. immigration policy, the reality is that individuals petitioning for legal residency on the basis of kinship, including parents and children, may have to wait years or decades for their applications to be processed and determinations made.

13. Cándida Rosa Gómez Suárez, personal communication, November 28, 2009.

14. Laleska's concerns echo the voices of immigrant children in the United States who reunify with migrant parents at the cost of estrangement from extended family in home countries (Suárez-Orozco and Suárez-Orozco 2001). Elsewhere, I have elaborated on this ambivalence that children of migrant mothers experience (Yarris 2014a).

15. In an ethnographic account of a visit back to a research field site after years of absence, Michael Jackson (2011) brings his son along on the journey to accompany a friend and former research participant, Sewa, from London to Sierra Leone. This self-reflective and deeply moving monograph reveals the complex emotional dynamics facing migrants (and the returning anthropologist) as they are confronted by the expectations of kin and other villagers for material contributions and ritual participation while they simultaneously feel distanced from extended family and community members because of the distance and time inherent to migration.

Conclusion

1. The National Domestic Workers Alliance has advocated for basic labor protections for all domestic workers in the United States, regardless of immigration status. A victory in this campaign was realized in California in 2013 when Governor Jerry Brown signed the Domestic Worker Bill of Rights into law. In 2015, Oregon became the fifth U.S. state (along with California, New York, Massachusetts, and Hawaii) to pass a domestic worker bill of rights. See Adler 2013; Southward 2015. While these laws include antidiscrimination clauses, it is unclear whether their protections will be de facto extended to undocumented workers.

2. Nonetheless, examples of advocacy to streamline family reunification in the United States include the project Moms for Family Unity, organized by mothers to support policy reform for immigrant mothers. See http://reformimmigrationfor america.org/77entre-nos-moms-for-family-unity-campaign/.

3. On August 24, 2010, seventy-two Central and South American migrants were massacred in the Mexican state of Tamaulipas by a Mexican drug and human-trafficking gang, raising international awareness about the treacherous journey through Mexico risked by thousands of undocumented Central American migrants each year. See "Migrant Misery" 2010. Unfortunately, additional horrendous attacks have happened in the ensuing years.

4. This concern led Nicaragua and the other Central America–4 countries (El Salvador, Honduras, and Guatemala) to bring a case against Mexico in the Inter-American Court of Human Rights for alleged complicity in the violence, kidnapping, and killing of Central American migrants.

References

Abad, Vicente, and Elizabeth Boyce. 1979. "Issues in Psychiatric Evaluations of Puerto Ricans: A Socio-cultural Perspective." *Journal of Operational Psychiatry* 10 (1): 28–39.

Abrego, Leisy. 2009. "Economic Well-Being in Salvadoran Transnational Families: How Gender Affects Remittance Practices." *Journal of Marriage and Family* 71:1070–1085.

———. 2014. *Sacrificing Families: Navigating Laws, Labor, and Love Across Borders.* Stanford, CA: Stanford University Press.

Adler, Lisa. 2013. "Breaking and Beautiful News: Victory for Domestic Workers in California!" Jobs with Justice, September 26. http://www.jwj.org/breaking-beautiful -news-victory-for-domestic-workers-in-california.

Aguilara, Amparo. 2010. "Migración nica a España tiene rostro femenino." *El Nuevo Diario*, July 25. http://www.elnuevodiario.com.ni/especiales/79699.

American Psychiatric Association. 2013. *Diagnostic and Statistical Manual of Mental Disorders.* 5th ed. Washington, DC: American Psychiatric Association.

Andersen, Lykke E., and Bent Jesper Christensen. 2009. "The Static and Dynamic Benefits of Migration and Remittances in Nicaragua." Institute for Advanced Development Studies Working Paper No. 05/2009. http://www.inesad.edu.bo/pdf/ wp05_2009.pdf.

Andersson, Ruben. 2014. *Illegality, Inc.: Clandestine Migration and the Business of Bordering Europe.* Berkeley: University of California Press.

Arregui, Edur Velasco, and Richard Roman. 2005. "Perilous Passage: Central American Migration Through México." In *Latino Los Angeles: Transformations, Communities, and Activism*, edited by Enrique C. Ochoa and Gilda L. Ochoa, 38–62. Tucson: University of Arizona Press.

Asamblea Nacional de la República de Nicaragua. 1992. Ley de Alimentos (Ley No. 143). http://legislacion.asamblea.gob.ni/normaweb.nsf/($All)/52CF21BC4B462F9F0625 70A100577C2E?OpenDocument.

Babb, Florence. 2001a. *After Revolution: Mapping Gender and Cultural Politics in Neoliberal Nicaragua*. Austin: University of Texas Press.

————. 2001b. "Nicaraguan Narratives of Development, Nationhood, and the Body." *Journal of Latin American Anthropology* 6 (1): 84–119.

————. 2003. "Out in Nicaragua: Local and Transnational Desires After the Revolution." *Cultural Anthropology* 18 (3): 304–328.

Baldassar, Loretta. 2007. "Transnational Families and the Provision of Moral and Emotional Support: The Relationship Between Truth and Distance." *Identities* 14 (4): 385–409.

Baldassar, Loretta, and Laura Merla. 2014. "Introduction: Transnational Family Caregiving Through the Lens of Circulation." In *Transnational Families, Migration and the Circulation of Care: Understanding Mobility and Absence in Family Life*, edited by Loretta Baldassar and Laura Merla, 3–24. New York: Routledge.

Baumeister, Eduardo. 2006. *Migración internacional y desarrollo en Nicaragua*. Santiago, Chile: Centro Latinoamericano y Caribeño de Demografía (CELADE).

Belli, Gioconda. 2002. *El país bajo mi piel: Memorias de amor y guerra*. New York: Vintage Español.

Bello, Oknan. 2008. *Remesas y tipo de cambio real en Nicaragua*. Managua: Banco Central de Nicaragua.

Benyamini, Yael, and Ellen Idler. 1999. "Community Studies Reporting Association Between Self-Rated Health and Mortality: Additional Studies, 1995–1998." *Research on Aging* 21:392–401.

Bibler Coutin, Susan. 2005. "The Formation and Transformation of Salvadoran Community Organizations in Los Angeles." In *Latino Los Angeles: Transformations, Communities, and Activism*, edited by Enrique C. Ochoa and Gilda L. Ochoa, 155–177. Tucson: University of Arizona Press.

Biehl, João G. 2007. "Pharmaceuticalization: AIDS Treatment and Global Health Politics." *Anthropological Quarterly* 80 (4): 1083–1126.

Boehm, Deborah A. 2008. "'For My Children': Constructing Family and Navigating the State in the U.S.-Mexico Transnation." *Anthropological Quarterly* 81 (4): 777–802.

————. 2012. *Intimate Migrations: Gender, Family, and Illegality Among Transnational Mexicans*. New York: New York University Press.

Boehm, Deborah A., and Heidi Swank. 2011. "Introduction." *International Migration* 49 (6): 1–6.

Boris, Eileen, and Rhacel Salazar Parreñas. 2010. "Introduction." In *Intimate Labors: Cultures, Technologies, and the Politics of Care*, edited by Eileen Boris and Rhacel Salazar Parreñas, 1–12. Stanford, CA: Stanford University Press.

Bourgois, Philippe. 1989. *Ethnicity at Work: Divided Labor on a Central American Banana Plantation*. Baltimore: Johns Hopkins University Press.

Brijnath, Bianca. 2009. "Familial Bonds and Boarding Passes: Understanding Caregiving in a Transnational Context." *Identities* 16 (1): 83–101.

Brown, Anna, and Eileen Patten. 2013. "Hispanics of Nicaraguan Origin in the United States, 2011." Pew Research Center, June 19. http://www.pewhispanic .org/2013/06/19/hispanics-of-nicaraguan-origin-in-the-united-states-2011.

Bryceson, Deborah F., and Ulla Vuorela. 2002. "Transnational Families in the 21st Century." In *The Transnational Family: New European Frontiers and Global Networks*, edited by D. F. Bryceson and U. Vuorela, 3–30. Oxford: Berg.

Buch, Elana. 2014. "Troubling Gifts of Care: Vulnerable Persons and Threatening Exchanges in Chicago's Home Care Industry." *Medical Anthropology Quarterly* 28 (4): 599–615.

Cardenal, Fernando. 2015. *Faith and Joy: Memoirs of a Revolutionary Priest*. Maryknoll, NY: Orbis Books.

Carsten, Janet. 2000. *Cultures of Relatedness: New Approaches to the Study of Kinship*. Cambridge: Cambridge University Press.

Centeno Orozco, Rebeca Dolores, and Martha Olivia Gutiérrez Vega. 2007. *La migración internacional y el desarrollo: ¿Un vínculo posible?* Managua: Informe Final, Fondo Mink'a de Chorlaví.

Coe, Cati. 2011. "What Is Love? The Materiality of Care in Ghanian Transnational Families." *International Migration* 49 (6): 7–24.

———. 2015. "The Temporality of Care: Gender, Migration, and the Entrainment of Life-Courses." In *Anthropological Perspectives on Care: Work, Kinship, and the Life-Course*, edited by Erdmute Alber and Heike Drotbohm, 181–205. New York: Palgrave.

Cohen, Jeffrey. 2011. "Migration, Remittances, and Household Strategies." *Annual Review of Anthropology* 40:103–114.

Cohen, Sheldon, Tom Kamarck, and Robin Mermelstein. 1983. "A Global Measure of Perceived Stress." *Journal of Health and Social Behavior* 24:385–396.

Cole, Jennifer. 2014. "The *Téléphone Malgache*: Transnational Gossip and Social Transformation Among Malagasy Marriage Migrants in France." *American Ethnologist* 41 (2): 276–289.

Cole, Jennifer, and Deborah Durham. 2007. *Generations and Globalization: Youth, Age, and Family in the New World Economy*. Bloomington: Indiana University Press.

Constable, Nicole. 1999. "At Home but Not at Home: Filipina Narratives of Ambivalent Returns." *Cultural Anthropology* 14 (2): 203–228.

Cornelius, Wayne A. 2006. "Impacts of Border Enforcement on Unauthorized Mexican Migration to the United States." *Border Battles: The U.S. Immigration Debates*, September 26. http://borderbattles.ssrc.org/Cornelius/printable.html.

De Genova, Nicholas. 2002. "Migrant 'Illegality' and Deportability in Everyday Life." *Annual Review of Anthropology* 31:419–447.

Dirección General de Migración y Extranjería. n.d. "Residencias." http://www.migra cion.go.cr/extranjeros/residencias.html (accessed January 11, 2017).

Donato, Katherine M. 1993. "Current Trends and Patterns of Female Migration: Evidence from Mexico." *International Migration Review* 27 (4): 748–771.

Dreby, Joanna. 2010. *Divided by Borders: Mexican Migrants and Their Children.* Berkeley: University of California Press.

Duque-Páramo, Maria Claudia. 2010. "Understanding Experiences and Health Problems of Children Living Parental Migration." Paper presented at "The Doors of Perception: Viewing Anthropology Through the Eyes of Children" conference, University of Amsterdam, September 30.

Ehrenreich, Barbara, and Arlie Russell Hochschild. 2004. *Global Woman: Nannies, Maids, and Sex Workers in the New Economy.* New York: Henry Holt.

El Guindi, Fadwa. 2004. *Visual Anthropology: Essential Method and Theory.* Lanham, MD: Altamira Press.

Escobar, Arturo. 1994. *Encountering Development: The Making and Unmaking of the Third World.* Princeton, NJ: Princeton University Press.

Farmer, Paul. 2003. *Pathologies of Power: Health, Human Rights, and the New War on the Poor.* Berkeley: University of California Press.

Finkler, Kaja. 1994. *Women in Pain: Gender and Morbidity in Mexico.* Philadelphia: University of Pennsylvania Press.

Fog Olwig, Karen. 2003. "'Transnational' Socio-cultural Systems and Ethnographic Research: Views from an Extended Field Site." *International Migration Review* 37 (3): 787–811.

———. 2007. *Caribbean Journeys: An Ethnography of Migration and Home in Three Family Networks.* Durham, NC: Duke University Press.

Folbre, Nancy. 2001. *The Invisible Heart: Economics and Family Values.* New York: New Press.

Fouratt, Caitlin. 2012. "Por el amor y la tierra: Las inversiones emocionales de los migrantes nicaragüenses." *Anuario de Estudios Centroamericanos* 38:193–212.

Garcia, Angela. 2010. *The Pastoral Clinic: Addiction and Dispossession Along the Rio Grande.* Berkeley: University of California Press.

Garro, Linda C. 2005. "'Effort After Meaning' in Everyday Life." In *A Companion to Psychological Anthropology: Modernity and Psychocultural Change,* edited by Conerly Casey and Robert B. Edgerton, 48–71. Malden, MA: Blackwell.

———. 2011. "Enacting Ethos, Enacting Health: Realizing Health in the Everyday Life of a California Family of Mexican Descent." *Ethos* 39 (3): 300–330.

Garro, Linda, and Carolina Izquierdo. 2003. "Studying Health and Well-Being in the Everyday Lives of Families." UCLA Sloan Center on Everyday Lives of Families Working Paper No. 25. http://www.celf.ucla.edu/pages/view_abstractf9c5.html?AID=28.

Garro, Linda, and Kristin Yarris. 2009. "'A Massive Long Way': Interconnecting Histories, a 'Special Child,' ADHD, and Everyday Family Life." *Culture, Medicine and Psychiatry* 33:559–607.

Ginsberg, Faye D., and Reyna Rapp. 1995. "Introduction." In *Conceiving the New World Order: The Global Politics of Reproduction*, edited by Faye D. Ginsburg and Rayna Rapp, 1–18. Berkeley: University of California Press.

Glenn, Evelyn Nakano. 2007. "Caring and Inequality." In *Women's Labor in the Global Economy: Speaking in Multiple Voices*, edited by Sharon Harley, 46–61. New Brunswick, NJ: Rutgers University Press.

———. 2010 *Forced to Care*. Cambridge, MA: Harvard University Press.

Gobierno de Reconciliación y Unidad Nacional. 2007. "Cifras municipales." http://www.inide.gob.ni/censos2005/CifrasMun/tablas_cifras.htm.

Goldade, Kathryn. 2009. "'Health Is Hard Here' or 'Health for All'? The Politics of Blame, Gender, and Health Care for Undocumented Nicaraguan Migrants in Costa Rica." *Medical Anthropology Quarterly* 23 (4): 483–503.

"Grupos de inmigrantes intensifican campaña de boicot contra Western Union." 2007. *Vida Nueva*, December 11. http://vida-nueva.com/grupos-de-inmigrantes-intensi fican-campana-de-boicot-contra-western-union.

Guerrero Nicaragua, Ricardo. 2014. "Remesas van por nuevo récord." *El Nuevo Diario*, June 3. http://www.elnuevodiario.com.ni/economia/321369-remesas-van-nuevo -record.

Habed López, Nasere. 2007. "Solidaridad, virtud del Nicaragüense." *El Nuevo Diario*, November 22. http://www.elnuevodiario.com.ni/opinion/2463-solidaridad-virtud -nicaraguense.

Han, Clara. 2012. *Life in Debt: Times of Care and Violence in Neoliberal Chile*. Berkeley: University of California Press.

Heidbrink, Lauren. 2014. *Migrant Youth, Transnational Families, and the State Care and Contested Interests*. Philadelphia: University of Pennsylvania Press.

Held, Virginia. 2006. *The Ethics of Care: Personal, Political, and Global*. Oxford: Oxford University Press.

Heumann, Silke. 2014. "Gender, Sexuality, and Politics: Rethinking the Relationship Between Feminism and Sandinismo in Nicaragua." *Social Politics* 21 (2): 290–314.

Hinton, Devon E., and Roberto Lewis-Fernandez. 2010. "Idioms of Distress among Trauma Survivors: Subtypes and Clinical Utility." *Culture, Medicine and Psychiatry* 34:209–218.

Hinton, Devon, Ria Reis, and Joop de Jong. 2015. "The 'Thinking a Lot' Idiom of Distress and PTSD: An Examination of Their Relationship Among Traumatized Cambodian Refugees Using the 'Thinking a Lot' Questionnaire." *Medical Anthropology Quarterly* 29 (3): 357–380.

Hirsch, Jennifer S. 2003. *Courtship After Marriage: Sexuality and Love in Mexican Transnational Families*. Berkeley: University of California Press.

Hirst, Joel. n.d. "A Guide to ALBA." *Americas Quarterly*. http://www.americasquarterly .org/hirst/article (accessed January 11, 2017).

Hochschild, Arlie Russell. 1983. *The Managed Heart: Commercialization of Human Feeling*. Berkeley: University of California Press.

———. 2000. "Global Care Chains and Emotional Surplus Value." In *On the Edge: Living with Global Capitalism*, edited by W. Hutton and A. Giddens, 130–146. London: Jonathan Cape.

Holmes, Seth, and Heide Castañeda. 2016. "Representing the 'European Refugee Crisis' in Germany and Beyond: Deservingness and Difference, Life and Death." *American Ethnologist* 43:12–24.

Hondagneu-Sotelo, Pierrette. 2001. *Doméstica: Immigrant Workers Cleaning and Caring in the Shadows of Affluence*. Berkeley: University of California Press.

Hondagneu-Sotelo, Pierrette, and Ernestine Avila. 1997. "'I'm Here, but I'm There': The Meanings of Latina Transnational Motherhood." *Gender and Society* 11 (5): 548–571.

Horton, Sarah. 2008. "Consuming Childhood: 'Lost' and 'Ideal' Childhoods as a Motivation for Migration." *Anthropology Quarterly* 81 (4): 925–943.

———. 2009. "A Mother's Heart Is Weighted Down with Stones: A Phenomenological Approach to the Experience of Transnational Motherhood." *Culture, Medicine and Psychiatry* 33:21–40.

Howe, Cymene. 2013. *Intimate Activism: The Struggle for Sexual Rights in Postrevolutionary Nicaragua*. Durham, NC: Duke University Press.

Jackson, Michael. 1996. *Things as They Are: New Directions in Phenomenological Anthropology*. Bloomington: Indiana University Press.

———. 2009. *The Palm at the End of the Mind: Relatedness, Religiosity, and the Real*. Durham, NC: Duke University Press.

———. 2011. *Life Within Limits: Well-Being in a World of Want*. Durham, NC: Duke University Press.

———. 2013. *The Wherewithal of Life: Ethics, Migration, and the Question of Well-Being*. Berkeley: University of California Press.

Jenkins, Janis H., and Martha Valiente. 1994. "Bodily Transactions of the Passions: El Calor Among Salvadoran Women Refugees." In *Embodiment and Experience: The Existential Ground of Culture and Self*, edited by Thomas J. Csordas, 163–182. Cambridge: Cambridge University Press.

Kaiser, Bonnie, Kristen E. McLean, Brandon A. Kohrt, Ashley K. Hagaman, Bradley H. Wagenaar, Nayla M. Khoury, and Hunter M. Keys. 2014. "Reflechi Twòp—Thinking Too Much: Description of a Cultural Syndrome in Haiti's Central Plateau." *Culture, Medicine, and Psychiatry* 38:448–472.

Kaiser, Bonnie, Kristen E. McLean, Brandon A. Kohrt, Ashley K. Hagaman, Bradley H. Wagenaar, Nayla M. Khoury, and Hunter M. Keys. 2015. "'Thinking Too Much': A Systematic Review of a Common Idiom of Distress." *Social Science and Medicine* 147:170–183.

Kampwirth, Karen. 2004. *Feminism and the Legacy of Revolution: Nicaragua, El Salvador, Chiapas.* Athens: Ohio University Press.

Kinzer, Stephen. 2015. "Daniel Ortega Is a Sandinista in Name Only." *Al Jazeera America*, April 6. http://america.aljazeera.com/opinions/2015/4/daniel-ortega-is-a-sandinista-in-name-only.html.

Kirmayer, Laurence J. 2008. "Empathy and Alterity in Cultural Psychiatry." *Ethos* 36 (4): 457–474.

Kleinman, Arthur. 1992. "Pain and Resistance: The Delegitimation and Relegitimation of Local Worlds." In *Pain as Human Experience: An Anthropological Perspective*, edited by Mary-Jo DelVecchio-Good, Paul E. Brodwin, Byron J. Good, and Arthur Kleinman, 169–197. Berkeley: University of California Press.

———. 2006. *What Really Matters: Living a Moral Life Amidst Uncertainty and Danger.* New York: Oxford University Press.

Kleinman, Arthur, and Bridget Hanna. 2008. "Catastrophe, Caregiving, and Today's Biomedicine." *BioSocieties* 3:287–301.

Lamb, Sarah. 2014. "Permanent Personhood or Meaningful Decline? Toward a Critical Anthropology of Successful Aging." *Journal of Aging Studies* 29:41–52.

Lancaster, Roger N. 1992. *Life Is Hard: Machismo, Danger, and the Intimacy of Power in Nicaragua.* Berkeley: University of California Press.

Lee, Sang E. 2010. "Development or Despair? The Intentions and Realities of South–South Migration." *Revista Encuentro de la Universidad Centroamericana* 87:6–25.

Leinaweaver, Jessaca B. 2010. "Outsourcing Care: How Peruvian Migrants Meet Transnational Family Obligations." *Latin American Perspectives* 37:67–87.

———. 2013. *Adoptive Migration: Raising Latinos in Spain.* Durham, NC: Duke University Press.

Leinaweaver, Jessaca B., and Linda J. Seligmann. 2009. "Introduction: Cultural and Political Economies of Adoption in Latin America." *Journal of Latin American and Caribbean Anthropology* 14 (1): 1–19.

Levitt, Peggy. 1998. "Social Remittances: Migration Driven Local-Level Forms of Cultural Diffusion." *International Migration Review* 32 (4): 926–948.

Levitt, Peggy, and Nina Glick Schiller. 2004. "Conceptualizing Simultaneity: A Transnational Social Field Perspective on Society." *International Migration Review* 38 (3): 1002–1039.

Lion, Katherine C., Ndola Prata, and Chris Stewart. 2009. "Adolescent Childbearing in Nicaragua: A Quantitative Assessment of Associated Factors." *International Perspectives on Sexual and Reproductive Health* 35 (2): 91–96.

Martínez Ramírez, Arnoldo. 2009. "La paz precisa de justicia, liberad, equidad y solidaridad." *El Nuevo Diario*, May 11. http://www.elnuevodiario.com.ni/opinion/47430-paz-precisa-justicia-libertad-equidad-solidaridad.

Massey, Douglas. 1990. "Social Structure, Household Strategies, and the Cumulative Causation of Migration." *Population Index* 56 (1): 3–26.

Mendenhall, Emily. 2012. *Syndemic Suffering: Social Distress, Depression, and Diabetes Among Mexican Immigrant Women*. Walnut Creek, CA: Left Coast Press.

Mendenhall, Emily, Kristin Yarris, and Brandon Kohrt. 2016. "Utilization of Standardized Mental Health Assessments in Anthropological Research: Possibilities and Pitfalls." *Culture, Medicine, and Psychiatry* 40 (4): 726–745.

Menjívar, Cecilia. 2006. "Liminal Legality: Salvadoran and Guatemalan Immigrants' Lives in United States." *American Journal of Sociology* 111:999–1037.

Mezzich, Juan E., Arthur Kleinman, Horacio Fabrega, and Delores Parron. 1996. *Culture and Psychiatric Diagnosis: A DSM IV Perspective*. Washington, DC: American Psychiatric Press.

"Migrant Misery, in Mexico." 2010. *Los Angeles Times*, August 27. http://articles.latimes.com/2010/aug/27/opinion/la-ed-mexico-20100827.

Montoya, Rosario. 2002. "Women's Sexuality, Knowledge, and Agency in Rural Nicaragua." In *Gender's Place: Feminist Anthropologies of Latin America*, edited by Rosario Montoya, Lessie Jo Frazier, and Janise Hurtig, 65–88. New York: Palgrave Macmillan.

Moran-Taylor, Michelle. 2008. "When Mothers and Fathers Migrate North: Caretakers, Children, and Child Rearing in Guatemala." *Latin American Perspectives* 35 (4): 79–95.

Murchison, Julia. 2010. *Ethnography Essentials: Designing, Conducting, and Presenting Your Research*. San Francisco: Jossey-Bass.

Navarro, Marysa. 2002. "Against Marianismo." In *Gender's Place: Feminist Anthropologies of Latin America*, edited by Rosario Montoya and Janise Hurtig, 257–272. New York: Palgrave Macmillan.

NicaNet. 2009. "NDI Trains Young Political Leaders; FSLN Absent." *Nicaragua Network Hotline*, September 22. http://www.nicanet.org/?page=blog&id=24198.

Nichter, Mark. 1981. "Idioms of Distress: Alternatives in the Expression of Psychosocial Distress—a Case Study from South India." *Culture, Medicine and Psychiatry* 5: 379–408.

———. 2010. "Idioms of Distress Revisited." *Culture, Medicine and Psychiatry* 34: 401–416.

OIM (Organización Internacional para las Migraciones). 2013. *Perfil migratorio de Nicaragua 2012*. Managua: Organización Internacional para las Migraciones.

Orozco, Manuel. 2002. "Globalization and Migration: The Impact of Family Remittances in Latin America." *Latin American Politics and Society* 44 (2): 41–66.

Orr, Brianne. n.d. "From Machista to New Man? Omar Cabezas Negotiates Manhood from the Mountain in Nicaragua." http://www.lehman.cuny.edu/ciberletras/v22/orr.html (accessed January 11, 2017).

Pan American Health Organization. 2017. "Nicaragua eHealth Country Profile." http://www.paho.org/ict4health/index.php?option=com_content&view=article&id=9741%3Anicaragua&catid=5646%3Aehealth-country-profiles&Itemid=0&lang=en.

Parreñas, Rhacel Salazar. 2000. "Migrant Filipina Domestic Workers and the International Division of Reproductive Labor." *Gender and Society* 14:560–580.

———. 2001. *Servants of Globalization: Women, Migration, and Domestic Work.* Stanford, CA: Stanford University Press.

———. 2005. *Children of Global Migration: Transnational Families and Gendered Woes.* Stanford, CA: Stanford University Press.

Pedersen, David. 2013. *American Value: Migrants, Money, and Meaning in El Salvador and the United States.* Chicago: University of Chicago Press.

Pérez, Arlen. 2013. "Crisis en España no frena migración nica." *El Nuevo Diario,* August 12. http://www.elnuevodiario.com.ni/nacionales/294070-crisis-espana-no-frena-migracion-nica.

Pessar, Patricia R. 2003. "Anthropology and the Engendering of Migration Studies." In *American Arrivals: Anthropology Engages the New Immigration,* edited by Nancy Foner, 75–98. Santa Fe, NM: School of American Research Press.

Pribilsky, Jason. 2012. *La Chulla Vida: Gender, Migration, and the Family in Andean Ecuador and New York.* Syracuse, NY: Syracuse University Press.

Rae-Espinoza, Heather. 2011. "The Children of Émigres in Ecuador: Narratives of Cultural Reproduction and Emotion in Transnational Social Fields." In *Everyday Ruptures: Children, Youth, and Migration in Global Perspective,* edited by Cati Coe, Rachel R. Reynolds, Deborah A. Boehm, Julia Meredith Hess, and Heather Rae-Espinoza, 115–138. Nashville, TN: Vanderbilt University Press.

Randall, Margaret. 1995. *Sandino's Daughters: Testimonies of Nicaraguan Women in Struggle.* New Brunswick, NJ: Rutgers University Press.

Rebhun, Leslie A. 2007. "The Strange Marriage of Love and Interest: Economic Change and Emotional Intimacy in Northeast Brazil, Private and Public." In *Love and Globalization: Transformations of Intimacy in the Contemporary World,* edited by M. B. Padilla, J. S. Hirsch, M. Muñoz-Laboy, R. E. Sember, and R. G. Parker, 107–119. Nashville, TN: Vanderbilt University Press.

Robbins-Ruszkowski, Jessica C. 2013. "Challenging Marginalization at the Universities of the Third Age in Poland." *Anthropology and Aging Quarterly* 34 (2): 157–169.

Rocha, José Luis. 2006. *Una región desgarrada: Dinámicas migratorias en Centroamérica.* San José, Costa Rica: Servicio Jesuita para Migrantes Centroamérica.

———. 2008. *Central Americans: Redefining the Borders*. Managua: Universidad Centroamericana.

———. 2009. "Migración y desarrollo: Temas e implicaciones desde una perspectiva Centroamericana." *Envío* 7 (23): 6–11.

Safa, Helen. 2005. "The Matrifocal Family and Patriarchal Ideology in Cuba and the Caribbean." *Journal of Latin American Anthropology* 10 (2): 314–338.

Sales, Esther. 2003. "Family Burden and Quality of Life." *Quality of Life Research* 12 (suppl. 1): 33–41.

Sandoval-Cervantes, Iván. 2015. "Unfinished Lives: The Affect of Migrants' Unfinished Houses." Paper presented at the American Anthropological Annual Meeting, Denver, CO, November 20.

Sassen, Saskia. 1998. *Globalization and Its Discontents*. New York: New Press.

Saunders, Mitzi M. 2008. "Factors Associated with Caregiver Burden in Heart Failure Family Caregivers." *Western Journal of Nursing Research* 30 (8): 943–959.

Scott, Mary Alice. 2012. "Paying Down the Care Deficit: The Health Consequences for Grandmothers Caring for Grandchildren in a Mexican Migrant Community of Origin." *Anthropology and Aging Quarterly* 33 (4): 142–151.

Seider, Rachel. 2001. "War, Peace and Memory Politics in Central America." In *The Politics of Memory, Transitional Justice in Democratizing Societies*, edited by Alexandra Barahona de Brito, Carmen Gonzalez Enriquez, and Paloma Aguilar, 161–189. Oxford: Oxford University Press.

Selka, Stephen. 2010. "Morality in the Religious Marketplace: Evangelical Christianity, Candomblé, and the Struggle for Moral Distinction." *American Ethnologist* 37 (2): 291–307.

Servicio Jesuita para Migrantes de Centroamérica. 2009. "Una mirada desde la acción a los derechos humanos de los migrantes deportados." http://enlaceacademico.ucr .ac.cr/sites/default/files/publicaciones/Monitoreo_ddhh_migrantes_equipo_SJM.pdf.

Simpson, Sergio. 2010. "La oposición Sandinista a Daniel Ortega." *El Nuevo Diario*, March 18. http://www.elnuevodiario.com.ni/opinion/70589-oposicion-sandinista -daniel-ortega.

Sirias, Tania. 2008. "'Impunidad e injusticia' en caso Natividad Canda." *El Nuevo Diario*, September 12. http://www.elnuevodiario.com.ni/nacionales/26802-impunidad -e-injusticia-caso-natividad-canda.

Soronellas Masdeu, Monserrat, ed. 2010. *Familias en la migración: Emociones, solidaridades y obligaciones en el espacio transnacional*. Barcelona: Icaria, Centre de Cooperación per al Desenvolupament Rural.

Southward, Brandon. 2015. "Oregon Becomes Fifth State to Pass Domestic Worker Bill of Rights." *Statesman Journal*, June 18. http://www.statesmanjournal.com/ story/news/2015/06/19/oregon-becomes-fifth-state-pass-domestic-worker-bill-rights/ 28961597.

Stephen, Lynn. 2007. *Transborder Lives*. Durham, NC: Duke University Press.

Stevenson, Lisa. 2014. *Life Beside Itself: Imagining Care in the Canadian Arctic*. Berkeley: University of California Press.

Stoll, David. 2010. "From Wage Migration to Debt Migration? Easy Credit, Failure in El Norte, and Foreclosure in a Bubble Economy of the Western Guatemalan Highlands." *Latin American Perspectives* 37 (1): 123–142.

———. 2012. *El Norte or Bust! How Migration Fever and Micro Credit Produced a Financial Crash in a Latin American Town*. Lanham, MD: Rowman and Littlefield.

Suárez-Orozco, Carola, and Marcelo Suárez-Orozco. 2001. *Children of Immigration*. Cambridge, MA: Harvard University Press.

Taylor, Edward J. 1999. "The New Economics of Labour Migration and the Role of Remittances in the Migration Process." *International Migration* 37 (1): 63–88.

Taylor, Janelle S. 2014. "Care: Integration." *Cultural Anthropology*, April 30. http://www.culanth.org/fieldsights/525-care-integration.

Thelen, Tatjana. 2015. "Care as Social Organization: Creating, Maintaining and Dissolving Significant Relations." *Anthropological Theory* 15 (4): 497–515.

Ticktin, Miriam. 2011. *Immigration and the Politics of Humanitarianism in France*. Berkeley: University of California Press.

Torres, Olimpia, and Milagros Barahona. 2004. *Las migraciones de nicaragüenses al exterior: Un análisis desde la perspectiva de género*. Managua: United Nations Population Fund.

Tronto, Joan. 1993. *Moral Boundaries: A Political Argument for an Ethic of Care*. New York: Routledge.

U.S. Citizenship and Immigration Services. 2016. "Bringing Children, Sons and Daughters to Live in the United States as Permanent Residents." http://www.uscis.gov/family/family-us-citizens/children/bringing-children-sons-and-daughters-live-united-states-permanent-residents.

Vogt, Wendy. 2013. "Crossing Mexico: Structural Violence and the Commodification of Undocumented Central American Migrants." *American Ethnologist* 40 (4): 764–780.

Willen, Sarah S. 2007. "Toward a Critical Phenomenology of 'Illegality': State Power, Criminalization, and Abjectivity Among Undocumented Migrant Workers in Tel Aviv, Israel." *International Migration* 45 (3): 8–38.

———. 2012. "Migration, 'Illegality,' and Health: Mapping Embodied Vulnerability and Debating Health-Related Deservingness." *Social Science and Medicine* 74 (6): 805–811.

World Bank. 2006. *Global Economic Prospects 2006: Economic Implications of Migration and Remittances*. Washington, DC: World Bank.

Yarris, Kristin Elizabeth. 2011. "The Pain of 'Thinking Too Much': *Dolor de Cerebro* and the Embodiment of Social Hardship Among Nicaraguan Women." *Ethos* 39 (2): 226–248.

————. 2014a. "'Pensando Mucho' ('Thinking Too Much'): Embodied Distress Among Grandmothers in Nicaraguan Transnational Families." *Culture, Medicine and Psychiatry* 38 (3): 473–498.

————. 2014b. "'Quiero Ir y No Quiero Ir' (I Want to Go and I Don't Want to Go): Nicaraguan Children's Ambivalent Experiences of Transnational Family Life." *Journal of Latin American and Caribbean Anthropology* 19 (2): 284–309.

————. 2017. "Sacrifice or Abandonment? Nicaraguan Grandmothers' Narratives of Migration as Kin Work." In *Transnational Aging and Reconfigurations of Kin Work*, edited by Parin Dossa and Cati Coe, 61–82. New Brunswick, NJ: Rutgers University Press.

Yarris, Kristin, and Heide Castañeda. 2015. "Introduction." In "Discourses of Displacement and Deservingness: Interrogating Distinctions Between 'Economic' and 'Forced' Migration." Special issue, *International Migration* 53 (3): 64–69.

Yeates, Nicola. 2005. "A Global Political Economy of Care." *Social Policy and Society* 4 (2): 227–234.

————. 2012. "Global Care Chains: A State-of-the-Art Review and Future Directions in Care Transnationalization Research." *Global Networks* 12 (2): 135–154.

Zelizer, Viviana A. 2005. *The Purchase of Intimacy*. Princeton, NJ: Princeton University Press.

Zigon, Jarrett. 2011. "A Moral and Ethical Assemblage in Russian Orthodox Drug Rehabilitation." *Ethos* 39 (1): 30–50.

Index